W9-CFS-010

SAMURAI
The Warrior Tradition
STEPHEN TURNBULL
Illustrations by James Field

ARMS AND
ARMOUR

Arms and Armour Press
An Imprint of the Cassell Group
Wellington House, 125 Strand
London WC2R 0BB

Distributed in the United States by Sterling Publishing Co Inc
387 Park Avenue South, New York, NY 10016-8810

Distributed in Australia by
Capricorn Link (Australia) Pty Ltd
2/13 Carrington Road, Castle Hill, NSW 2154

This is an omnibus edition of *Samurai Warriors* (1987)
and *Samurai Warlords* (1989) published by Blandford Press

British Library Cataloging in Publication Data:
a catalogue record of this book is available from the British Library

ISBN 1-85409-359-2

Printed and bound in Slovenia by printing house
Mariborski tisk by arrangement with Korotan Ljubljana.

Frontispiece (overleaf): Hajikano leads the Takeda army to Odawara
This plate reproduces a dramatic moment during the Takeda army's advance against the Hōjō family in 1569. As the army under Takeda Shingen (shown here wearing a red *jinbaori* surcoat) moved against the Hōjō's fortress of Odawara, their progress was halted by the swollen waters of the Sasaogawa river. One of Shingen's junior commanders, Hajikano Masatsugu, who bore the rank of *ashigaru-taishō* (general of foot-soldiers), volunteered for the dangerous task of assessing the depth of the raging river. He rode his horse into the water and, having first tested the depth with the shaft of his spear, rode on until for a brief moment only the *sashimono* flag on the back of his armour was visible above the surface. The design on the banner was one of the playing pieces in the Japanese board game of *shōgi*, representing a spear, which in *shōgi* can only move forward, and not retreat. Hajikano put this to Shingen as a reason for his confidence in advancing.

Hajikano Masatsugu is drawn according to his description in the account of the incident in the *Kōyō Gunkan*. The flags among the Takeda army are those of the two subordinate commanders who attended Shingen on this occasion, Naitō Masatoyo and Baba Nobuharu.

Contents

Acknowledgements *6*

Introduction *7*

Heian Period *9*

Kamakura Period *28*

Early Muromachi Period *44*

Sengoku Period – the Age of the Country at War *63*

Momoyama Period – Oda Nobunaga *79*

Momoyama Period – Toyotomi Hideyoshi *96*

Early Edo Period *115*

Later Edo Period *135*

Daimyō – The Samurai Elite *173*

Focus of Loyalty *191*

Commander-in-Chief *209*

The Cultured Warlord *227*

The Keeper of the Peace *244*

Sex and the Samurai *262*

Death and the Daimyō *282*

The Duty of Vengeance *302*

Appendix I The 1559 Hōjō Register *322*

Appendix II The 1575 Uesugi Register *324*

Appendix III Takeda Shingen *327*

Appendix IV Hashiba Hideyoshi *328*

Appendix V The Ii 'Red Devils' *329*

Bibliography *330*

Index *332*

Acknowledgements

This book draws upon 20 years of research into samurai history, armour and weapons and, using exclusively Japanese sources, paints a picture of the samurai in words, photographs and via specially commissioned artwork that is unique outside Japan itself.

Such use of rare materials could not have been entertained without the help and support of many individuals and organisations. In this context particular mention must be made of Mrs Nahoko Kitajima of Moriguchi City, Osaka, and her colleague Mr Nishikawa; and also Mr Yukito Kaiki and Miss Nobuyo Ichifugi, of Kanazawa. Much valuable information was also supplied by the helpful staff of the Tokyo Offices of the prefectures of Yamanashi, Shizuoka, Gifu, Shiba, Ishikawa and Aichi. Museums and collections that opened their doors to us include the Nagashino Castle Preservation Hall, the Minatogawa Shrine Museum, Kobe, the Ieyasukan at Okazaki, the Gifu City Historical Museum, the Sanada Museum, Matsushiro, Ueda Castle Museum, Osaka Castle Museum, Hamamatsu Castle Museum, the Nampian Kannon-ji at Kawachi-Nagano, the Memorial Hall at Nakamura Park, Nagoya, and the Takeda Museum at the Erin-ji, Enzan, in addition to well-known national collections such as the Tokyo National Museum. The staff of the Oriental Collections at the British Library, particularly Mrs Yu-Ying Brown, have been most helpful.

It has been a pleasure to work with James Field and see my notes and ideas translated into his splendid paintings.

Introduction

The samurai were the military elite of old Japan, and the daimyō were the elite of the samurai.

Using original Japanese works such as those of Yoshihiko Sasama, the first part of this omnibus edition deals with the costume, equipment, training and tactics of the samurai warriors, their country's equivalent to the military knights of medieval Europe. As historians have long been fascinated with the codes by which the latter operated so, by access to this type of original research, they have been able to become better acquainted with these special fighters from the East.

There are many similarities in the two themes. Like the knights of Britain, they secured their status by dint of hard training and battle experience which separated them from the standard foot soldier. Then, by internal competition, demonstrable excellence in martial skills and success in combat, the very best forced themselves to higher positions and responsibilities, and so became the 'crème de la crème'.

This ultimate elite were the daimyō. Their military achievements brought wealth and property, land which they defended with loyal forces of samurai. From these original warlords grew great dynasties which enjoyed a symbiotic existence with the central government of the Shōgun until all were swept away in the upheavals of the 1850s which gave birth to modern Japan.

There is a popular theory, nowadays, that one reason the Japanese are so successful in the modern world is that they give to their company, and to their country, that same loyalty which once they gave to the daimyō. In the pages that follow we shall see of what that fierce loyalty consisted.

The second part of the book examines in depth a particular role which the daimyō was required to play. We shall see him as a warrior, as a commander and as a focus for that legendary loyalty which still amazes one even today. We shall examine his other demanding duties as the founder of a dynasty, as the keeper of the peace and as the patron of the arts. To be a daimyō was a demanding life, and the demands did not stop with the warlord's death, for he then entered on a new and strange role as spiritual guardian of the family, to be honoured, and if necessary, bloodily revenged.

In a sense, this portion of the book is about two very different types of people, the *Sengoku-daimyō*, the warlords of the Sengoku Period, or the 'Age of War' (which is roughly the same as the sixteenth century AD), and the daimyō of the Edo Period, the three centuries that followed, which were marked by the almost total absence of war. The lives of these two groups were very different but closely related, because it was the experience of life in the Age of War, or at the very least the tradition passed on from their ancestors, that prepared the later daimyō to survive the different demands of the Age of Peace. It is this thread of tradition of self-sacrifice, of the needs of the group, of identification with a leader, that tells us so much about Japan today.

This book is based entirely upon Japanese sources, and compiled with the generous assistance of many friends made during various trips to Japan.

Heian Period

The samurai were the knights of Medieval Japan. Like their counterparts in Europe, they began as a military élite and became a social élite, their prize being the triumph which their swords had won for them. The history of the samurai is very much the history of Japan itself, so for convenience we will follow a chronological sequence based on the traditional divisions of the Japanese historical eras. The 'Heian Period' (during which the word 'samurai' is first used) derives from the name by which the capital city, Kyoto, was known at the time: 'Heian-kyo' or the city of heavenly peace.

The Early Warriors

There is no doubt as to when the samurai officially ceased to exist as a separate class. The decisive date must be 1876, when the wearing of swords was forbidden to all except the national conscript army of the new Japan. What is at issue is how the samurai began. Exactly how did a military élite emerge? This is a problem of Japanese history that has still not been adequately explained. In terms of the long history of the Japanese people the samurai are comparative newcomers. The word itself hardly pre-dates the eleventh century AD and follows a millennium of years of war. *Samurai* means, literally, 'those who serve', implying the rendering of honourable military service by an élite to an overlord, which is effectually what the samurai existed to provide until the time when the class was abolished in the 1870s. These three factors: military prowess, élitism and service to another, are the keys to identifying the origin of the samurai.

Ancient records give us some clues as to the samurai antecedents. Within the *Nihongi*, the *Chronicles of Japan*, compiled sometime during the first decades of the eighth century AD, may be found the term *bugei*, or 'martial arts', so no doubt some degree of military specialism existed in the armies of the period, whether they were under the control of the central government or local officials. The early history of Japan was as much a time of conflict as any of the 'samurai centuries' that followed.

In the year AD 672 we are given a hint of one role which the future samurai were to make very much their own, that of the mounted archer, a form of warfare, which, it would appear, was already achieving an élite status. In AD 671 the Emperor Tenchi died, his death causing one of those succession disputes with which samurai history is littered. Emperor Tenchi had apparently promised the throne to his brother, who had declined the honour and subsequently become a monk, so that on Tenchi's death his son ascended to the throne. This was, however, only within a month of the uncle renouncing the world, and the opportunity to take up that which he had recently discarded must have proved very tempting. As a result the brother left the monastery and revolted against his nephew. What is interesting from a military point of view is that he made good use of the rapid striking power of a force of mounted archers. The coup was successful, and he ascended the throne as Emperor Temmu. The accounts of Temmu's coup, and the achievements of his reign, come from the above-mentioned *Nihongi*, which was compiled under the jurisdiction of Temmu's daughter, so its claims for Temmu's military accomplishments may have to be regarded with some scepticism. Nevertheless, this is the first written account of the mounted archer in action, a model of military accomplishment that was to be the mark of the élite samurai.

Rivalry such as this between Imperial princes was far less common as a reason for war than the continuing need for campaigns against the aboriginal inhabitants of the Japanese islands, the Ainu. The old accounts make it quite clear that the suppression of these people was seen almost as a moral duty and an act of spreading civilisation, as it is referred to in the *Chronicles* as *emishi no seiobatsu* or 'punishment of the emishi'. *Emishi*, which

PLATE 1   *A samurai of the time of the Later Three Years' War*

In contradiction to its title, this war lasted from 1083 to 1087, and was one of the several 'little wars' in which the Minamoto clan rose to prominence by defeating rebels.

The samurai wears a suit of armour of the classic *yoroi* style, laced with thick silken cords. The *yoroi* is the typical samurai armour of the time and is derived from Asiatic styles of lamellar armour, whereby an armour plate is made up of several small plates fastened together in some way, rather than using single large plates of metal or leather. The plate of a *yoroi* would be made by binding a row of scales together with leather thongs, then lacquering the whole to make a waterproof, light and tough protection. A number of these plates would then be fastened together by cords, overlapping slightly in concertina fashion. The *yoroi* is the style which we will meet time and time again as we go through samurai

history. The box-like body-armour, or *do*, hangs from the shoulders and is fastened around the waist. Only the plate under the right arm is separate. There is a leather covering, beautifully patterned, on the front of the armour, called the *tsurubashiri*, which gives the appearance of a breastplate. The two appendages, called the *sendan-no-ita* and the *kyubi-no-ita*, which hang in front, are designed to protect the cords holding the armour from severance by swordstrokes.

For an indication of what this armour would look like from the rear, consult the illustration on p. 20.

The helmet worn with a *yoroi* was made from a number of iron plates riveted together. We can see the large rivet heads left protruding from the helmet surface, in the style known as a *hoshi-kabuto*. His hair has been gathered into a pigtail on top of his head inside an *eboshi* cap, which protrudes through the *tehen*, the

hole formed where the ends of the helmet plates meet, thus providing a padding for the weight of the helmet. He wears a *kote*, or armoured sleeve, on his left arm only, thus leaving the right freer for drawing a bow, for at this period in Japanese history the samurai was essentially a mounted archer. His sword is suspended from a belt beside a *tanto*, or dagger.

The figure is based on an illustration in the *Gosannen no eki emaki (Scroll of the Later Three Years' War)* in Tokyo National Museum, with additional details of the armour being taken from a *yoroi* of the period preserved in the Oyamazumi Shrine Museum, Omishima (Hiroshima Prefecture). The common soldier beside him has much simpler armour called *do-maru*, or 'body-wrappers', made of similar lamellar construction.

A map showing the general outline of Japan and its main islands, and also its position in relation to the Asiatic mainland.

is probably a variant of the Ainu word for 'man', was used in the sense of 'barbarian', implying the disdain of a civilised state, much as the word was used by the Romans against the Celtic tribes of Europe. *Emishi* was actually the politest term their enemies used for them, as the indigenous population are elsewhere variously referred to as 'earth spiders'.

The *emishi* proved to be stubborn fighters and early Emperors very soon made a habit of recruiting pacified *emishi* for their armies, a practice that had on occasions already been adopted by rebels against the throne, for whom these discontented and rebellious people were an obvious source of

12

Prince Yamato-Takeru, slayer of serpents and semi-mythological hero of early Japan. Yamato's career, as the brave individual warrior, sets the tone for the most cherished ideals of the samurai. His statue is in the Kenroku-en Gardens, Kanazawa.

support. They proved to be worthy of their hire, and many of the military traditions which later became associated with the samurai had their origins in these warriors. Even the curved sword, so much a symbol of the samurai, probably owes its origin to the weapons carried by *emishi* who were recruited as guards for the Imperial Court in the latter part of the ninth century. But, most important of all, it was the *emishi* campaigns, which were fought against soldiers who were familiar with their territory, that provided the practice for the wars of later years when the samurai would take on their own kind in struggles for the fertile lands of Japan.

For an explanation of the élite nature of the samurai we must look elsewhere than the barbarian *emishi*. There was a clearly defined tendency for certain families to acquire reputations for military excellence from the earliest centuries. Examples are the Otomo in the eighth century, who held the post of hereditary palace guards, and the Sakanoue in the ninth, but it is not until the tenth century that we see tl emergence of 'warrior houses' of samurai. The formation of these units, based on the possession of land rather than patronage, was the most important social development during these early years. Typically, such a unit would be based around a central familial core, often with aristocratic connections. In many cases there was an actual lineage from a scion of the Imperial House, an honoured ancestor who had left Kyoto for the distant provinces to open up new rice-lands, pacify barbarians, and generally make a name for himself. The members were bound together by ties of loyalty and reward. These 'warrior houses', or 'clans' (either translation gives the reader a good mental picture of their fundamental nature), prospered best in areas remote from the capital, where they were able to grow at the expense of rivals and had the constant threat from the *emishi* to keep them in trim.

These developments are illustrated by the revolt of Taira Masakado in AD 935. Masakado, as his name implies, came from a branch of the Taira clan, which was to achieve great power in the following century. His rebellion, which went as far as Masakado proclaiming himself as a rival Emperor, produced a serious challenge both to the ruling house and to the other law-abiding members of the Taira family. It was in fact his own clan which was instrumental in bringing about his death in AD 940. *Konjaku Monogatari*, the twelfth-century chronicle which covers the rebellion, includes in its narrative some important guidelines as to how the idea of an élite samurai class was emerging and what its values were. One theme that comes over is the move towards a certain exclusivity of the samurai class, membership of which is a privilege so universally accepted that it is felt necessary to make some comment when this factor is absent. One example is the comment on a particular samurai that 'although he did not belong to a

---

PLATE 2 *A provincial samurai, in a poor quality armour, ca 1160*

The samurai who fought for the Minamoto cause in the early campaigns of the Gempei War were regarded as rough and vulgar characters by the more sophisticated Taira clan. This plate, which is based on a section of the *Heiji Monogatari Emaki* in the Museum of Fine Arts, Boston, Massachussetts, is an attempt to realise such a rough, unshaven warrior. His heavy helmet (copied from an extant specimen in the Oyamazumi Shrine Museum, Omishima, Hiroshima Prefecture) with its wide *fukigayeshi* (turnbacks) and *shikoro* (neckguard) has a minimum of decoration, the finish of the metal bowl being a natural coating of rust. His suit of armour is the simple *do-maru*, lacking the leather breastplate of his betters, but he enjoys a better protection than a common footsoldier by wearing two large *sode* or shoulder-plates. His pole-arm is a very plain *naginata*, which he is carefully sheathing after use. Note that, even though his main weapon is not the bow, he wears no armour on his right sleeve, in true samurai tradition. His armour is laced with leather thongs.

A warrior from the period between the fifth and seventh centuries AD wearing a *tanko,* the solid plate form of body-armour that preceded the adoption of lamellar styles. This statue is in the Gifu Historical Museum.

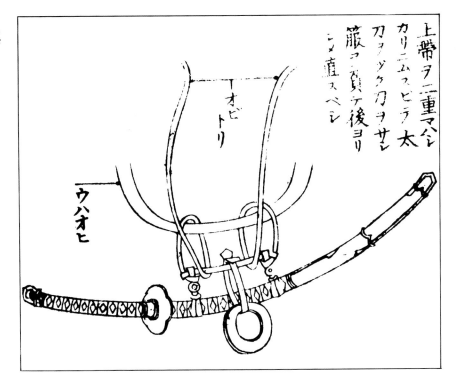

上帯ヲ二重マ八シ
カリニムッピテラ太
ワァ、ゾク刀ヲサレ
巌ッ頁ヲ後ヨリ
ニ直スベレ

オビ
トリ

ウハオヒ

One way recommended by the *Gunyoki* for wearing the slung sword, the *tachi*, and the reel holding a spare bowstring. The cords of the sword are looped around a belt, the *uwaobi*, thus giving additional support.

warrior house, he was courageous and accomplished in the Way of Bow and Arrow'. This latter phrase, *kyusen no michi*, otherwise rendered as *kyuba no michi*, 'The Way of Horse and Bow', is the obvious precursor of the much later *bushido*, 'The Way of the Warrior', and implies the existence of certain standards of conduct and accomplishment which are by rights the prerogative of an élite, though not, as yet, the élite's exclusive possession. A further example is found in the *Shoyuki*, the diary of the venerable old Fujiwara Sanesuke (957–1046). Here Sanesuke refers disparagingly to a distant relative called Fujiwara Norimoto, who killed one of his own vassals. 'Norimoto enjoys the martial arts', writes Sanesuke, 'but people do not approve. He is not of warrior blood.'

The struggle for land is a fundamental theme throughout samurai history. Sometimes it was gained by outright warfare, but territory could often be acquired by being granted a high office of state with lands attached, and the conflicts for such appointments could be as bitter as direct campaigns for the acquisition of territory. Taira Masakado's revolt occurred because he was refused the important office of *kebiishi*, an appointment concerned with the arrest and punishment of criminals. An order given by the *kebiishi* carried with it the full weight of Imperial authority and many warrior houses gained their early reputations by delivering the heads of criminals to Kyoto and collecting rewards such as provincial governorships. To become a provincial governor made a samurai into a petty prince, taking his considerable share of the produce of the lands entrusted to his care. *Kebiishi* was thus a coveted position.

Provincial governors were not always benevolent. One notorious example is Taira Korehira, son of the vanquisher of Masakado, who at various times was granted governorships of the provinces of Ise, Mutsu, Dewa, Izu, Shimotsuke, Sado, Kozuke and Hitachi. Not that he governed any of them very well. His successor in Hitachi complained that the people were starving and Korehira eventually ended his disappointing career by making open war against his kinsman Muneyori. For this he was apprehended and was exiled to the island of Awaji in the Inland Sea.

The Classical Samurai

The most important series of events in the history of the samurai was the process by which these élite, land-owning fighters transformed their condition from being the servants of Emperors and quellers of rebels and barbarians to being the *de facto* government of Japan, reducing the Emperor to a mere figurehead under their military dictatorship. This revolution happened during the latter part of the twelfth century AD, and is centred around a civil war between two clans, the Minamoto and the Taira, called the Gempei War.

Both the Minamoto and the Taira descended from branches of the Imperial family. Both had ancestors whose valiant exploits had set the standard against which their samurai measured their own accomplishments, and both were enormously ambitious. Each clan held numerous rice-lands and provided a focus for the adherents who served them as farmers and samurai and occasionally married into the family. The strength of the Taira was concentrated in the West of Japan. Their 'family temple' was the beautiful Itsukushima Shrine built out onto the sea of the island of Miyajima in the Inland Sea. They had great influence at Court, bought by years of service to succeeding Emperors.

PLATE 3   *A warrior monk from Mount Hiei, ca 1170*

A prominent feature of the warfare of eleventh-and twelfth-century Japan was the use of armies of *sohei*, or warrior monks, by the great Buddhist foundations of Kyoto and Nara. The *sohei* shown here wears a costume typical of these fierce fighters. The long white monk's robe, which is gathered at the ankles, is augmented by a simple footsoldier's *do-maru* armour, consisting of a tube-like corselet of lacquered leather or iron plates laced together with leather or cord thongs. It has seven *kusazuri*, or skirt pieces. On top is worn a thin black, gauze-like outer robe, and the sword hangs outside it, through the deep slashes at the waist. The traditional headgear was either a knotted towel around the shaven pate, or the elaborate headcowl shown in this illustration, which reached almost to nose level and was tied behind the head. He carries the traditional weapon of the warrior monks – the *naginata* – and is depicted standing outside one of the hundreds of shrines on Mount Hiei, to the North-West of Kyoto. The main foundation of Mount Hiei, the Enryaku-ji, was a Buddhist temple, but the mountain was also sacred to a Shinto deity, Sanno, the Mountain King, hence the *torii* gateway behind him.

The picture is based on several sources, notably the scrolls *Tengu Zoshi emaki* (Tokyo National Museum) and *Kasuga Gongen Reikenki* (Imperial Household Collection).

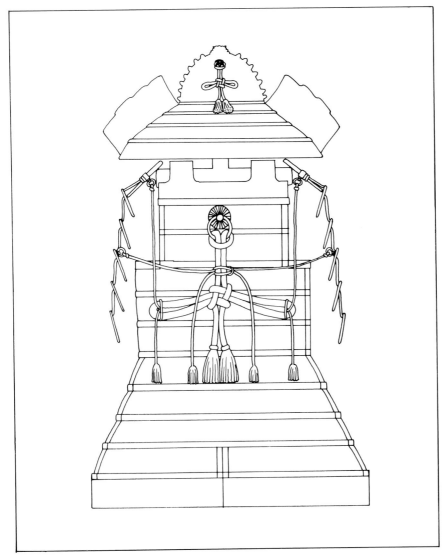

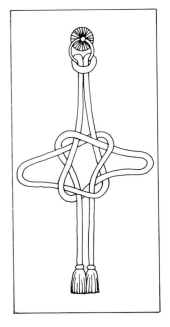

The Minamoto's power lay in the less-civilised East where there were still *emishi* to fight. Their family temple was the striking Tsurugaoka Hachiman Shrine in Kamakura, dedicated to Hachiman, the Shinto God of War. These 'Eastern Warriors' were spoken of disparagingly by the more sophisticated West and, in the early days of the clans' struggle, the differences were probably quite marked. The troops of Minamoto Yoshinaka (1154–1184), for example, were regarded as rough mountain men, whose appearance and manners alone alarmed the people of the capital and did much to erode his support. Yoshinaka's own uncouth and ambitious presence eventually led to his death at the hands of his cousin Yoritomo.

By contrast the Taira samurai are often portrayed as accomplished poets and refined courtiers. Nor was this far from the truth, for by the 1170s the

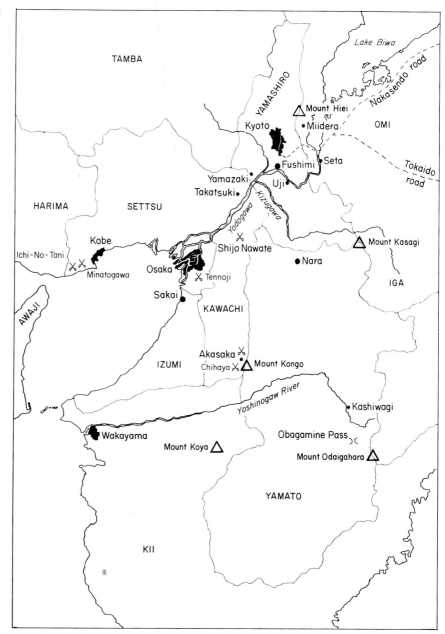

The 'Home Provinces' of Japan. Until modern times this central area of Japan between Kyoto and Osaka, bordered to the north-east by Lake Biwa, and to the south by the mountains of the Kii peninsula, was the pivot around which much of Japanese history revolved.

Taira had risen to a point of political pre-eminence by the straightforward process of marrying their daughters to Imperial princes. There was nothing particularly revolutionary about this – the Fujiwara clan had been doing it for centuries, and the Taira was merely the first other family to try the same game. It meant, however, that the Taira, in the person of the clan head, Taira Kiyomori, an astute politician, had gained political power by using and manipulating existing political institutions which they served as loyal samurai. It was the Minamoto who were to provide the samurai revolution.

The early samurai battles of the Gempei War are notable for the presence of a third force – contingents of warrior monks, or *sohei*. Several of the great monasteries of Kyoto and Nara maintained armies for defence in the lawless times, and would readily use them against rival temples or samurai armies. The fiercest coterie of warrior monks belonged to the Enryaku-ji, the main temple on Mount Hiei, which lies to the North-East of Kyoto, an area regarded as the abode of several very powerful *kami*, the Shinto word for a spiritual divinity. Mount Hiei also provided a natural fortress, and a standing army of several thousand monks, and we will see regular references to support being sought from the warrior monks of Mount Hiei as late as the sixteenth century. They were formidable warriors, though unreliable as allies, for they always put the interests of their temples first. In their early disputes the fear of the *kami* they represented was often enough to frighten the Imperial Court into granting their demands. They would march on Kyoto carrying the sacred *mikoshi*, or portable shrine, in which the *kami* was supposed to dwell. If the Imperial Court would not grant their wishes, which were usually concerned with land rights or prestige, the *mikoshi* would be left in the city street until a different decision was reached. Few samurai had such fear of the monks, but they would earn great approbation for standing up to them.

The war between the Taira and the Minamoto was a struggle for supremacy into which all social classes were drawn. The first Taira/Minamoto struggle in which the monks fought was the First Battle of Uji in 1180. The veteran warrior, Minamoto Yorimasa, raised the flag of rebellion against the Taira while he was still based in Kyoto – a very risky operation. His monkish support came from the temple of Onjo-ji, or Miidera, which lies at the foot of Mount Hiei and had a long history of stubborn independence from the Enryaku-ji on the summit. When Yorimasa's plot

PLATE 4   *A general being dressed by a page in a fine* yoroi, *ca 1180*

This plate provides a direct comparison between the military costume of the highest and lowest ranking samurai of the Gempei War Period. The *taisho* (general) is completely armed except for his helmet. Note that instead of the hair being gathered into a pigtail it has been let down. The stiff *eboshi* cap will be removed before the helmet is placed on to the head. This may indicate that the helmet has a separate lining. The *yoroi* armour is little different from that shown in Plate 1, except that it is more richly ornamented with gilt fittings, as befits the wearer, and is based on an

extant specimen in the Oyamazumi Shrine Museum, Omishima (Hiroshima Prefecture). His *yoroi-hitatare*, or armour robe, is richly embroidered and ornamented with pom-poms. His attendant is tying the general's quiver securely round his waist in such a position that arrows may be easily withdrawn with the right hand. The arrows are held in place in the basket-like quiver by twisted cords that are wound round the quiver's back. As the general is of such exalted rank he has been depicted wearing footwear while indoors! The interior design is based on the contemporary Genji

Monogatari Scroll.

The attendant's costume, which appears to change little for four centuries, is based on the simple *do-maru* we noted on the warrior monk. His black *eboshi* cap, tied with cords, is of similar design to the general's. When going into battle it would be augmented by the face-mask seen in Plate 5. His small shoulder-protectors are of padded cloth, possibly strengthened within by metal or leather plates. As he is not an archer he wears two *kote* (armour sleeves) which are simple cloth bags with metal plates sewn on at strategic places.

was discovered he and his warrior monks decided to retreat South, across the Uji River, to join forces with the warrior monks of the Kofuku-ji at Nara. The Uji River, which flows out of Lake Biwa to join the Yodo River, entering the sea near Osaka, has always been a natural moat to Kyoto, and the two bridges at Seta and Uji were strategic prizes for any army wishing to take the capital or, as in Yorimasa's case, safeguard his flight from it. The Taira forces followed in pursuit, so the Minamoto tore up the planking of the Uji bridge and prepared to make a stand until the Nara monks could join them. After much fierce fighting, and gallant acts of swordsmanship while balanced on the beams of the broken bridge, the Taira samurai succeeded in crossing the river and Yorimasa, completely surrounded, committed suicide.

The act of suicide when faced with certain defeat is a well-known tradition concerned with samurai warfare. Suicide could also be taken as an alternative to execution, as a means of apologising for a wrong deed while saving one's honour and, more rarely, as a highly dramatic act of protest. Yet suicide was never an automatic act. We frequently hear of samurai fleeing, withdrawing and, occasionally, surrendering, though the latter is very often followed by the suicide of the captive. As we shall see in the following pages the omission of suicide is sometimes more surprising than its commission.

Minamoto Yoshitsune

A large part of the accounts of the Gempei War is taken up by descriptions of the long campaigns of Minamoto Yoshitsune, the Minamoto's ablest general, and one of the most famous samurai who ever existed. He is best known for his battles against the Taira, but he began his career by defeating his cousin, the rough man from the mountains, Minamoto Yoshinaka.

Yoshinaka had in fact served the Minamoto cause well, by defeating the Taira at the Battle of Tonamiyama (or Kurikara) in 1182, where he had succeeded in forcing the Taira army into a dead-end valley by stampeding a herd of cattle, enraged by tying lighted torches to their horns. As a result he succeeded in being the first of the Minamoto to enter the capital in triumph, where his men behaved very badly. It was probably Yoshinaka's very success that set his cousins against him, rather than any genuine concern for the inhabitants whom his men had abused. Yoshitsune was sent to the West to chastise him and met Yoshinaka's force at the Uji River. Unlike Yorimasa in 1180, however, who was fighting off an attack from the capital, Yoshinaka attempted to use it in reverse. But once again a successful crossing was made and Yoshinaka withdrew with a handful of followers, until his horse crashed through the ice of a frozen paddy field. As Yoshinaka turned in the saddle an arrow hit him in the face. Two samurai ran up and struck off his head.

Kebiki-odoshi **lacing – detail**
This shows the way in which the
cords of a *kebiki-odoshi* (laced
armour) interrelated. The outer line
of cords was often of a multicoloured
weave, known as 'woodpecker
braid'.

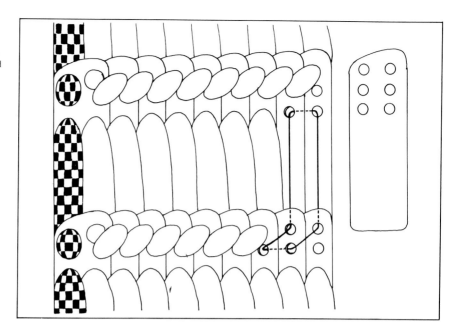

With Yoshinaka's personal ambitions out of the way the main branch of
the Minamoto could concentrate on the defeat of the Taira, who had
possession of the child Emperor, grandson of Taira Kiyomori. To be seen to
be acting in the name of the Emperor, even if he was virtually a hostage,
was an important guarantee of support. The other great strength of the
Taira was their command of the sea. They had their own fleet and a network
of bases along the Inland Sea. On three occasions they withstood attacks
from Yoshitsune while based either on the sea or very near to it. The first
was the Battle of Ichi-no-tani in 1184. Ichi-no-tani was a stockade-type
fortress on the shore of the Inland Sea near to the present-day city of Kobe.
It was defended on two sides by palisades, while the third was open to the
sea where the escape craft lay, and the rear was defended by steep cliffs.
Yoshitsune's attack shows his imagination and daring. While two groups of
samurai attacked from the sides, he led a picked band of men down a
precipitous path at the rear and took the Taira completely by surprise.
There was no wild panic for the boats – samurai honour would not have
permitted that. Instead a number of individual combats took place on the
shore, several of which, such as the death of the young Taira samurai,
Atsumori, quickly entered the pantheon of samurai heroics as being perfect
examples of the death of the brave, lone warrior – an image cherished
throughout samurai history. But the bulk of the Taira escaped, taking with
them the child-Emperor Antoku, whose capture was their main aim.

A few months later Yoshitsune pursued them to Yashima on the island
of Shikoku. Here the battle was fought in the shallows which divided the
then island of Yashima from Shikoku. It was fiercely contested, but one
celebrated incident which occurred during the fighting shows that the
tradition of the samurai as an élite mounted archer was still as strong as

25

ever. During a lull in the fighting the Taira had tied a fan to the mast of one of their ships and challenged the Minamoto to shoot it down, hoping thereby to encourage them to waste their ammunition. The challenge was accepted by Nasu Munetaka, a young samurai retainer of the Minamoto, who took careful aim as the fan fluttered in the breeze and shattered it with his first shot, which greatly improved the Minamoto morale.

The Battle of Yashima was as indecisive as Ichi-no-tani had been, as the child Emperor was once again spirited away by sea. But it served to illustrate that the Minamoto were determined to pursue the Taira wherever they led. The final reckoning came in April 1185, when both armies met in a sea battle at Dan-no-Ura in the Straits of Shimonoseki, the narrow gap of water that divides Honshu from Kyushu. The fighting was long and hard, and a sea battle only in the sense of two armies using ships as fighting platforms for archers and swordsmen, for there is very little of naval manoeuvring to be discerned. Dan-no-Ura ended with the utter defeat of the Taira, and one of the largest mass suicides in samurai history as the Taira reeled from an overwhelming attack. The child-Emperor Antoku was drowned and the replica Sacred Sword, one of the three items that comprise the Japanese Imperial Regalia, was lost forever. So terrible was the eclipse of the Taira clan at Dan-no-Ura that many legends grew up concerning ghosts, seas of blood, and crabs with the spirits of samurai within them. It is still regarded as one of the most decisive battles in Japanese history.

Minamoto Yoshitsune, however, was not the clan member who benefited from the defeat of its rivals. His elder brother Yoritomo was head of the clan, and it was Yoritomo who was to take over where the Taira had left off, and found a dynasty to rule the country in the name of the Emperor. Where Yoritomo's achievement differed from that of the Taira, however, was that instead of making use of existing institutions of Imperial government, and marrying daughters into the family, Yoritomo founded a new system of hereditary military government under a dictator known as the *shogun*, a word that is nowadays as familiar as *samurai*. In 1192 Minamoto Yoritomo became the first Minamoto Shogun, ruling by means of a Shogunal government or *bakufu*. The Minamoto triumph was complete, as was the total ascendancy of the samurai military élite.

PLATE 5   *A footsoldier in a* do-maru, *ca 1184*

This common footsoldier is taken directly from an illustration in the scroll *Kasuga Gongen Reikenki*. He is on guard duty outside a samurai headquarters in Kyoto. His costume is very similar to that of the footsoldiers in Plates 4 and 6 except that he wears a metal face-protector that covers the forehead and cheeks, and provides some defence against a sword slash. His shoulder-protectors are covered by a dyed leather similar to that used for the 'breastplate' of a samurai's armour. Details of the scenery are taken from the Heiji Monogatari Scroll.

Kamakura Period

The establishment of Minamoto Yoritomo's Shogunate, or *bakufu*, marks the beginning of the 'Kamakura Period' in Japanese history, from 1192 until 1333, as the city of Kamakura was the seat of the Shogun and thus the administrative capital of Japan.

The Fall of the Minamoto

The Kamakura *bakufu* was never all-powerful, in spite of the dramatic way it had been formed, and had to face a continued resistance to the Shogunal power from the Imperial family. As we shall see, it was to be the power of an Emperor that finally brought about its downfall. There is one other remarkable feature about the Kamakura Period: that the Minamoto, the family whose triumph seems so complete in 1192, should so soon be vanquished as thoroughly as they had destroyed the Taira.

In view of the tremendous achievement of Yoritomo in raising his family to the highest position in the land, it is strange that their dynasty should turn out to be so short-lived. Apart from the earlier destruction of Yoshinaka, the first feuding within the family was Yoritomo's personal rivalry with his brothers Yoshitsune and Noriyori, whose military skills had helped him gain the position of Shogun. Both were driven from office and pursued to death. Perhaps fittingly Yoritomo himself enjoyed only 7 years as Shogun, dying in 1199, at the age of 52, when he was thrown from a horse while returning in state from a public ceremony. His death was accidental, untimely, and threw the whole *bakufu* into confusion. His 18-year-old son Yoriie immediately succeeded to his late father's civil offices, but there was a long delay in having him appointed Shogun. Many Kamakura officials had expressed genuine concern about the young man's ability to govern, but in fact the whole of the government had been so thoroughly shaken by Yoritomo's unexpected death that it was left to his widow, Masa-ko, to form a provisional government together with her father Hojo Tokimasa.

Masa-ko comes over as a very strong-willed woman. She had entered the religious life on her husband's death, as was the custom of the times, but her vows do not seem to have diminished her political skills and ambi-

One of the most historic places associated with the samurai is the Tsurugaoka Hachiman Shrine at Kamakura. It is always thronged with visitors. It is dedicated to Hachiman, the God of War, and was particularly honoured by the Minamoto clan, although this picture illustrates two tragic aspects of the history of that great samurai family. In the foreground is the dancing platform where Shizuka Gozen, the lover of the fugitive Minamoto Yoshitsune, was forced to dance for Yoshitsune's brother, Yoritomo, the first Shogun of Japan. Shizuka defiantly sang a song in praise of Yoshitsune, an act which enraged the dictator, and when she gave birth to a male child he had the baby murdered. To the left is a very large, and very old gingko tree, which may well be the actual one behind which lurked the assassin of the third and last Minamoto Shogun, Sanetomo, one snowy day in 1219.

tions, for she is referred to as *ama shogun*, the 'Nun Shogun'. Her provisional government, however, was not a success in bringing about the unity the country required and, when Yoriie was eventually proclaimed Shogun in 1202, little had been done to assist the headstrong young man in his rule of the warriors. Then Yoriie became gravely ill and within a year had been forced to retire, sick and humiliated, from the post of Shogun. He withdrew totally from public life and entered a monastery, only to be assassinated in 1204, probably at the instigation of his grandfather, Hojo Tokimasa.

Yoriie had a son, but the Hojo influence in the *bakufu* was so strong that his succession was passed over in favour of Yoriie's younger brother Sanetomo, who was then only 12 years old. Sanetomo became the third and last Minamoto Shogun and, as he was a minor, a Regent was necessary, a role Hojo Tokimasa was ready to fulfil. Tokimasa therefore became the first of a long line of *shikken*, the Hojo Regents, who ruled behind a nominal Shogun for a century and a half.

But even with the power of the Minamoto so dramatically curtailed, Sanetomo was doomed to enjoy for a very short time the honours of office. In the New Year of 1219 Sanetomo proceeded to the Tsurugaoka Hachiman Shrine in Kamakura to give thanks to Hachiman, the patron deity of the Minamoto, for the favours which his clan had received. As he was walking down the snow-covered steps of the shrine, a figure jumped out from behind a gingko tree and stabbed him to death. He was 26 years old. Legend has embellished the facts of his murder, which was as much a tragedy for Japanese culture as it was for the family of Minamoto.

Sanetomo was a noted poet, and legend tells of how he was warned of the threat to his life, but declined his attendant's suggestion that he should wear armour under his robe. Instead he wrote a farewell poem, and left a lock of his hair behind as a memento.

His nephew Kugyo, whose succession had been ignored, was the natural suspect for instigating the murder plot, and the deed provided the perfect excuse for having him, the last in the Minamoto line, executed. This was the final act of the blood-letting that makes the clan of Minamoto sound like the subjects of Greek tragedy. For the next 100 years power was kept by the 'Nun Shogun's' family, the Hojo, who had so thoroughly eclipsed them.

The Jokyu War

The establishment of the Shogunate may have weakened the Imperial power, but little could negate the magic in the name of the divine Emperor, and we see throughout samurai history successive Emperors of Japan, sometimes manipulated and reduced to ceremony, sometimes defiant and proud, but always exerting the charisma that comes from unquestioned legitimacy. The fall of the Minamoto showed the comparatively weak base of any alternative ruler.

The great problem which faced the rule of the Hojo *shikken* was to find a succession of suitable candidates for Shogun, in whose names they could rule as Regent, so it was almost inevitable that the Imperial family should

PLATE 6 *Hojo Yasutoki, in 'half-armour', inspects heads after the Jokyu Rebellion, 1221*

From ancient times the surest proof that a samurai had performed the task with which he had been entrusted was for him to return to his master bearing the severed head of the enemy. Elaborate rituals grew up over how heads were presented, prepared and examined. The business of preparing severed heads was traditionally done by the women of the clan, and there exist accounts of how the heads were washed, drained of blood and mounted on a spiked wooden board. The hair would be neatly combed from the mess which battle would have caused and tied with white paper into the traditional samurai pigtail. The heads would be anointed with perfume by waving an incense burner under them, and cosmetics applied to recreate the colours they would have possessed in life. The final touch was provided by tying a slip of paper to each pigtail, giving the name of the dead samurai, the name of the samurai whose 'trophy' the head had become, and any other relevant details. In the case of a shaven-headed monk the absence of a pigtail meant that a hole had to be made in the ear-lobe to take the identifying document!

Head-viewing ceremonies could be very elaborate, as they were an important part of public relations. By head-viewing, a victorious general was given the opportunity of commenting upon an ally's achievements and making a forcible point to newly subordinate clans of the folly of opposing such a glorious band of samurai.

This plate is a reconstruction of the head-viewing ceremony that must have taken place following the collapse of ex-Emperor Go-Toba's Jokyu Rebellion of 1221. The victorious general, Hojo Yasutoki, sits on a tiger-skin rug on a camp stool in 'undress armour', which shows what was worn under the main body-armour of the *yoroi*. The extent of the sleeve bag on the left arm is clearly seen, and also how the separate portion of the *yoroi* fitted under the right arm. His *eboshi* is a courtier style, which is much larger than that normally worn under a helmet. The footsoldiers wear simple body-armours.

The label on the monk's head reads 'The head of a brave warrior monk: Hojo Yasutoki'. The other labels credit their trophies to Yasutoki's uncle, Hojo Tokifusa, who also took part in the downfall of Go-Toba's rebellion.

try to take advantage of this potential weakness whenever possible, and the early thirteenth century provided such a challenge in the person of the ex-Emperor Go-Toba. The Emperor Go-Toba had succeeded to the throne in 1184, at the age of 4, and soon learned the lesson of all Emperors that true power only came about following abdication, when they could rule behind the scenes, freed from the long round of religious ritual, which, as living god, the Emperor was required to perform. He was still too young to become such a Retired, or 'Cloistered' Emperor when Go-Shirakawa died in 1192, and 1192 was also the year when Yoritomo achieved the Shogunate, reducing all Imperial power to a very low ebb. He eventually managed to abdicate in 1198, and tested his new powers by appointing his infant son, Tsuchimikado, to the vacant throne without asking permission from Kamakura. Yoritomo was much annoyed, but before he could assert his Shogunal authority he had suffered the fatal accident which was eventually to destroy the Minamoto clan. Go-Toba played a careful game through the troubled years of Yoriie and Sanetomo and was, in fact, on very good terms with the latter, as he shared his love for poetry, but when Sanetomo was murdered Go-Toba realised that the Hojo's need for a puppet successor to the Shogunate might provide an opportunity for the throne to assert itself more strongly than it had for half a century.

The first suggestion the Regent Hojo Yoshitoki made was that one of Go-Toba's own sons should become Shogun. Go-Toba refused the apparent honour, as he saw the potential danger that could arise if there was a succession dispute when an Imperial prince was Shogun. He then turned down a candidate from the Fujiwara family and, in fact, managed to frustrate for several years every one of the Hojo's attempts to have a Shogun appointed. In the meantime he openly courted the favour of any rival samurai families who might one day join him in armed struggle against the Shogunate for the restoration of Imperial power. There were a number of clans in the Western half of the country who could be persuaded to support him. Some were the remnants of the once mighty Taira, others mere opportunists who had suffered from the Minamoto or Hojo ascendancy. But they were only one factor in Go-Toba's scheme. The other involved seeking support from that most dangerous and unreliable of weapons: the warrior monks.

The armed clergy had been very peaceful during Yoritomo's lifetime. The first Shogun had been generous with his gifts towards rebuilding temples

PLATE 7   *A samurai commander awaits the Mongol Invasion in 1274*

His armour has altered to no appreciable degree since the time of the Gempei War, evidence that, until the coming of the Mongols, there was little to challenge any samurai assumptions about the nature of warfare. He is seated on an armour box, into which his *yoroi* would be packed for careful storage.

damaged during the Gempei War, but in common with every other faction in the land they had become rebellious when the Shogunate was seen to be weakening. In 1219 the old rivalry between the Enryaku-ji and Miidera once more flared into life, and the Kofuku-ji of Nara also began to rediscover its warlike traditions. A land dispute provided the excuse for the Mount Hiei monks to try their mettle against Go-Toba, and in the manner which had been so successful with his predecessors they descended on Kyoto to lay their grievances before the throne with threats and riot. But times had changed. Instead of being cowed by the threats of divine vengeance Go-Toba scattered their incursion by a well-timed assault from the palace samurai. However, in further contrast, he followed up this lesson not with a revenge attack on the Enryaku-ji, but with a carefully worded call to arms against the Shogun on the Emperor's behalf, asking them to unite against the warriors from the East who had shown so little respect for the monks' militant and religious tradition.

Go-Toba began an open revolt against the *bakufu* on 6 June 1221, when by solemn decree the Regent Hojo Yoshitoki was declared to be an outlaw. Three days later a further statement was made decreeing the whole of the Eastern half of the country to be in a state of rebellion. Both announcements were designed to catch Kamakura unawares, but a relay of fast messengers had managed to warn Yoshitoki of the former proclamation by the day the latter was issued, and he immediately took steps to assure himself of the loyalty of neighbouring samurai. His support was solid, and plans were quickly made.

Their first consideration was one of defence, of closing the passes of Ashigara and Hakone, in the Mount Fuji area, to prevent any advance on Kamakura by the Tokaido Road. But bolder spirits argued that attack would be the better response to the Imperial forces, so a plan was drawn up involving a march on Kyoto by means of the three practical routes: the Tokaido along the Sea Coast, the Nakasendo through the central mountains, and a wide sweep off the Nakasendo going round Lake Biwa to approach Kyoto from the north. This third column met with the most resistance. There were still several clans in the Hokurikudo region who had not accepted Kamakura rule, and the Hojo forces were held for a while at Tonamiyama, the site of Yoshinaka's fierce battle in the Gempei War, but this fighting in Echizen Province proved to be the only serious resistance Kamakura faced and, by the time the Hokurikudo column had fought its way down from the mountains, the capital was already in *bakufu* hands. The Imperial troops were largely inexperienced and had little will to fight the warriors from the East, whose fathers' reputations had preceded their advance Westwards. Many of the defenders fled from their positions in Mino and Omi Provinces, putting their trust in the natural moat of the Uji River, so for the third time in half a century the two bridges of Uji and Seta echoed to the din of war. But this time there were no warrior monks to stride nimbly with their *naginata* across the broken planking, for in spite of all Go-Toba's pleas the *sohei* of the Enryaku-ji remained on Mount Hiei,

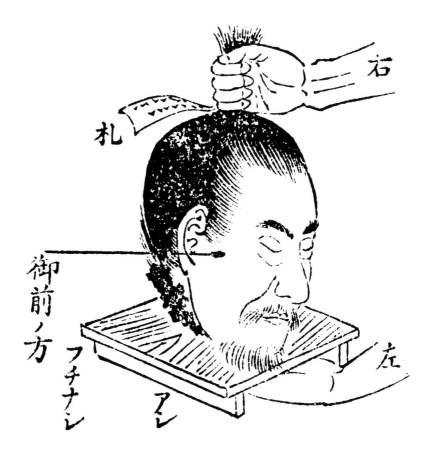

This illustration from the *Gunyoki* is one of several recommended ways of displaying a severed head. Note the carefully delineated positions of the hands, the identification label, and the spiked wooden board.

and it was an almost totally secular force that attempted to hold the line on 5 July. The fighting of this, the Third Battle of Uji, lasted all through a hot summer's day, but by nightfall Hojo Yasutoki's men had taken Seta, in spite of heavy losses, and the road to Kyoto was open.

Hojo Yasutoki (who was Yoshitoki's eldest son) made a grand entrance on the following day, 6 July, his scouts having prepared the city for his arrival. Unfortunately many of the retreating troops, and some of the Hojo's advance guard, had burned and looted as they went, and the Imperial capital presented a sorry spectacle when the *bakufu* army received the surrender of Go-Toba.

Thus ended the brief Jokyu Rebellion, so called from the era name of Jokyu (1219–1221). The *bakufu's* triumph was due largely to its boldness in advancing. Had their original consideration of a defensive strategy been put into effect it is quite likely that Go-Toba's support would have continued to grow to an extent dangerous to the Shogunate. In the event Go-Toba was exiled and the *bakufu* confiscated the largest area of defeated enemies' lands since the fall of the Taira. The Minamoto may have passed away, but even without the figurehead of a Shogun to lead them, the Hojo *shikken* proved that the institution of warrior government which Yoritomo had established was sufficiently sound to withstand even a challenge from an ex-Emperor. It was to be 50 years before any other military threat arose and, when it came, it was very different from anything the samurai had faced before.

The Mongol Invasions

The attempts to invade Japan made in the thirteenth century by the Mongol Emperor of China, Kublai Khan, are unique events in Japanese history. The ferocity with which the attacks were launched, the strength and bravery of the resistance, and the final, sudden and spectacular end of the Mongol fleet by a typhoon fill some of the noblest pages in the history of the samurai.

Kublai Khan, it must be admitted, had reasons for invading Japan other than mere personal ambition. The pressing demands of various civil wars had caused *bakufu* officials in Kyushu responsible for maintaining law and order to turn a blind eye towards a frequent abuse of their authority – overseas piracy. The coastal areas of China and Korea were frequently ravaged by Japanese pirates and Kublai Khan's first letter to the Japanese government was simply a request that such activities be curtailed. It was only when he received no reply to this demand that his theme became one of demanding tribute from the Japanese people. It was fortunate for Japan that it faced the challenge under the Hojo Regent Tokimune, the seventh of the *shikken* and a capable and resourceful samurai. It was also free from civil strife so it was possible to make a positive response to the threat.

PLATE 8   *Kusunoki Masashige defends Chihaya castle, 1333*

The mid-fourteenth century is dominated by the epic struggle of the War Between the Courts. This plate depicts the greatest hero of that war, the loyal samurai, Kusunoki Masashige (1294–1336). He is shown conducting operations in the forests around Mount Kongo, where he established his bases of Akasaka and Chihaya, and defied the Kamakura *bakufu*. His defence of Chihaya, in particular, is regarded as one of the three classic sieges of samurai history when defenders withstood enormous odds and never capitulated.

Kusunoki Masashige is wearing what is basically a *yoroi* armour, but with several developments. First, the *yoroi* has lost something of its stiff, box-like appearance and fits the body more closely, like a footsoldier's *haramaki*. It still has the

tsurubashiri, the leather 'breastplate', and Masashige's is very beautifully decorated. An *agemaki* bow would connect all the pieces from the rear.

The helmet's *shikoro* is now much flatter, which would allow the wearer to turn his head more easily, while its greater sweep still allows good protection. His helmet bowl is neater. The conical rivets have disappeared, and it is ornamented by a particularly fine set of *kuwagata*.

It is in his leg protection that we notice the greatest difference. The *suneate* are much heavier and extend up higher to surround the knee. The thighs are now protected by an early form of *haidate*, or thigh-guards, which are of exactly similar construction to the plates of the body-armour, and fasten behind the leg. Bearskin boots have given way to the more practical *waraji*, straw

sandals, and *tabi*, the traditional Japanese sock with a divided toe.

The long, red-lacquered bow is well represented here, for even though horsemanship is irrelevant in the wooded mountains, the samurai is still an archer. Note the waterproof quiver, and the arrow being brought to the bow from the righthand side, in the Japanese style of archery.

The figure is based on the modern statue of Kusunoki Masashige at the Kanshin-ji near Chihaya, where Masashige's head is buried, and painted scrolls kept at the Nampi-an Kannon-ji, also near Chihaya. Details of his body-armour are taken from a *yoroi* of the period preserved in the Kasuga Shrine at Nara which is supposed to have been owned by Masashige. Details of accessories and leg-armour are taken from a sketch by Sasama.

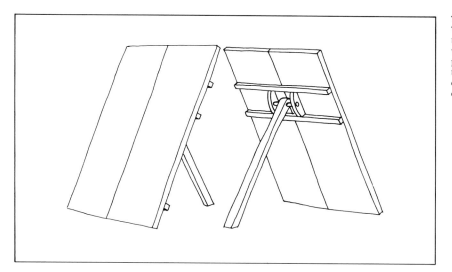

The wooden shield
This type of wooden shield was used throughout the samurai period. It was planted in the ground, and provided protection for missile troops. Contemporary illustrations often depict them with *mon* painted on the front.

The first attack came in 1274. The Khan swelled his army with sub-servient Koreans and packed them into several hundred ships. They first attacked Tsushima, the island mid-way between Japan and Korea, where the garrison of 200 men under So Sukekuni, grandson of Taira Tomomori, who was drowned at Dan-no-Ura, fought bravely until they were overwhelmed. The next island, Ikishima, suffered a similar fate. Their attempt on the Japanese mainland (in fact the large Southern island of Kyushu) took place near the present-day city of Hakata. The Japanese resistance was fierce, in spite of several surprises that the Mongols were able to inflict on the defenders, for their military traditions were totally different from the samurai. The Japanese were used to a style of warfare that laid great emphasis on individual combat, while the Mongols con-trolled, by drum and gong, huge bodies of troops packed together in phalanxes, and fired arrows in huge random showers. There were no noble opponents to challenge to individual combat, just an anonymous alien horde of Mongols, Chinese and Koreans. Their enemies also had some form of fire-bomb, flung by catapult, which is illustrated in a painted scroll of the period. The samurai very quickly adapted to all these new threats and their fighting skills forced the Mongols into a tactical withdrawal. A storm caught the fleet as it left, causing much damage, and the first invasion came to a end.

The Mongols returned in 1281 with a much bigger armada. By this time coastal defences had been strengthened, including the building of a long stone wall, and the Japanese also managed to harass the fleet as it approached the coast. They sailed out in little ships and mounted daring hit-and-run raids under the cover of darkness. On one occasion thirty samurai swam out to a ship, cut off the heads of the crew, and swam back. Apart from the direct damage the raids were able to inflict, these raids also had the considerable benefit of forcing the Mongol fleet to remain for long periods lying safely offshore in the stifling heat of summer. As the days wore on, the typhoon season approached and, on 15 August 1281, the Japanese prayers were answered when a fierce storm, the *kami-kaze,* blew up. It surpassed in intensity the storm that had damaged the fleet in 1274 and smashed the Mongol fleet so totally that they never returned.

Few episodes in Japanese history are as proudly recalled as the defeat of the Mongols. To the defeat of the Mongols we owe the phrase *kami-kaze* (divine wind), an expression which came to have such a different meaning in 1945, when it linked the threat of an American invasion with the failed attempts of 1274 and 1281, inspiring a new generation to resist an assault on the homeland. It has in it all the finest elements of Japanese tradition. There are noble samurai, united against a common enemy, and fired by a common spirit which later manifests itself in the cataclysm of the holy typhoon. For once in their history the samurai are not fighting each other, but become Japanese before anything else.

The War of Emperor Go-Daigo

The defeat of the Mongols saw the samurai united as never before, yet within two generations they were to be divided on the most fundamental issue of their tradition: that of the legitimacy of their divine Emperor. The attempts of a young Emperor, Go-Daigo, to rule, rather than merely to reign, caused a schism in the Imperial House, and a long civil war.

The destruction of the Mongol fleet may have been a military victory for the *bakufu,* but one long-term result was to produce severe economic strain on the government. No one could be sure that the Mongols would not return, so they faced the need to be prepared against foreign invasion for half a century. Rewards also had to be paid to samurai who had fought in the wars, and there were no freshly conquered lands to redistribute, as would have been the case in a civil war. Numerous claims were made. One samurai even had a long narrative scroll painted depicting his exploits as an aid to his demands. Temples and shrines too, mindful of the miraculous intervention of the *kami-kaze,* put in claims for reward as a mark of appreciation of their spiritual efforts. Hojo Tokimune, whose leadership had proved such an inspiration to the samurai, died in 1284, and his successors failed completely to inherit his abilities and drive. As at the time of Jokyu, the Imperial family saw the *bakufu's* weakness as their opportunity.

From 1318 the incumbent of the throne had been the Emperor Go-Daigo, or 'Daigo the Second'. He had succeeded at the age of 30, and made it quite clear that he was a proud and ambitious man. It is difficult to tell at what stage Go-Daigo began to think of achieving his aim of absolute control by overthrowing the *bakufu,* but there is circumstantial evidence from the very beginning of his reign. On the day of his accession he sent his son, Prince Morinaga, to be a monk at Mount Hiei. There can have been no reason for removing his heir from the mainstream of politics other than to use him as a way of gaining support from the warrior monks, and this was confirmed in 1328 when he promoted Prince Morinaga to be Abbot of Mount Hiei. Prince Morinaga, an accomplished samurai warrior, is referred to as 'The Prince of the Great Pagoda' in the *Taiheiki*, the great war chronicle of the time.

In 1321 Go-Daigo abolished the hallowed tradition of the Cloistered Emperor, making clear his determination to rule directly as Emperor. Contemporary chroniclers speak well of the reforms he introduced, and contrast the lack of action the *bakufu* took against them with their speedy reaction to Go-Toba's similar attempts at independence of thought and action. There was an equally sluggish reply when the *bakufu* received hard evidence that Go-Daigo was preparing to challenge the *bakufu* rule by force. When they eventually sent an army from Kamakura, Go-Daigo had full knowledge of their approach and sufficient time to plan accordingly. As well as courting Mount Hiei he had made generous offerings to the Buddhist institutions of Nara, a wise move, considering that the *bakufu* controlled a much higher proportion of the land than had been the case under Go-Toba. In fact the governors of over half the provinces in Japan were Hojo kinsmen, so armed support from monks would be crucial.

Go-Daigo's plots were revealed to the *bakufu* in September 1331, and Go-Daigo left Kyoto for the safety of the Todai-ji in Nara. He took with him the symbols of his sovereignty – the Imperial Regalia, or at least that part of them he was able to secure. As the legitimacy of the Imperial claimant was inseparable from the question of the possession of the 'Crown Jewels', it is worth spending a little time discussing what these regalia are. They consist of three objects: the Mirror, the Sword and the Jewels. The Mirror and the Sword that are actually transmitted from one Emperor to another have been, from ancient times, replicas of the originals, which are kept respectively at Ise and the Atsuta Shrine near Nagoya. In 1185, as noted previously, this 'replica' Sword was lost at the Battle of Dan-no-Ura and, in 1210, another replica had to be made. But to all intents and purposes these replicas were treated as if they were the real thing. They were, after all, the actual objects that had passed from hand to hand as the legitimate sign of kingship. The Imperial Jewels, however, were never copied, and it was with the original Jewels, and the other 'official copies' that Go-Daigo fled to Nara.

The Todai-ji monks expressed concern that they could not withstand an attack by the *bakufu*, so Go-Daigo moved on to Kasagi, a mountain some 600 feet high overlooking the Kizugawa. It, too, was the home of warrior monks, who welcomed him and strengthened their position against an expected attack. The *bakufu* forces however first concentrated their attacks on Mount Hiei and 'The Prince of the Great Pagoda', and overcame their initially slow response to the crisis by forcing Prince Morinaga to flee for his life, thus isolating Go-Daigo at Kasagi. While the attacks continued on Kasagi, the *bakufu* made moves in the political sphere and tried to negotiate, hoping to persuade Go-Daigo to abdicate and enter a monastery.

When he refused to do so the drastic decision was made to raise another member of the Imperial family to the throne. Go-Daigo had therefore been officially deposed, but he still had the Regalia, so the actual enthronement ceremony had to be postponed until the items were recaptured.

It is at this point in the war that we first hear the name of Kusunoki Masashige, a samurai whose skill in warfare, and above all his loyalty to the legitimate Emperor, make him the model of perfection for all samurai. Little is known of his background, except that he was from an obscure warrior family in Kawachi. He suddenly enters history as Go-Daigo's staunchest supporter, and fights for him from a stronghold called Akasaka in Kawachi, a fortified encampment ('castle' is a misleading description) in the Western foothills of Mount Kongo. Here he was joined by Prince Morinaga, who helped Kusunoki defend it against a determined attack by the *bakufu*. The loyalists were short of troops and soon only the terrain frustrated the attackers' attempts. The 'castle' fell on about 20 November 1331 but, instead of making a last-ditch stand and an honourable suicide, Kusunoki Masashige and Prince Morinaga both escaped, the latter to a monastery in Nara where, according to legend, he hid in a large wooden chest. But bad news awaited them. On his way to join them in Akasaka, Go-Daigo had been captured and taken to Rokuhara, the *bakufu* headquarters in Kyoto. A few months later, in 1332, he was exiled to the island of Oki. It appeared to all that Go-Daigo's revolt had been crushed as thoroughly as that of Go-Toba, and that further resistance was useless.

Had it not been for Kusunoki Masashige and Prince Morinaga this latest attempt at Imperial restoration would indeed have been over. However, Prince Morinaga, who had by now abandoned his monkish habit and returned to the life of the son of the legitimate sovereign, based himself with an army of warrior monks in the mountainous district of Yoshino, far to the South of Kyoto, and sent out calls to arms to any samurai clans who would support him. Meanwhile his former comrade in arms, Kusunoki Masashige, continued to demonstrate how successful a continuing resistance to the *bakufu* might be. He built a new stronghold at Akasaka, Kami-Akasaka, higher up the mountain than the previous one, and inflicted such damage on the *bakufu* armies attempting to take it that orders were issued for the execution of the Prince and Kusunoki, rescinding previous commands merely for their capture.

The resistance greatly surprised the *bakufu*. Early in 1333 three armies left Kamakura to chastise the Imperial rebels. The first, commanded by a Hojo kinsman called Aso, was to attack Kami-Akasaka along the Kawachi road. The second, under Osaragi, was to attack Yoshino. Both were ultimately successful, though Kami-Akasaka only fell when its water supply was cut, and Prince Morinaga fled to Koya-san, a remote and peaceful monastery, the centre of the Shingon sect of Buddhism. The two victorious *bakufu* armies then joined the third force (under Nagoshi) for a full-scale assault on Kusunoki's newest fortification at Chihaya, to which he had withdrawn.

Chihaya was also on Mount Kongo but much stronger than Kami-Akasaka and, to the *bakufu's* amazement and chagrin, held out against every attempt to take it. The great army of the Hojo was practically immobilised in front of this makeshift mountain fortress. All of Kusunoki Masashige's skills were brought to bear in enticing the enemy to attack him in places where the terrain, with which Kusunoki's men were familiar, proved as much of a hindrance as the loyalists' arrows. Huge boulders were balanced on cliff edges, ready to be dislodged into a pass full of *bakufu* soldiers. The *bakufu* samurai were tempted into night attacks and picked off at will. Pits were dug across paths, felled trees provided almost insurmountable obstacles and, with every day that the *bakufu* spent frustrated in the forests round Chihaya, more and more samurai clans were shown that Kamakura could be challenged, and encouraged to try their hand.

In fact Chihaya was never captured and its continuing existence inspired the exiled Go-Daigo to return in the Spring of 1333. He landed in Hoki Province, on the Japan Sea coast West of Kyoto, and the local response to his return so alarmed Kamakura that the *bakufu* sent to oppose him two of their ablest generals: Nagoshi Takaie, a Hojo kinsman, and Ashikaga Takauji, who was descended from Minamoto stock and leader of one of the wealthiest families in the East.

They set out separately from Kyoto but, on his way to Hoki, Nagoshi was attacked by a guerrilla army similar to Kusunoki's under Akamatsu Norimura and was killed. His troops fled back to Kyoto, where they were absorbed by Takauji, who now had sole command of all the *bakufu* forces in Western Japan. Takauji realised what an opportunity had come his way. Unlike any other of Go-Daigo's supporters his Ashikaga family had the lineage which would enable them to accept the position of Shogun from a captive, or merely grateful, Emperor. Takauji's future lay with Go-Daigo, not the Hojo Regency. Kusunoki's defence of Chihaya was daily exposing the weakness of the Hojo state, so, declaring himself to be for the Emperor, Ashikaga Takauji turned from a pursuit of Go-Daigo and launched his army against the *bakufu's* Kyoto headquarters at Rokuhara. The surprise element was total and he succeeded in capturing the city for the rightful Emperor. Go-Daigo, still apparently in possession of the Imperial Jewels, returned in state to his throne. He generously allowed the Hojo-nominated Emperor to abdicate peacefully and retire to estates Go-Daigo made available to him, and set about restoring his previous position.

When the news of the *bakufu's* collapse in the West reached Chihaya, the siege was abandoned and many of the samurai went over to the Imperial camp. The Hojo strength was now largely confined to Eastern Japan and its doom was almost complete. In June 1333 a warrior called Nitta Yoshisada joined the Imperial supporters. He collected other opportunistic clans about him in Kozuke Province and descended from the mountains on to the *bakufu* capital of Kamakura. He divided his army into three and the columns slowly forced their way through the narrow passes that act as a natural defence for the city. Nitta Yoshisada is credited with obtaining

Samurai warrior, armed with a sword. His quiver is covered with a cloth bag to protect the arrows from rain. (From the *Gunyoki*)

Footsoldier archer, wearing a *do-maru*. (From the *Gunyoki*)

divine intervention from the Sun-Goddess, who, in response to Yoshisada's offering of his sword, caused the sea to roll back so that his army could attack Kamakura from the coastal route. After 5 days of fighting through the man-made tunnels and cuttings of Kamakura, the last of the Hojo *shikken*, along with several hundred of his men, withdrew to a small Buddhist temple, where they committed suicide as Kamakura blazed about them.

The fall of Kamakura marked the end of the Hojo Regency and the eclipse of Kamakura as the administrative capital. From now on the focus would be the Imperial capital of Kyoto. Go-Daigo's restoration of the Imperial power was complete.

Footsoldier archer, wearing a *do-maru* and carrying a bow. (From the *Gunyoki*)

Early Muromachi Period

The return of authority to Kyoto marks the beginning of the 'Muromachi Period' in Japanese history, because the seat of the subsequent Ashikaga *bakufu* was a palace on Muromachi Avenue in Kyoto. It is convenient to subdivide this long span of time into shorter units, the first of which may be regarded as ending with the Onin War in 1467, when the capital itself was the battlefield.

The Triumph of the Ashikaga

The destruction of Kamakura in 1333 confirmed Go-Daigo as supreme ruler – for a time. The Hojo *shikken* may have disappeared for ever, but the institution of *bakufu* rule, the government of the samurai by the samurai and largely for the samurai, had attractions that only began to be appreciated once it had ended. The crisis for Go-Daigo came when he was required to make rewards to the samurai warriors who had served him so well. There were many claimants and problems of finance similar to those that had undermined the Hojo after the Mongol Wars. Many were disappointed. None had more to gain than Ashikaga Takauji, and none was more dissatisfied with his reward.

Ashikaga Takauji, as we noted in the last chapter, was of Minamoto

PLATE 9   *A footsoldier in a stockade in the Yoshino Mountains, 1348*

The samurai of the War Between the Courts were supported, as samurai had always been, by large numbers of footsoldiers. In this plate we see one such footsoldier taking guard from a parapet of a fortress high in the mountains of Yoshino, where the Southern Emperors held sway. His body-armour is a *hara-ate*, a very rudimentary form of protection, which consists of the front section of a samurai's *do*, without any unnecessary appendages, to which are attached three short skirt pieces, or *kusazuri*, the longer of which is central to protect the groin area. The *hara-ate* had no back-plate and was tied diagonally at the rear by stout straps, which appear to be well padded across the shoulders.

He wears two simple *kote* on his sleeves and, as it is summer, he wears a rough pair of shorts and simple, heavy cloth *suneate* or shin-protectors. Bare feet are considered adequate by this hardy warrior.

His headgear is still the traditional *eboshi* cap and the metal face-protector. His *naginata* has a particularly fierce-looking blade. The figure is based on a sketch by Sasama, and the details of the *hara-ate* on contemporary illustrations.

The great hero, Kusunoki Masashige, bids farewell to his son Masatsura as he prepares to leave to fight his last battle at Minatogawa. This poignant moment, frequently reproduced in Japanese art, is made all the more moving by the knowledge that the young boy was to follow his father in death at the Battle of Shijo-Nawate only 12 years later. This relief painting is at the Kannon-ji near Chihaya-Akasaka, and is reproduced here by kind permission of the Chief Priest.

descent, which entitled his family to the position of Shogun. In late 1335 he was ordered to re-take Kamakura, which had been recaptured in the name of the Hojo by a surviving son of the late Regent. Takauji vanquished the rebel with little difficulty but, once established in the East, his behaviour became very suspicious and, in February 1336, he was reported to be marching on Kyoto to set himself up as a new Shogun. Takauji cleverly exploited the old rivalry of the warrior monks by allying himself with Miidera, which was currently enjoying one of its periodic squabbles

46

This vivid oil painting of the Battle of Minatogawa was completed during the Meiji Period, when the revival of interest in Kusunoki Masashige as the archetype of loyal service to the Emperor was at its height. The painting, which is much damaged, hangs in the museum of the Minatogawa Shrine on the site of the conflict.

with Mount Hiei. But his attempt was not a success. His advance Westwards was opposed by various loyalists and the Mount Hiei monks, and Takauji was defeated. He was driven out of the capital and pursued as far as the narrow straits that divide Honshu from Kyushu, where he was forced to cross to the Southern island for support.

In the majority of cases in samurai history such a severe defeat proves total, but Ashikaga began to play upon the grievances of Kyushu samurai against their contemporaries on Honshu. Some local clans eventually rallied behind him and his numbers swelled greatly after a victory at the Battle of Tadara Beach. By early June 1336 Ashikaga Takauji felt sufficiently confident to return to Honshu.

The advance of the Ashikaga host by sea and by land caused panic in the Court, and a fearful Go-Daigo ordered a stand to be made at the Minato River, where it flows into the sea at the present-day city of Kobe. Nitta Yoshisada had already taken his stand here to await the enemy, but Kusunoki Masashige warned Go-Daigo that to attempt to fight a pitched battle would lead to disaster. He suggested instead that Go-Daigo should leave Kyoto for Mount Hiei and its loyal monks, while Kusunoki conducted a campaign of harassment against the Ashikaga in much the same way that he had kept the *bakufu* forces at bay on Mount Kongo. These tactics had worked before, but one gets the impression that Go-Daigo's victory had made him much less inclined to flee from place to

47

place. The Court, with Go-Daigo's support, refused to accept Kusunoki's suggestion. They were decided upon a battle and, not wishing to take issue with the Emperor whom he had served so loyally, Masashige had no choice but to agree, and rode off to share in what he knew would be an inevitable defeat.

The Battle of Minatogawa

The Battle of Minatogawa took place on a hot, humid day. Kusunoki took a stand with his back to the Minato River against the advance of Takauji's son, Tadayoshi. The seaborne force, under Hosokawa, attempted to land to the loyalists' rear to cut off their retreat. Kusunoki's resistance was fierce and the battle could have gone either way, had it not been for a fatal error of judgement on the part of Nitta Yoshisada, who withdrew from the front line when Hosokawa succeeded in landing at his rear. Soon Nitta was driven from the field and the whole of the Ashikaga army closed in around Kusunoki Masashige. He committed suicide as soon as it was seen that the day was hopeless. It is interesting to note that, on several occasions before, Masashige had been defeated and returned to fight another day. Why was Minatogawa different? Why had the loss of Kami-Akasaka not obliged him to commit suicide to atone for his failure? The answer lies in the notion of samurai loyalty. In the campaigns around Mount Kongo it had been the will of the Emperor that Masashige should keep on fighting, fleeing from mountain to mountain. That was the nature of the loyal service that was required of him. But at Minatogawa such a course of action had been ruled out, and it was the inevitable consequence of the Emperor's decision that Masashige should fight to the last.

PLATE 10   *A samurai in leather-covered armour with a* no-dachi, *ca 1410*

The bitter days of the early fifteenth century are recalled in this plate, which illustrates armour contemporary with the murder of the Shogun Ashikaga Yoshinori by Akamatsu Mitsusuke (1388–1441).

This unusual leather-covered armour, the original of which is in the Tokyo National Museum, shows a perfectly logical development of armour in which all the outer surfaces of the plates, except the bottom one, were covered in a sheet of leather to protect the individual cords underneath. In a sense this style anticipates the more rigid solid plates that were to make their appearance in the following century.

The armour has a sombre, workaday appearance, and must have had much less flexibility than the traditional styles. The old *sendan-no-ita* and *kyubi-no-ita* of the *yoroi* have been replaced by two small appendages that are merely functional, and cover the cords that fasten the armour together on the collar bones against a sword stroke. Note the large *sode* still being worn, and the adoption of two armoured sleeves, any pretence of being a mounted archer having been completely discarded. His shin-guards are big and clumsy, and he has obviously decided that he has no need of *haidate*.

His helmet is quite remarkable. The wide sweeping *shikoro* has reached its ultimate level, being almost horizontal (cf. Plates 7 and 8), making the wearer include an additional, smaller set of leather(?) plates closer to the head.

His wicked-looking long sword is a *no-dachi*, which augments his *katana* and *tanto* in his belt. The *no-dachi*, which resembles a *naginata* more than it does a sword, was carried in a long scabbard over the shoulder. One of the characters in the famous film *The Seven Samurai* has a *no-dachi* as his preferred weapon, though his is not as large as this example, which is authentic.

He died as a true samurai, which is how he is remembered, motivated entirely by loyalty to the Emperor, in complete contrast to the machinations of Ashikaga Takauji, whose motives were solely ones of self-interest and the advancement of his family. This, at any rate, is how Kusunoki and Ashikaga have been represented throughout history, and there is no other samurai who can better represent the ideals of the warrior than Kusunoki Masashige.

The Emperors of Yoshino

Ashikaga Takauji, of course, had a different prize from that of immortality. It was to his family that the title of Shogun was to pass, but there was some more bitter fighting before he could be assured of his triumph. Takauji thus became the first Ashikaga Shogun. He had first-hand experience of the remoteness of Kamakura when independent-minded Emperors were abroad, so Takauji took the administrative seat of military government back to the home of the Imperial family and set up his headquarters in the Muromachi district of Kyoto.

After Minatogawa, Go-Daigo was forced to take refuge on Mount Hiei, just as Kusunoki had originally suggested. Takauji turned all his forces on to this mountain stronghold and, according to the chronicles, was only able to secure the person of Go-Daigo by means of trickery, as the *sohei* fought savagely. There were tricks on both sides, however, for Go-Daigo's supporters were to claim for the next half century that the Regalia which Go-Daigo surrendered to Takauji, and which were thereupon used for the enthronement of the Ashikaga nominee, the Emperor Kogon, were in fact counterfeit. Go-Daigo thus maintained that, even though he had been deposed for a second time, he was still the rightful Emperor and, in fact, made explicit statements of it in various written communications. In 1337 he frustrated the Ashikaga by managing to escape from custody to the mountains of Yoshino, where he and his successors were to reign as rival Emperors until 1392. The cherry-tree clad hills of Yoshino had been the temporary refuge of Prince Morinaga and had a terrain ideally suited to defence. Go-Daigo also discovered that he had considerable support, notably from the survivors of the Kusunoki family. Masatsura, Masashige's son, carried on the fight after his father's death until he was cut down at the Battle of Shijo-Nawate in 1348.

Go-Daigo died in 1339. Prince Morinaga had pre-deceased him, so his younger son, Prince Norinaga, became the second 'Southern Emperor' Fighting between the two lines continued around the country till 1392, but towards the end many of the combatants had forgotten why they were fighting and changed allegiance from 'Northern' to 'Southern' Court whenever it suited their personal aspirations to do so. The lines were finally united under the third Ashikaga Shogun, Yoshimitsu, a skilled politician who organised trade with China and enjoyed the respect of all. It is to Yoshimitsu that we owe the building of the famous 'Golden Pavilion' which symbolised the glory of the Ashikaga, but his greatest achievement occurred in 1392 when he persuaded the rival Emperors to reconcile their differences and proposed a scheme whereby Go-Kameyama, the Southern Emperor, would abandon his claim to the throne in return for a guarantee that the succession would then alternate between the two lines. Go-Kameyama agreed, and the war ended, but in fact the mechanism of alternation was never put into operation. In 1412 the Northern Emperor, Go-Komatsu, abdicated in favour of his son, Shoko (1401–1428), and, when the latter died, the succession passed to another Northern Emperor, Go-Hanazono (1419–1470). Go-Kameyama's son, Prince Ogura, claimed his right to the throne, but was ignored by the Ashikaga *bakufu,* who had no intention of honouring the agreement. In fact there was never to be another 'Southern Emperor', and the Northern Court has provided every Emperor down to the present day.

Even though the reconciliation provided a much-needed peace, the supporters of the Yoshino Emperors knew they had been cheated and, no less than three times' in the next century, stubborn loyalists to the Southern Court attempted to restart the war, using the line of 'Southern Pretenders' which Prince Ogura was to produce. The first revolt, in 1413, was led by Kitabatake Mitsumasa on behalf of Prince Ogura himself, but the move was soon crushed. In 1428, with the accession of Go-Hanazono, Kitabatake tried again, supported by the latest in a long line of Kusunoki samurai, Mitsumasa. The plot involved assassinating the fifth Ashikaga Shogun, Yoshinori, but the scheme was discovered and Kusunoki was beheaded in 1429. The third, and final, attempt proved much more successful and, although a little known incident in Japanese history, it adds its own bizarre appendix to the story of Go-Daigo and the tales of samurai loyalty.

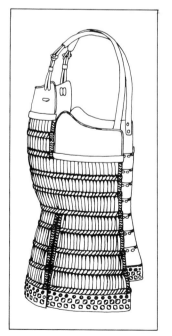

A *hara-ate*
A type of body armour, protecting only the torso and groin, suspended from cords at the shoulders. It was used by footsoldiers between *c.* 1300 and 1550.

The Heavenly King

By the fourth decade of the fifteenth century the Ashikaga Shogunate was entering a period of decline. Yoshimitsu had set it on a glittering peak of achievement, which his successors Yoshimochi and Yoshikazu consolidated, and it appeared that the sixth Shogun, Yoshinori, was also destined for glory. Yoshinori's end came, however, when he tried to curtail the growing power of the Akamatsu clan by transferring some territories from the then head of the clan, Mitsusuke (1381–1441), to Yoshinori's homosexual lover, Akamatsu Sadamura, a kinsman of Mitsusuke and his rival for clan leadership. To forestall this measure, Mitsusuke plotted the Shogun's death and, in the summer of 1441, invited Yoshinori to a celebration at his Kyoto mansion to mark the Akamatsu's recent defeat of the Yuki clan. The unsuspecting Shogun accepted the invitation and, when the party was at its height, two Akamatsu retainers released all the horses from the stables into the garden, where they kicked and bit each other and created a great uproar. Under cover of the confusion the Akamatsu samurai set on the Shogun and relieved him of his head. The assassins then calmly withdrew from Kyoto to their territories in Harima, leaving behind them (according to the chronicler of this so-called 'Kakitsu Affair') 'none to disembowel themselves and none to pursue', suggesting that the Akamatsu were not alone in their plotting. It was 3 days before a force could be assembled to ride off to bring them to justice, and even then the expeditionary force hesitated at the provincial border. Yamana Sozen (1404–1474) was the only samurai leader who decided to 'break ranks' and advance against the rebels, and was rewarded by being granted the Akamatsu's territories of Harima, Bizen and Mimasaka.

Yoshinori was succeeded by his son Yoshikatsu, who succeeded at the age of 8 and died at the age of 10, to be followed by his younger brother Yoshimasa, also 8 years old. Yoshimasa enjoyed a long 30-year reign as Shogun, filled with many aesthetic advances, much of which was to be offset by the virtual collapse of Shogunal authority. However, to return to the death of Yoshinori, one group that took advantage of the Akamatsu's appalling crime was the Southern Court adherents, then under the leadership of a certain Hino Arimitsu. On 16 October 1443, they broke into the Imperial Palace, set fire to some buildings and, in the confusion, made off with two items of Regalia, the replica Sword and the Jewels. They were hotly pursued and the Sword was recaptured after a skirmish near the Kiyomizu temple. They succeeded in presenting the Jewels to the heir of the Southern Court, Prince Takayoshi, sometimes known as Prince Manju-ji, who was living under the protection of the *sohei* of Mount Hiei. (There is in fact some confusion as to who the actors in this drama actually were. The 'Young Pretender' is referred to elsewhere as Prince Takahide. Other accounts credit the raid on the palace to Kusunoki Jiro Masahide, of whom little is known.) The immediate result of their efforts was a *bakufu* attack on Mount Hiei, which resulted in the Pretender's death. The Jewels were

PLATE 11 *A samurai, wearing a* haramaki, *enters a village, ca 1440*

This rear view of a group of samurai entering a village shows several points of detail about armour which are relevant from about 1440 to 1500. The helmet is of multi-plate construction, with a wide *shikoro*, though not so grotesquely so as Plate 10. His body armour is a *haramaki*, and the rear view shows the separate *kusazuri* that make it so different from a *yoroi*. This particular style of armour fastened down the middle of the back. The fastenings cannot be seen because they are concealed under the separate plate known as the *sei-ita*, referred to sometimes, for obvious reasons, as the 'coward's plate'. Tied to the ring of the *sei-ita* is an *agemaki* bow, which still performs its traditional function of holding the *sode* (the shoulder-plates) in place. As the *sode* are much smaller, and contoured to the arm, there seems little need for the *agemaki*, and in time its use will become purely decorative, until it disappears altogether with the invention of the *sashimono*, the identification flag worn at the back of armour, the carrier for which leaves no room for an *agemaki*.

He wears two *kote*, as is now universal, and also wears a strange form of *haidate* (thigh-guards), which are basically armour-plated shorts! His *suneate* are still quite large, but the wearing of ordinary straw sandals, rather than any specialised footwear, is now standard.

His sword is suspended *tachi*-style, with the cutting edge downwards, as it has always been, and he has a *tanto* tied securely above it. His main weapon, however, is a *naginata*.

Site of the final resistance to the Northern Court, Sannoko Canyon, deep within the mountains of Yoshino, was the hiding place for the Imperial Regalia taken by supporters of the Southern Emperors in 1443. They managed to hold out for 14 years.

taken away by the Kusunoki family to Yoshino where they proclaimed the Pretender's son, Prince Kitayama, as Emperor (referring to him as 'The Heavenly King') and set up his brother Tadayoshi as Shogun.

This dramatic raid was a serious challenge to the Ashikaga *bakufu*'s declining authority, for as we have seen before, great store was laid on the legitimacy provided by the possession of the Regalia. The Shogunate rallied its support and fierce attacks forced the Southern Court to retreat from Yoshino, deeper into the forested mountains around Mount Odaigahara, where they raised a palace for the 'Heavenly King', and hid the Jewels in a cave. From here this 'unofficial' Southern Court managed to hold out for another 14 years.

Their eventual defeat was almost as theatrical as their initial success. The Akamatsu clan had been in disgrace since the murder of Yoshinori, but the Shogun Yoshimasa made it clear that they would be restored to favour if they destroyed the Southern Court. Some retainers of the Akamatsu therefore made the dangerous journey to the Sannoko River, where the rebels had their base, and presented themselves as sympathisers come to join their cause. As the Akamatsu were the former destroyers of a Shogun the loyalists were completely fooled. One night the new arrivals turned on their host and slew the Southern Emperor (who was either the former Prince Kitayama referred to above, or a successor called Takamasa), then made off in two groups through the snow, one with his head and the other with the Jewels. Legend adds a colourful touch to their escape, for as the group with the head, under Nakamura Taroshiro, were crossing the Obagamine Pass they were attacked by samurai from Yoshino. They buried the Emperor's head in the snow, meaning to retrieve it afterwards, but in the midst of the fighting the head sent up a spurt of blood and the loyalists were able to recapture it. The Jewels, however, were safely returned to the capital.

That was the end of the Southern Court. During the Onin War of 1467–77 the Yamana clan briefly displayed a 'Southern Emperor' to offset the Hosokawa's manipulation of the Emperor Go-Tsuchimikado, but found no Kusunoki to support him, and from then on such figures disappear from history. However, as a footnote to the story of the *Nambokucho* or 'Wars

---

PLATE 12   *A samurai, wielding an iron club, fights in the Onin War in 1467*

The Onin War, which began in the First Year of Onin, 1467, and lasted intermittently for another 10 years, marked the final collapse of the Ashikaga Shogunate as an institution with any real power, and the emergence of a number of land-owning *daimyo* who ruled their provinces with little regard for anything beyond their own immediate concerns. The Onin War began in the city of Kyoto, where rival samurai clans burnt each other's mansions and fought street battles. This plate attempts to illustrate these unhappy early days.

The samurai, whose appearance is based almost entirely on a sketch by Sasama, wears a *do-maru* armour, which opens at the right side, and is otherwise almost identical to a *haramaki*. His *sode* have a gentle curve, and are of medium size, so they would probably be anchored to an *agemaki* at the rear. Two small metal plates protect the suspensory cords on the chest, as in Plate 10, and he also sports a sensible innovation, the *nodowa*, or throat-protector, which fastened round the neck and hung in front of the neck. His *do* has seven *kusazuri*. His helmet is of similar style to the one with the wide-sweeping neckguard shown in Plate 10, but he has eschewed *kuwagata*, and his long black hair hangs down inside it. His helmet cords are twisted securely around his chin.

A long belt, the *uwa-obi*, pulls the loose *do-maru* into his waist, taking some of the weight off the shoulders. This problem of the distribution of the armour's weight was only solved by the introduction of a tapered waist in the sixteenth century. His *kote* are surprisingly modern. Gone are the simple cloth bags to which plates have been sewn. Instead we see an early form of chain-mail protection, which was to become universal during the following century. The metal plates are fastened with thongs. His *haidate* are similar to those seen from the rear in Plate 11, and his heavy metal *suneate* complete what is a good example of plain, undecorative, fifteenth-century battledress.

He is certainly taking no chances with personal armament, having two *tanto* (daggers) in addition to his sword. His main weapon is, however, an enormous studded iron club, with which he appears to have caused havoc!

Between the Courts', we may mention that in 1945 no less than seventeen 'Pretenders' claimed to be the rightful Emperor and objected to Hirohito's surrender to the United States of America. One man, a shopkeeper from Nagoya called Kumazawa Kando, who claimed to be descended from the Southern line, attracted a great deal of attention and even came to the notice of General MacArthur. Some are still around. A new religious sect in Japan owes its allegiance to a lady who claims to be descended from the rightful line. In her case, however, she goes further than rejecting the settlement of 1392 and claims descent from Susano-o, the thunder God, the Goddess Amateratsu's elder brother and thus the founder of the real line of Emperors of which she is the first claimant!

The Kongo-ji in Kashiwagi, at the head of the Kono Valley, is the traditional site of the palace of the rival Shogun, the younger brother of the last of the 'Southern Pretenders', whose tomb appears in this picture. The destruction of the remnants of the Southern Court proved the means whereby the Akamatsu clan was restored to favour after the Kakitsu Incident, when the Shogun Yoshinori was murdered.

The Onin War

Ashikaga Yoshimitsu, who had united the Imperial lines, had built a

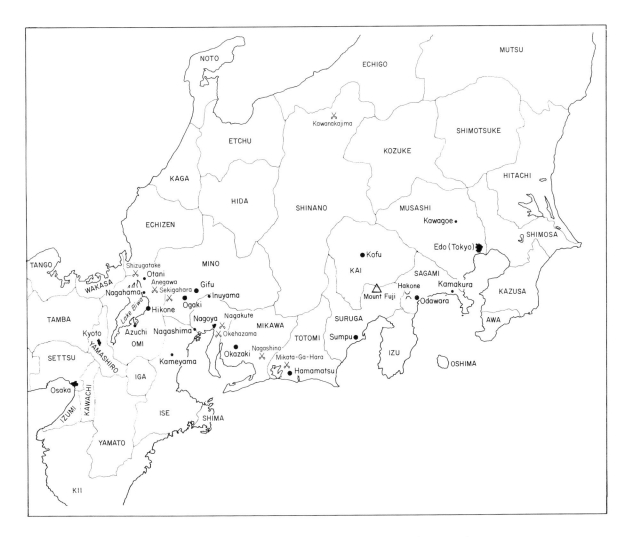

Central Honshu, showing the provinces that lay between Kyoto and Edo (Tokyo), major battlefields and towns. The major landowning daimyo are shown in the territories they controlled in the latter half of the sixteenth century.

Pavilion of Gold. His grandson, the aesthete Yoshimasa, was to attempt to emulate him by constructing a Silver Pavilion in 1483, and wept when the troubled times made it impossible to finish the work, so that the building stood gaunt and black, as fitting a symbol of the new age as the glorious gold had been of a previous generation.

Between the times of building of the Gold and the Silver Pavilions, the samurai had fought the war named after the Year of Onin in which it had begun. What began as a succession dispute between samurai clans turned into a fragmented civil war. Even a nation so used to violence found the Onin War particularly terrible, for the city of Kyoto was its first battlefield, where bands of samurai challenged each other from among the blackened ruins of what had once been houses, shops and temples. Peasant riots and armed monks had brought their own destruction in the past, but attacks like these ended as precipitately as they arrived. During the war of Onin the agony went on and on, with no respite over 10 years for the rebuilding of homes and the reconstruction of a shattered society. Only the eventual spread of the war to distant provinces ultimately gave Kyoto the breathing space it needed. The merchants and craftsmen returned, the temples were rebuilt once again, and the cycle of death and rebirth went on.

Three of the clans mentioned previously in this chapter became prominent by their involvement in the Onin War. Within 10 years of the Akamatsu's restoration of fortune by defeating the Heavenly King they took part in the bitter conflict. Akamatsu Masanori (1455–1496) was a well-known general. He was the grandson of Akamatsu Mitsusuke, the murderer of the Shogun Yoshinori. The Yamana, who had profited by their revenge of Shogun Yoshinori's death, were represented in the Onin War by the same Yamana Mochitoyo, known by his Buddhist name of 'Sozen', and nicknamed the 'Red Monk' because of his fiery complexion. The Red Monk's chief enemy was his son-in-law, Hosokawa Katsumoto, showing that clan issues as such over-rode all humanitarian considerations. All that mattered was survival. Hostages were given for good behaviour and frequently met an untimely end.

By the end of the Onin War in 1477 the power of the Shogun as a military force had collapsed entirely. He was now honoured as a figurehead, as an Emperor without the attendant divinity, respected only for the legitimacy of the Imperial commission-to-rule which only a family descended from the Minamoto could possess. Real power now lay elsewhere, as new families replaced old ones. There had been strong, independent samurai clans before, but precious few managed to make the transition from

PLATE 13   *Hosokawa Sumimoto leads a charge, ca 1510*

We enter the sixteenth century with Hosokawa Sumimoto (1496–1520), whose life bears so many of the hallmarks of the Sengoku Period – the Age of the Country at War. His father, Hosokawa Masamoto (1466-1507), was the son of the great general, Katsumoto, who fought in the Onin War. In 1493 he acted as kingmaker and deposed the rightful Shogun Ashikaga Yoshitane. Masamoto was childless, and adopted three sons to carry on the Hosokawa name. This Sumimoto was the second of the three, and was only 11 years old when his adoptive father died. A dispute broke out almost immediately and young Sumimoto took refuge with the Sasaki family in Omi Province. The powerful Miyoshi Nagateru supported Sumimoto and disposed of his elder 'brother', Sumiyuki. This enabled Sumimoto to take possession of the domains intended

for him on Shikoku Island and attain the high office of Kwanryo in Kyoto. His triumphs were soon put into reverse when the Shogun, whom his father had deposed, returned to Kyoto under the protection of Ouchi Yoshioki. Hosokawa Sumimoto intended to stop him in Settsu Province but, seeing the size of his army, fled to Shikoku. Ouchi Yoshioki entered Kyoto, restored the Shogun and took Sumimoto's title of Kwanryo. Sumimoto's eventual return marked the beginning of a series of battles between him and the Shogun's supporters, which eventually ended in Sumimoto's defeat and final withdrawal to Shikoku, where he died in 1520.

In this plate Sumimoto is seen leading a desperate charge across a rice-field. His *do-maru* is almost identical to the one shown in Plate 12, but his helmet has a deeper *shikoro*, making it look almost old-

fashioned. His *nodowa* is unusual in that he has tucked it under the top of his *do*. His *sode* are large, and would be tied at the rear via an *agemaki* bow similar to that depicted in Plate 11. His armour is completely laced in black except for the bottom row of his *haidate*. His *suneate*, which are of a russet-iron finish, are very large indeed.

Two items proclaim his status as a commander: his whip, slung casually across his *tanto*, and his signalling fan. There were several varieties of these. Sumimoto has a flat wooden one called a *gumbai uchiwa*, which was reserved for commanders. Note that horse furniture has not changed appreciably over the centuries.

The source for these details is a contemporary painting on silk of Hosokawa Sumimoto in a private collection in Japan.

Shogun's man before the Onin War to their own man after it. Some, like the Shimazu in the far South of Kyushu, achieved it with the help of their geographical remoteness from the capital. Other noble houses died out as completely as their burned mansions that had once graced the Kyoto skyline. Yamana, Isshiki and Hatakeyama disappeared from history. Takeda, Uesugi and Saito, the new *daimyo*, or 'warlords', who replaced them, were almost invariably lower-class opportunists who had seized the moment and made the transfer of power a reality for themselves.

The wars that followed Onin became spread throughout the country in a very different way from the war between the Courts. There were no sides to choose in these wars, just the terrible realisation that every clan had to fight to survive. Smaller clans allied themselves with larger until they were able to confront their erstwhile protectors. Ambitious leaders of samurai put more and more men into battle, so that even the despised peasants were given spears and swords to fight with beside the samurai élite and were called *ashigaru*, or 'light feet', because the leaders could not afford armour for them. Soon the most ignorant village blacksmith had become a swordmaker, mass-producing spear heads for the samurai and crude swords for the *ashigaru*, so that the quality of work plummeted to a crude and shameful level. The poorly-tempered, brittle blades shattered against armour and such was the mistrust placed in these inferior swords that a samurai forced by poverty to depend upon them would take five or six with him into battle, ready to be discarded at will. The glory of the Ashikaga, and its most potent symbol, the peerless samurai sword, were both passing away.

Sengoku Period
– the Age of the Country at War

In view of the number of battles we have described in the preceding pages the dubbing of the years from 1477 to 1576 as the *Sengoku-jidai* or 'Age of the Country at War' may seem an unnecessary appellation to give to any one time in Japanese history. The reason this latter half of the Muromachi Period is so-called, however, is better explained by a more exact translation of the term. Sengoku-jidai is in fact a way of making a direct comparison between the condition of Japan at the time and the 'Period of Warring States' in Ancient China. Unlike the Wars Between the Courts, and the Gempei War, there was no real conflict over Shogunal or Imperial authority – such a centralised power simply did not exist. Both institutions continued but, as noted in the previous chapter, real power lay elsewhere. The wars of the Sengoku Period were fought between contingents representing two different sorts of military grouping: the *daimyo,* or samurai warlords, and the peasant leagues, or *ikki.*

The Army of the Holy Lotus

As we have seen on several previous occasions any apparent weakening of Shogunal authority was a signal to other groups to try their hand. More

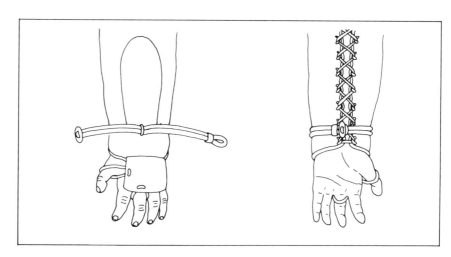

Armour for the sleeve
The means of attaching the *kote* (armoured sleeve) to the hand changed little through the centuries in spite of changes in the *kote* design. There was a loop round the wrist, fastened with toggles, and two smaller loops, one around the thumb, and another around the middle finger.

than Emperors were willing to challenge the Shogunate after the Kakitsu Affair, the murder of the Shogun Yoshinori in 1441. This not only provided a stimulus for the Southern Court supporters to try their last desperate attempt at power, but also provided the ideal conditions of confusion in Kyoto to enable peasant rioters, in leagues called *ikki*, to descend with impunity upon the capital, a trend that is first discerned in the mid-fifteenth century, but reaches its peak in the confusion following the Onin War.

The grievances of country-dwellers after Onin were directed against the rich pawnbrokers and rice-dealers of the city who had grown fat at the farmers' expense. As the finances of these *doso*, or merchants, were indispensable to the humble shopkeepers and artisans who lived beside them no support was found for the peasants among their urban counterparts. Instead there grew up a strong measure of urban solidarity against the peasant *ikki* and, as the *bakufu* became increasingly unable or unwilling to defend them against such incursions, this solidarity took the form of armed intervention. This military resistance to the *ikki* was in fact the beginning of a heady period of virtual self-government for the people of Kyoto. More than occupation divided them from the rural *ikki*, for their religious differences were paramount. The esoteric sects of Buddhism, such as the Tendai of the warrior monks of Mount Hiei, had made little headway with the simple-minded townsfolk. Their mainstay was the sect founded by the monk Nichiren, known either by the name of its founder, or as the *Hokke-*

PLATE 14   *Yamamoto Kansuke prepares to join in the Fourth Battle of Kawanakajima, 1561*

Yamamoto Kansuke takes us into the most exciting period of samurai history, the *Sengoku-jidai*, the 'Age of the Country at War'. The one-eyed Kansuke was a trusted advisor to the great *daimyo* Takeda Shingen (1521–1573) and one of the Takeda's renowned 'Twenty-Four Generals'. Takeda Shingen and his arch-rival, Uesugi Kenshin, fought five battles in the flat plain of Kawanakajima, near the present-day city of Nagano in Nagano Prefecture. This plate is based on the most famous of these encounters, which was fought in 1561.

We are standing on the hills overlooking Shingen's fortress of Kaizu (now Matsushiro) down in the valley. The battle has begun across the Chikuma-gawa towards Hachiman Plain. Kansuke's personal retainers begin the descent towards the conflict. Their *sashimono*, the little flags on their backs, are characteristic of the period now

under discussion. They bear Kansuke's *mon*, or badge, which is also seen in modified form as a *maedate*, the badge on the front of his helmet. When the battle was joined, Yamamoto Kansuke created havoc in the Uesugi ranks by charging singlehanded with his long spear, an act that almost certainly saved the Takeda from a crushing defeat. Eventually, overcome by wounds from arquebus fire, Kansuke retired and committed *hara-kiri*. (For a full, detailed account of the Battle of Kawanakajima see *Battles of the Japanese Samurai* by the present author.)

His helmet is an excellent example of the way a simple 'battle-dress' suit of armour, so typical of the age, could be made to look spectacular. This helmet is one of several known from the sixteenth century that sported enormous wooden buffalo horns. (Kuroda Nagamasa possessed the best-known example,

which is illustrated in Plate 25. See also the author's *The Samurai – a Military History* for the one owned by Tokugawa Ieyasu.) Similar basic helmets will be noted in most of the plates that follow, but the reader will appreciate the tremendous difference in overall design between this and preceding illustrations. The *fukigayeshi* have shrunk to small projections, and the *shikoro* is very simple. Note the very basic *hoate*, a face-mask, which at this stage of development is little more than an anchoring plate for the helmet cords. As Kansuke was a Buddhist monk, like Shingen, he wears the monk's *kesa* over his armour. The rear view of the armour would be very similar to those illustrated in Plate 27.

The sources for the illustration are materials displayed in the museums at Kawanakajima and Matsushiro, and numerous contemporary illustrations.

shu, or Lotus sect, from the fundamental importance Nichiren attached to the teachings enshrined within the Lotus Sutra. By about 1500 there were twenty-one Nichiren temples in Kyoto, several of which were very sensibly surrounded by moats and earthen embankments for protection.

By placing their reliance on their own efforts the craftsmen and merchants of Kyoto had clearly rejected the traditional role of the samurai to protect them, and formed their own self-governing, self-defending organisations that had as little regard for class or pedigree as had the new *daimyo* of the distant provinces. United in their need for protection, and inspired by their brash, tub-thumping Buddhism, these townsmen armies made the samurai of the Shogun seem archaic in their obsession with rank, honour and the self-destructive demands of samurai glory.

Their biggest challenge came in 1528. Not even the presence of townsmen armies could dissuade the Shogun from fleeing before the advance of a huge army on Kyoto. It was not an army of samurai as the Shogun understood the term – there was no pedigree to inspect, no worthy opponents to challenge. Nor was it a rabble of *sohei* monks from one of the old monasteries of Nara or Mount Hiei, who had attacked the city in the past. It was instead the first united attack upon Kyoto by the Ikko-ikki, or 'Single-minded League', adherents of the Jodo-Shinshu sect of Buddhism, who believed that death in battle guaranteed heaven, while retreat promised eternal damnation.

An armour of *haramaki* style, which opens down the middle of the back. It has a large *nodowa*, the protector for the throat, and curved shoulder-plates, or *sode*.

The Rise of the Ikko-ikki

It is a mistake to think of the Ikko-ikki as warrior monks analogous to the *sohei* of Mount Hiei. They were rather more of a social movement, far more developed than the ordinary *ikki*, with a religious basis uniting them even more fiercely than the townsmen's Nichiren sect. Some may have shaved their heads, but the majority dressed, fought and died like the samurai they opposed. Jodo-Shinshu, the sect to which the Ikko belonged, which is today the largest Buddhist denomination in Japan, was an offshoot of the Jodo, or 'Pure Land' sect, and placed its faith in the Vow of Amida Buddha to save all mankind, rather than restricting salvation to those with the leisure and the intellect to explore the spirituality of the esoteric creeds such as the Tendai of Mount Hiei. Jodo-Shinshu was given a much-needed revival under Rennyo (1415–1499), who succeeded in uniting the many diverse independent groups of adherents (known as *monto,* hence the alternative name for the Ikko as the Monto sect) under his leadership.

The emergence of the Ikko-ikki as a military force reached its consummation with their conquest of the province of Kaga in 1488, a territory they managed to hold until 1580. Such political power inevitably encouraged a shift from the collective, egalitarian organisation they had been, whereby oaths were signed in a circle so that no one took precedence over another. On some occasions these *ikki* documents were then burned, the

66

Samurai, wearing armour typical of the mid-sixteenth century, attack a house.

ashes dissolved in water, and the resulting liquid drunk by the confederates. By the middle of the sixteenth century the Ikko-ikki form of organisation had become largely indistinguishable from that other form of collective security: the *daimyo* domain, the territory of a warlord. As noted above, unlike the townsmen's Lotus sect, their support came from the country-side, where disaffected peasants saw in the salvation promised by Shinshu, and the more earthly benefits conveyed by the Ikko-ikki, a splendid alter-native to service to any samurai family, new or old. By 1520 they controlled three provinces from their huge fortress of Ishiyama Hongan-ji in Osaka, which they defended with an army as formidable as any of the *daimyo,* and it was only a matter of time before they turned their attentions to the rich pickings of the newly prosperous Kyoto.

In their 1528 campaign they had, however, reckoned without the resourceful townspeople of Kyoto. As the army of the Ikko-ikki approach-ed the capital, the army of the Hokke-shu began to mobilise with a rapidity which would have astonished even samurai. Swords, armour and banners appeared from nowhere, and for weeks a force of thousands paraded through the streets under the flag of Nichiren, chanting the Lotus Sutra. The Ikko-ikki were driven off. There then began a successful, if somewhat grudging, alliance between the 'Old Guard' of the samurai class and their fellow human beings outside it. In 1533 the Lotus army joined forces with Hosokawa Harumoto (1519–1563) for an attack on the Ikko-ikki's huge 'fortress cathedral' of the Ishiyama Hongan-ji, which stood on the site of present-day Osaka castle. So secure did their joint efforts make Kyoto that the Shogun Yoshiharu returned in 1534 to the city from which he had fled in 1528 and, within months, the gardens of the Shogun's Palace rang once again to the sound of music and song.

But the peace was illusory. The townsmen of the Hokke-shu had been altogether too successful in filling the temporary vacuum of authority which existed in Kyoto. Their intolerant religious fundamentalism, as much as their assertion of proprietorial rights, particularly offended the monks of Mount Hiei. After securing the neutrality of the townsmen's erstwhile ally, Hosokawa Harumoto, and the approval of the Ikko-ikki at Ishiyama Hongan-ji, the *sohei* of Mount Hiei descended in a surprise attack on the city with a ferocity that they had not even exercised at the height of the Gempei War. All twenty-one Nichiren temples were burned to the ground and the conflagration took much of the rest of the city with it. Thus one of the forms of social organisation which had emerged out of the ashes of the Onin War came to a violent end. The self-governing structure of Kyoto lasted a few more years after the destruction of its Nichiren nuclei, until it was all swept aside in the triumph of Oda Nobunaga. The Ikko-ikki shared in the victory, but it was the other trend mentioned briefly above, the *daimyo* domain, that really prospered. As it was a *daimyo* who was to to bring about the Ikko-ikki's downfall it is to this final manifestation of Sengoku military power that we must now turn.

The Warlords of Western Japan

The development of the *daimyo* is best illustrated by tracing the careers of

---

PLATE 15   *The war-drum of the Takeda summons the troops, c. 1564*

The most important signalling devices in any army were the war-drums. This is the particularly large version which would be mounted in a drum-tower of a castle. A burly *ashigaru*, or footsoldier, hammers out the call to war for the Takeda clan. He is wearing the most straightforward of all 'battle-dress' armours, the *okegawa-do*, which consists of two sections, front and back, connected by a hinge and fastening under the right armpit by a cord. The *kusazuri* (or *gesan*), the tassels that hang down over the thighs, are of simple construction laced in *sugake-odoshi* (paired cords). Many samurai armours of the period are nothing more than ornamented *okegawa-dos*.

Drumming is hot work – so the drummer has dispensed with all other items of clothing except for his *fundoshi*, or loincloth, which is visible through the cords of his *kusazuri*.

The castle may look a rudimentary construction to those who are familiar with pictures of the stone structures of Himeji and Hikone, but this is the authentic style of the period. Some stone was used, but the vast sweeping stone walls of Odawara and Edo would not be found in the mountains of Kai Province. Nor did Takeda Shingen prefer to place great reliance on castles. The loyal people of his province were his castle. Wood is therefore the main material of this typical mid-sixteenth century fortress.

Ascending the stairs behind the drummer comes a member of Takeda Shingen's *tsukai-ban*, or messenger corps, an army unit maintained by every *daimyo* of note. 'Aide-de-camp' is probably the best translation. The Takeda aides-de-camp were distinguished by the very appropriate device of a busy centipede on their *sashimono*. Behind him comes a samurai who wears the *sashimono* of one of Shingen's greatest generals, Baba Nobuharu, who was to meet his death at the cataclysmic Battle of Nagashino in 1575. The flags of some other Takeda generals' troops are seen down in the courtyard. There are the six black rings on red of Sanada Yukitaka, the first of the Sanada to serve Shingen; the Takeda *mon* on blue of Takeda Nobukado, Shingen's brother; the red octagon on white of Obata Masamori; the black zig-zag of Baba; the black design on white of Hara Masatane, who was to be killed during the charge at Nagashino, and the white flower on black of another victim of Nagashino – Yamagata Masakage.

The sources for the heraldic designs are materials collected by the author from Kofu in Yamanashi Prefecture, which was formerly Shingen's capital. Every year local people dress up in authentic costume for the 'Shingen-ko matsuri', to commemorate the district's most famous son.

representative examples, and history provides us with many from which we can choose. The Western end of Honshu furnishes us with the case of how the ancient clan of Ouchi were overthrown by the Mori in a classic case of *gekokujo*, 'the low overcome the high', which is the phrase used to describe how one *daimyo*, often of a highly prestigious family, might be overcome by his inferiors, who could even be his own samurai.

The Ouchi had an impressive pedigree, claiming descent from a Korean prince who came to Japan in 611, and the record of their achievements reads like a potted history of Japan. Ouchi Hiroyo was one of the many samurai leaders who changed allegiance during the Wars Between the Courts, eventually siding with the Ashikaga in 1364 and receiving from them the provinces of Nagato and Iwami. His son, Yoshihiro (1355–1400), fought for the third Ashikaga Shogun, Yoshimitsu, builder of the Golden Pavilion, and was Yoshimitsu's chief negotiator in the talks which led to the settlement of the claims of the rival dynasties. Several years later he backed the wrong horse by supporting a rival Shogun and perished in battle, leaving his domains to his 5-year-old son. The child thrived under the protection of a benevolent uncle and, on achieving maturity, became one of the avengers of the murdered Shogun Yoshinori, which enhanced the family's reputation. He died without issue and the succession passed eventually to his nephew's grandson, Yoshioki (1477–1528), under whom the clan reached the height of its powers. Yoshioki's greatest achievement was restoring the deposed Shogun Ashikaga Yoshitane to his rightful place,

The 'Parable of the Arrows'. Mori Motonari, avenger of Ouchi and eventual inheritor of his domains, had three sons. As a lesson to them he invited each one to break an arrow, and then demonstrated how difficult it was to break three arrows held together. 'So it must be with you', he added, and the three branch families of Mori, Kobayakawa and Kikkawa showed great loyalty to each other for many decades. Admirers of the Japanese cinema will note that Kurosawa includes an incident similar to this in his film *Ran*.

causing the powerful Hosokawa Sumimoto, whose father had deposed him, to flee before the Ouchi's advance.

Yet, as in so many other cases, the son of this valiant father neglected his military responsibilities and Ouchi Yoshitaka (1507–1551) indulged too freely and unwisely in literature, art and pleasure. Eventually, hearing of the treacherous designs of one of his retainers, Sue Harukata, he called his samurai to arms, only to find that his appeal was ignored by most of them. He then left his castle, where he felt too unsafe, and retired to the temple of Hosen-ji. This too he soon left and fled towards Nagato, where he landed and sought refuge. Here the wretched man was besieged by Sue Harukata and committed suicide. When his son followed suit, 900 years of the Ouchi came to an end.

The rider to the story of Ouchi's downfall is that Sue Harukata did not live long to enjoy his success, but was himself vanquished by another former vassal of the Ouchi, Mori Motonari, at the Battle of Itsukushima (Miyajima) in 1555. Mori Motonari enticed Sue Harukata into making a base on the island, where the Mori destroyed him by a surprise attack. The Mori, having avenged their late masters the Ouchi, went on to become one of the leading *daimyo* in Japan. Such was the nature of *gekokujo*.

The Warlords of the Kanto

As the Ouchi were giving way to the Mori at one end of Honshu, a fierce struggle was continuing 600 miles to the East, in a four-cornered fight for power between the clans of Uesugi, Takeda, Hojo and Imagawa. To a large extent all four represent a more developed form of *daimyo* control than that illustrated by the ancient Ouchi. Of the four mentioned above, only the Imagawa had anything like an illustrious pedigree. The Takeda and the Uesugi were classic examples of post-Onin *gekokujo*. The rise to power of Takeda Shingen (1521–1573), one of the most colourful characters in Japanese history, came about when the youthful Harunobu, as he was known until shaving his head in 1551, discovered that his father planned to disinherit him in favour of a younger brother. Harunobu revolted against his father and placed him in the custody of his father-in-law Imagawa Yoshimoto. Shingen took over the Takeda domain completely, which he ruled efficiently and well. He was one of the few *daimyo* who managed a workable compromise between the need to maintain a large army of reasonably trained troops under experienced samurai, without denuding the rice-fields of agricultural workers. He soon began to expand his territory, largely at the expense of his neighbour, Uesugi Kenshin (1530–1578), with whom he had several military contests where their lands met at at a place called Kawanakajima. There were five 'Battles of Kawanakajima' between 1553 and 1564.

Kenshin, incidentally, in true Sengoku style, was nothing to do with the original Uesugi clan. The Uesugi were an ancient family located around the

The great general Takeda Shingen (1521–1573), as represented by this modern statue in his capital of Kofu. He wears the Buddhist *kesa* over his armour, and a long-sleeved *haori* jacket. His helmet is set off with a horse-hair plume.

site of present-day Tokyo. The clan was, however, almost wiped out by the fourth name mentioned above, the Hojo, who, it must be noted, had nothing to do with the original Hojo! The reason for this confusing scenario is that it was quite common for samurai to change their names, but only the *daimyo* of the Sengoku Period seemed to have appropriated other samurai's names because they sounded better! Both Hojo Soun (1432–1519) and Uesugi Kenshin gave themselves new family names which they felt would improve their social positions. In the case of Hojo Soun (formerly Ise Shinkuro), he married his son to a descendant of the former Hojo *shikken*, who in the past had controlled Shoguns, so as a family name it looked auspicious. As for Kenshin, in 1551 the last of the old Uesugi, Uesugi Norimasa, took refuge with his former vassal after his defeat by the Hojo. The samurai accepted his old master on condition that Uesugi would adopt him as his son and give him the title of Lord of Echigo Province. Norimasa had little choice but to agree and the great *daimyo* Uesugi Kenshin was 'born'.

Changing names was only one of several devices by which a *daimyo* of the Sengoku-jidai could consolidate a position which his sword had won

The tombs of Takeda Shingen and his wife, at the Erin-ji, Enzan, Yamanashi Prefecture.

for him. Other ways were the giving and receiving of hostages and the use of adoption and marriage. We have mentioned hostages before. They were often young children given to an ally as an expression of trust, or demanded from a newly conquered *daimyo* as a guarantee of good behaviour. So blatantly political were adoptive and marriage alliances that they can often be regarded as no more than an extension of the hostage system. No stranger example of adoption exists than that furnished by the Takeda, Hojo and Uesugi. The seventh son of Hojo Ujiyasu (1515–1570), Ujihide, was sent at the age of 10 to be adopted by Takeda Shingen, and, as Takeda Saburo, symbolised and confirmed the alliance between the two clans. When the alliance folded, the Takeda had no further use for him, so he was returned to the Hojo. The Hojo were at that time courting support from the Uesugi, so the young man was sent in turn to Uesugi Kenshin, who adopted him in 1569 as Uesugi Kagetora, the great hope of the Hojo/Uesugi alliance. All went well for Kagetora until Kenshin's death in 1578. It had been Kenshin's wish that his domain be divided equally between Kagetora and his nephew Kagekatsu, but Kagekatsu was greedy and hounded the wretched Kagetora until he committed suicide in 1579.

Marriage was an equally cruel weapon and, among the families of Imagawa, Takeda and Hojo, we may note that Shingen's son, Takeda

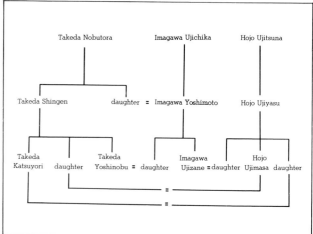

A *ninja* drops from the ceiling on to his victim. This wax dummy hangs menacingly from the ceiling in the Ninja Museum at Iga-Ueno.

Family tree of the Takeda, Imagawa and Hojo families
Marriage was much used in the days of the samurai as a way of cementing military alliances. This diagram shows the remarkably complex relationships that existed between the three families of Takeda, Imagawa and Hojo.

Yoshinobu (who was later forced to commit suicide for opposing his father), married Imagawa Yoshimoto's daughter. Imagawa Yoshimoto was himself married to Shingen's sister, who produced the Imagawa heir, Ujizane, who married a daughter of Hojo Ujiyasu. Another daughter of Ujiyasu married Takeda Katsuyori, Shingen's heir, while his son Ujimasa married Shingen's daughter (see above for a diagram of this incredibly complicated system). Uesugi Kenshin, who seems to have kept his vows of celibacy far more rigidly than Shingen, does not seem to have gone in for the marriage market as a means of advancement. There is a strange tradition about Kenshin that 'he' in fact was a woman, but there is no real evidence for such a bizarre twist to the history of the competing *daimyo*. Even stranger are the legends concerned with Kenshin's death, which is supposed to have come about as the result of a totally unexpected swordthrust delivered by a *ninja* who had concealed himself beneath Kenshin's lavatory. The assassin was apparently a dwarf who lived for days among the filth of the closet, waiting for his chance to strike. (The official version was that Kenshin died from an apoplectic fit, which was probably how it looked to attendants who rushed to aid the stricken warlord.)

Of the four warlords here discussed the Hojo were ultimately the most successful, and the longest to last in power. In an age which demanded bigger and better armies a *daimyo's* success began to depend on how skilfully he could turn ignorant tillers of rice-fields into firers of arquebuses and wielders of spears. The Hojo promoted numerous military regulations to this end; the following, on the raising of troops, is a good example:

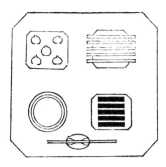

An illustration from the *Gunyoki* depicting the traditional farewell meal taken before battle. It consists of cooked chestnuts, dried *awabi*, *kombu* (seaweed) and *sake* to drink. The whole would be served on a tray to the departing general.

Sashimono must be black and new.

Helmet crests may be either gold or silver. [One assumes that lacquer, and not actual precious metal, is intended.]

The shaft of the pike [spear] must be covered in leather.

Children are not to be brought to camp.

Shields are to be two and a half feet long, one foot wide, and half an inch thick. [This must refer to the wooden shields planted in the ground as a protection for the arquebus troops, though they sound unusually narrow.]

Armour is not to be rolled up. It is to be placed in an armour box. The haori *[jacket] should also be cared for and ready for use.*

Mounted warriors should ride a horse worth one-third of your grant. Although having a horse is troublesome, you must not starve it.

As for your equipment, take care so that it will not be damaged by the elements. The haori *should be made of black cotton. Torn flags and rusty pikes are strictly forbidden.*

It was men such as those to whom the above orders were addressed that helped keep the Hojo supreme in the Kanto until their surrender to Hideyoshi's huge army in 1590.

How different was the fate of the Imagawa! They were ancient and aristocratic, and ruled their domain from their provincial capital of Sumpu (now Shizuoka city) as if it were a miniature version of Kyoto, where they held poetry contests, flower ceremonies and moon-viewing parties.They

PLATE 16   *Oda Nobunaga watches his army march past in 1570*

This plate depicts Oda Nobunaga (1534-1582) watching his army march back to Kyoto after the Battle of the Anegawa in 1570, where he defeated the Asai and Asakura clans. Nobunaga is the pivotal figure in the samurai history of the sixteenth century. Although a very minor *daimyo* compared to the Takeda or the Uesugi it was he who seized the initiative with his victory of Okehazama in 1560. It is also more than likely that it is to Nobunaga that we must look for the impetus in changing the organisation of a samurai army from being a collection of small units under separate, but loyal, commanders, to being a homogeneous force under one commander, divided by function, such as swordsmen,

arquebusiers etc, rather than allegiance to clan vassals.

The two samurai on the left wear *sashimono* bearing the Oda *mon*. This *mon*, in black on yellow, was also worn by Nobunaga's *Go-Umawari-shu*, his personal bodyguard. The second samurai has a *sashimono* with another Oda *mon*, a design of Japanese coins. The *ashigaru* behind wear typical smart *okegawa-do*, and support their long *nobori* banners in leather pouches fastened at the waist. The *nobori* were a universal feature of the armies of the time, and tended to indicate units of an army, in contrast to the *uma-jirushi*, the standard, which is illustrated in Plate 24, and is associated with the person of the commander.

Nobunaga is wearing a suit of

armour of rather 'old-fashioned' design, but of an elaboration in keeping with his status, and even full *yoroi* armours are found being worn by sixteenth-century commanders. It has *kebiki-odoshi* (close-spaced lacing) of blue silk and is a *do-maru*. The *haidate* are unusual as they consist of numerous metal hexagons sewn on to a cloth backing. His sword is carried *tachi*-style, and he has his *mon* as a *maedate* on his helmet. The armour is preserved in Kyoto, and a photograph of it appears in *The Book of the Samurai* by the present author.

Note the respectful attitude of the common people unlucky enough to have been caught out of doors as the procession marches by!

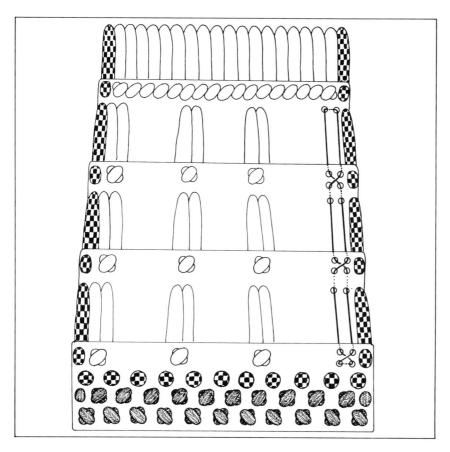

***Sugake-odoshi* lacing – detail**
Sugake (spaced lacing) was
introduced during the Muromachi
Period. This diagram shows how the
spacing was arranged, and illustrates
the separate lacing on the bottom
plate, which was usually red,
regardless of the colour of the rest of
the lacing.

were equally skilled in war and situated in much more favourable territory
than the mountains of Kenshin and Shingen. Their provinces were flat,
rich and bordered the Pacific Ocean, which gave them good lines of communication. In 1560 Imagawa Yoshimoto attempted to do what none of
the others had dared – to march on Kyoto and set himself up with a puppet
Shogun. He advanced Westward with a huge army, but as the host crossed
Owari Province they were observed by one of the upstart *daimyo* that great
families like the Imagawa so thoroughly despised. His name was Oda
Nobunaga, son of a former peasant warrior whose small territory had been
squeezed for a decade between the arms of the Imagawa and their rivals.
The Imagawa army, after a modest victory against one of Nobunaga's
frontier castles, had rested in a narrow gorge called Okehazama and, under
the cover of a fortuitous thunderstorm, the young Oda Nobunaga, outnumbered by twelve to one, attacked their encampment. So speedily did
he advance that at first Imagawa Yoshimoto thought a brawl had broken
out among his own men. As he rose bareheaded and unprotected from his
camp stool he saw a samurai advancing upon him with a drawn sword, and
there was no one to save him. The whole Battle of Okehazama took 15
minutes. It finished one clan forever, and threw another onto the forefront
of the stage. A new force was abroad – the samurai of Oda Nobunaga.

Momoyama Period – Oda Nobunaga

With the rise of Oda Nobunaga we enter the most exciting phase of samurai history. Strictly speaking we are still in the Muromachi Period, because the nominal seat of power remained at Muromachi until Nobunaga abolished the Ashikaga Shogunate in 1573, and the succeeding 'Azuchi-Momoyama' Period dates from Nobunaga's building of Azuchi castle in 1576. We are also quite definitely still in the 'Age of War'! Nevertheless, something happened in 1560 in that obscure little valley called Okehazama that was to change forever the political map of Japan and paved the way for a revolution in samurai warfare. Prior to Nobunaga, the aims of the *daimyo* were limited in scope but, from the time of his defeat of Imagawa, this young warlord acquired a vision of national conquest. Perhaps he was lucky being in the right place at the right time, but it is undoubtedly true that he, alone of all the *daimyo* at the time, knew what to do with such an opportunity when it presented itself.

The Rise of Nobunaga

The victory of Okehazama established Oda Nobunaga as a warrior of the first rank. As well as his undoubted military skills he also had the advantage that geography was on his side, because his province of Owari was set squarely in the fertile lowlands of the Nobi plain, near the present-day city of Nagoya. This also meant that he was quite near to Kyoto, should the opportunity ever arise of emulating Imagawa Yoshimoto's attempts to move on to the capital.

But Nobunaga was not only an accomplished new general, he was also as astute as any of his contemporaries about the need to seek and secure alliances. His victory of Okehazama impressed many, and one of the late Imagawa's generals, who had almost shared in the debacle of Okehazama, was among the first to make a pact with him. This was the famous Tokugawa Ieyasu, Lord of Mikawa, whose family were destined to rise to heights to which the humbly born Nobunaga could not aspire. Nobunaga was also a great believer in political marriages. He was himself married to the daughter of Saito Dosan, once an oil merchant and now the *daimyo* of Mino province, which was the next province between Nobunaga and the

Oda Nobutada, son of Oda Nobunaga, at the Battle of Nagashino 1575.
Oda Nobutada is identified by his *uma-jirushi* banner of a white rectangle within a gold border. This scene is from a modern copy of a well-known painted screen depicting the battle, painted originally for the Kuroda family.

PLATE 17   *A samurai of the Hojo clan rushes to his post in 1574*

Racing full tilt round the walls of Odawara castle comes a samurai of the 'yellow regiment', one of the élite units of the army of the Odawara Hojo. The commander of the 'yellow regiment' was Hojo Tsunanari, the son of an Imagawa retainer called Kushima, who was adopted into the Hojo family. Adoption, and marriage alliances, were very common in the Sengoku Period.

Details of these 'colour regiments' are taken from *Sengoku daimyo* by Sugiyama Hiroshi, who states that the other regiments wore red *sashimono* (under Hojo Tsunataka), blue (Tominaga), white (Kasawara – recruited from Izu Province) and black (Tame). These five commanders were called the five *karo*, or chief retainers. I have assumed that all the *sashimono* would also have borne the Hojo *mon* of a fish-scale design, which is supported by the presence in the Kanagawa Prefectural Art Museum in Yokohama of a red *sashimono* bearing a Hojo *mon* in white.

Our samurai is wearing a *go-mai mogami-do*, which is of solid horizontal plate construction with flanged upper edges, the sections being laced together with *sugake-odoshi*. There are four vertical hinges, giving the whole *do* the appearance of a rounded box. (For an 'exploded-view' see page 82, and for the *sashimono* holder see Plate 27.) The pouch at the front is an addition often found with this style of armour. It is made of blue cloth and fastens with a toggle. The helmet is a *suji-kabuto*, i.e. it has a ridged bowl, and is attractively finished, like the armour, in brown lacquer set off with gold. The gilded *maedate* badge bears the Hojo *mon*. Note the *kohire*, the padded shoulder-supports under the braces of the armour, the neat *ko-sode* (small-plates typical of the period). Note also the fully-developed *mempo* compared with the rudimentary *hoate* face mask in Plate 14. The mask bears snarling features and a bristly horse-hair moustache. A plate, the *yodarekake*, which is suspended from the *mempo*, provides

protection for the throat instead of a separate *nodowa*. His *katana* sword is thrust through his belt as it would be if he were not wearing armour, which is possible in a suit of armour, but means the samurai has to hold it in a comfortable position as he runs.

The *haidate* have now evolved into a standard form of chain mail and plates on cloth that was to become practically universal. They are tied behind the thighs. The *suneate*, with a leather pad where the legs touch the stirrup-carriers, will also be seen again. This figure also gives us a clear view of the *waraji*, or straw sandals. There were several ways of tying *waraji*, which were regarded as disposable items.

All in all, apart from various models for the *do*, many of which are illustrated in the following pages, this figure gives us an excellent example of the classic samurai 'battledress' of the late sixteenth century. It is based on several specimens in private collections and a drawing by Sasama.

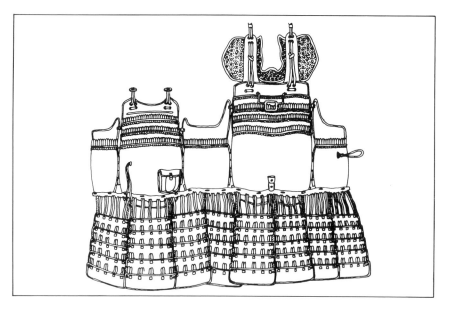

capital. Beyond Mino was Omi, ruled by Asai Nagamasa, so in the hope of securing his support or neutrality Nobunaga sent his younger sister O-ichi to be Nagamasa's wife. Finally, to protect his rear, Nobunaga promised his daughter in marriage to Takeda Shingen's son. This particular arrangement sealed forever the fate of the Imagawa house, for the threat of Takeda, Oda and Tokugawa being arraigned against him proved too much for Imagawa's heir, Ujizane. He abandoned all attempts at continuing his late father's struggle and sought refuge with his father-in-law, Hojo Ujiyasu, in Odawara castle.

Mino province was the next territory to fall to Nobunaga. In 1556 Saito Dosan was murdered by his son, Nobunaga's brother-in-law, which gave Nobunaga the perfect excuse for invading, on the grounds that he was avenging Dosan's death. He entrusted the campaign to one of the most able of his junior officers, Kinoshita Tokichiro, soon to be known as Toyotomi Hideyoshi, and who with Nobunaga and Tokugawa Ieyasu makes up the trio of the unifiers of Japan. Hideyoshi was a great strategist and showed his talent for assessing topographical features in the siege of Saito's fortress of Inabayama in 1564. Inabayama was built on top of a rocky hill and regarded as impregnable. Indeed, an attack upon it was logically impossible without a similar fortress nearby to act as a base and a refuge. Hideyoshi solved the problem very neatly by constructing the required fortress at Sunomata, under the very gaze of the defenders of Inabayama. His Oda colleagues considered his actions to be foolhardy, but Hideyoshi shamed them all by completing the castle with the help of a local robber chieftain and using it for a swift and successful assault on Inabayama. This placed Mino under Nobunaga's control and gave Hideyoshi a military reputation almost as great as his master's. Nobunaga transferred his capital from Kiyosu to Inabayama, which he re-named Gifu. It was an auspicious name,

Contrary to the popular image of the later Ashikaga Shoguns as idle, effeminate aesthetes, Ashikaga Yoshiteru put up a stout resistance to the attack on him by Miyoshi in 1565, then retired and committed *hara-kiri*.

as Gifu had been the place from which a Chinese warlord had begun his own campaign to unify a kingdom, and the allusion was not lost on Nobunaga's contemporaries. To make his intentions even clearer it was at this time that Nobunaga began using a seal which bore the motto *tenka fubu*, 'the realm covered in military glory'. If further recognition were needed it came the same year in the form of a letter from the Emperor Ogimachi, which began with a reference to Nobunaga as:

Famous general with no equal in any time, most superior in valour, and inspired by the Way of Heaven, since the provinces are now subject to your will it is certain that you will increasingly gain in victories.

The letter goes on to discuss such mundane details as the possibility of Oda Nobunaga repairing the Imperial Palace. Nobunaga, however, could not accept from any Emperor the supreme office of Shogun. For his dream of conquering the Empire to come true he would have to copy the technique of the Hojo *shikken* and rule through somebody else. All Nobunaga needed was a suitable puppet and an excuse to march on Kyoto, and in 1568 the perfect excuse arrived on his doorstep – Ashikaga Yoshiaki, the rightful Shogun.

This Yoshiaki had been a fugitive since the murder of his brother, the Shogun Ashikaga Yoshiteru, in 1565. The attack on Yoshiteru seems to have been every bit as savage and unexpected as the murder of the Shogun Yoshinori in 1441. Once again the conspirators were men close to their victim. One of them, Miyoshi Yoshitsugu, was in fact the commander of the Shogun's own army, which allowed him and his samurai to approach his victim without arousing much suspicion. The Shogun, we are told, fought bravely to the last and committed an honourable act of *hara-kiri*, a fact which contrasts nicely with the traditional view of sixteenth-century Shoguns as impotent, flower-viewing aesthetes. His young cousin Yoshi-hide, then living as a monk, was dragged from his cloisters and set up as the fourteenth Ashikaga Shogun, to rule in the name of the Miyoshi.

The true heir, Yoshiaki, who escaped, spent several years looking for a *daimyo* who was willing and able to support his cause. His first contact, Rokkaku Yoshisuke, was officially an ally of the Miyoshi and did not dare offend them. His second try, Takeda Shingen, fed him on hope for more than a year, then finally told him he was powerless to act on his behalf. Asakura Yoshikage, *daimyo* of Echizen, who had defeated an army of the Ikko-ikki in 1562 and was Nobunaga's main threat to the North of Kyoto, also refused to help Yoshiaki. Only Nobunaga himself would take the risk. Hideyoshi is supposed to have commented at the time that 'Nobunaga could do nothing without a name', and it was in the name of the Shogun Yoshiaki that Nobunaga began to conquer the Empire.

Nobunaga's first move was to secure his flanks by defeating Rokkaku Yoshisuke in Omi, who fled to Koya-san – a common enough refuge. He then turned his attentions towards the forces of Miyoshi and Matsunaga, whom his army met at the Battle of Sakai. This latter encounter is interesting in that it was described in great detail by one of the first European Jesuit missionaries to Japan, who was an eye-witness to the fighting and had the bizarre honour of celebrating Mass for Christian samurai from both armies during the period of truce prior to the battle. Nobunaga himself was not present, the victory being gained on his behalf by another of his able generals, Shibata Katsuie (1530–1583). The Jesuit account shows a keen appreciation of the political background to it:

After the truce had expired, the two armies marched out of the camps, and drew up in line of battle. Yoshitsugu commanded the right, and Hisahide the left. Both of

---

PLATE 18 *Arquebusiers in action at the Battle of Nagashino, 1575*

Nothing so well illustrates the trust Nobunaga was able to place in his well-disciplined *ashigaru* as his classic victory of Nagashino in 1575. For the Takeda clan it was a disaster. Three years before they had crushed Ieyasu's troops at Mikata-ga-hara with a well-timed cavalry charge, but by 1575 the great Shingen was dead, and it was his brave but foolhardy son, Katsuyori, who hoped to do the same at Nagashino. They charged out of the sun into the eyes, and the muzzles, of 3,000 men of the *teppo-shu*, or arquebus corps. It may be that the slow-loading *teppo* did not mow down hundreds of mounted samurai as is suggested by the popular accounts of Nagashino, but they certainly made an enormous contribution to the victory, if only by destroying the impact of the Takeda samurai advance and thus laying them open to the waiting blades of the swordsmen.

The *teppo-ashigaru* wear simple *okegawa-do* and iron *jingasa* helmets. From their belts hang bullet bags and powder flasks, and round their shoulders are slung ration bags. A coil of fuse is carried round the left arm, and the smouldering match end was not inserted into the serpentine until the last moment. The firing positions of the arquebusiers are taken from contemporary illustrations, which are supported by observations of arquebuses being fired by muzzle-loading enthusiasts in Japan who keep alive the traditions of the *teppo*.

The golden fan standard in the background indicates the presence of Nobunaga's ally, Tokugawa Ieyasu.

them marched through the ranks exhorting their men to signalise themselves this day, on which depended an Empire. They represented to them that Shibata had only a handful of raw and inexperienced men, that Nobunaga, having the Shogun in his power, made this only a sconce for his ambition ... that being a most bloody and ambitious tyrant, no quarter was to be expected, and so they must either conquer or die.

Shibata, being a great captain, drew up his army into two lines and animated his men to revenge the death of their master [i.e. Ashikaga Yoshiteru] the best of Princes, whom these two barbarous and unnatural rebels had assassinated....

Shibata, seeing his men resolute and determined, marched straight against the enemy, who was also well advanced to receive him. The shock was very rude and bloody, and the victory for a long time seemed doubtful, for the two rebels, seeing life and death depended on the action, played the parts of great captains and soldiers. Shibata, on his part, flew on every side to give necessary orders, and though his army in number proved far inferior to the enemy, yet they far surpassed them in valour and courage.

The victory being very dubious for some time, and Shibata's men beginning to give way, he marched up with a body of reserves, and fell upon Yoshitsugu's right wing with such resolution that he broke through the cavalry and put the infantry in an absolute rout....

The two rebels, seeing their own men upon the flight, followed sword in hand and forced them to wheel about. The cavalry also rallied again, returned to the charge, and the combat was immediately revived. Shame and confusion for the late disgrace spurred on the rebels to repair their honour. The others, on the contrary, puffed up with the late success, looked upon them as already conquered. In effect, after a slight skirmish they took to their heels, and the vanguard, falling upon the rear, put all to confusion. It was then nothing else but a downright butchery and slaughter; and as Shibata aimed principally at the two rebel commanders, he followed close, and charged in the rear; but they, by the help of good horses, saved themselves in the woods and thence retreated into their forts.

Most of the troops cried out for quarter, and went over to Shibata, the rest were all put to the sword.

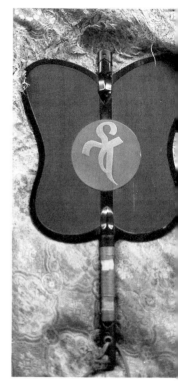

The war-fan of Takeda Shingen
Commanders of armies customarily carried fans as a means of signalling to troops. This is the rigid version, which is very similar to the ones used nowadays by the referees in sumo wrestling contests. This example was used by Takeda Shingen, and is preserved in the Takeda Museum at the Erin-ji at Enzan, (Yamanashi Prefecture). It is black, with a gold *bonji* on a red disc.

This vivid account paints a dramatic picture of sixteenth-century samurai warfare. Note the control both commanders seem to possess over their samurai until the closing stages and the willingness of some of the Miyoshi/Matsunaga troops to declare for Shibata when they see the cause is hopeless. Suicide was never an automatic choice in samurai warfare.

In the late autumn of 1568 Nobunaga entered Kyoto accompanied by Ashikaga Yoshiaki, who was proclaimed Shogun within the month. Miyoshi and Matsunaga fled before his advance.

The Battle of the Anegawa

In May 1570 Nobunaga moved against the Asakura clan, who threatened

him from the North. As noted above, Asakura Yoshikage was a formidable foe, having scored a notable victory over the Ikko-ikki in 1562, forcing them to be content with the province of Kaga as their domain, and sealing the agreement by giving his daughter in marriage to the Chief Priest of the sect. Nobunaga took the field with 30,000 men, including an army under Tokugawa Ieyasu, and captured two of Asakura's forts, Tezutsu-yama and Kamigasaki, to the North of Lake Biwa. He was about to lay siege to the Asakura fortress of Ichijo-ga-tani when he heard that Asai Nagamasa, Nobunaga's brother-in-law, had allied himself with the Asakura against him. This was a bitter disappointment, for Nobunaga had been relying on this alliance to guard his rear. At a council of his allies both Ieyasu and Matsunaga Hisahide (who had now joined Nobunaga) advised retreat, which they thought would be safe if executed immediately and at speed, for they did not rate Asai's capacity very highly. So Nobunaga started off with the vanguard. Fortunately Matsunaga had a friend who owned the castle of Kuchiki in Omi and went to him to ask for a guide to the by-roads that ran through the mountains to Kyoto via Ohara. Matsunaga went fully prepared to kill him if he refused, but he consented, and Nobunaga was able to lead his men safely back to the capital away from the main roads. Ieyasu and Hideyoshi formed his rearguard, which was harassed all the way and responded on several occasions by vigorous charges against Asakura's men.

Retreats, even when fought bravely and undertaken wisely, are not the most glamorous side of samurai warfare, but Ieyasu and Hideyoshi acquitted themselves well, and the retreat was accomplished with few losses, proving once again that samurai lives were precious and that there was no disgrace in choosing one's own time and place for a reckoning.

It was not long before Nobunaga issued from the capital once again against the Asai and Asakura. This time he advanced from Gifu up the Eastern side of Lake Biwa towards Asai's fortress of Odani, which he menaced by attacking Yokoyama castle on the left bank of the Anegawa to the South-East. This action forced Asai and Asakura into a pitched battle fought across this shallow river, the Battle of the Anegawa (1570). It resulted in a fine victory for Nobunaga with a toll of 3,170 heads, a large proportion of which were taken by the Tokugawa force.

The victory of the Anegawa, though not fully decisive, greatly relieved the pressure on Nobunaga from this quarter. It also meant that he could concentrate on the defeat of his greatest enemy – the adherents and allies

PLATE 19   *Warriors of the Ikko-ikki face Nobunaga in 1578*

There is much less material available about the appearance of the fanatical Ikko-ikki than the samurai who opposed them for 50 years. This plate is an attempt to reconstruct the 'feel', if not the actual appearance, of these staunch warriors. The main figure, who shows admirable disregard for the presence of an arrow through his arm, carries his long straight spear as he advances across the swampy ground of the Nagashima River delta towards Nobunaga's troops, to whom the Ikko-ikki were as contemptible as vermin. We have given him a very simple *hara-ate* of metal plates on cloth, and a white *hachimaki* headband strengthened with chain mail. His shaven head is growing hair again.

His fallen comrade in the foreground wears a folding version of samurai armour, which we know was worn by the defenders of the fortress-cathedral of Ishiyama Hongan-ji, and the stockades of Nagashima. He wears a *sashimono* that has been preserved, which bears the crudely-written slogan, 'He who advances is sure of heaven, but he who retreats will suffer hell.' Thousands of these flags must have existed. The other white flag bears a Buddhist slogan beginning 'Namu . . .' ('Hail to . . .'). The red flag with the *sotoba* design was carried by a contingent from the Zempuku-ji of Edo who supported the Ishiyama Hongan-ji against Nobunaga's attempts to destroy it.

The Nagashima area is still wild and mysterious to this day, in spite of being crossed by a railway line and several bridges over the reed swamps, and in misty weather one can easily conjure up images of the thousands of Ikko fanatics who were slaughtered here by Oda Nobunaga.

of the Ikko-ikki. The Ikko-ikki were the hub around which rolled a wheel of ever-changing alliances against Nobunaga, and a major part of his career was taken up by opposing this political focus that drew all opposition to Nobunaga into itself.

Nobunaga and the Ikko-ikki

The Ikko-ikki had continued to grow into the 1570s. Not only were the Ikko-ikki a powerful military force, they also had the ability to embarrass Nobunaga's *tenka* by various economic weapons, such as the withholding of taxes and rents. Their temples, also, existed ostentatiously as independent towns. What was of fundamental importance to Nobunaga was that the power of the Ikko-ikki was concentrated at the very places where *he* had to be powerful. There were Ikko strongholds in his native Province of Owari, in his early conquest, Mino, in the 'Home Provinces' that guarded Kyoto and in the strategic areas of Kaga and Echizen – all were vital to both interests, and there could be no compromise.

In his letters and despatches Nobunaga reserves his strongest language for the Ikko-ikki. They must be 'wiped out', 'eradicated', 'mown down'. No samurai honour was involved with this enemy. They would be searched out and destroyed *yama yama, tani tani*, 'on every hill and valley', as he wrote to the Governor of Kyoto in 1575, after massacring 20,000 of the sect's adherents in Echizen.

The religious nature of the Ikko-ikki attracted support from the older established organisations of militant clergy. In 1570 the Ishiyama Hongan-ji, the Ikko's fortified cathedral in Osaka, sent help to the Miyoshi faction, which was again stirring up trouble in Kyoto, and which was joined by *sohei* from Negoro in Kii Province, who included 3,000 arquebusiers in their ranks. Almost at the same time Asai and Asakura made an alliance with the veteran soldier monks of the Enryaku-ji on Mount Hiei, and Ikko-ikki from Ise Province threatened Nobunaga from the East. Nobunaga's tactics were reduced to holding the line from Kyoto to Gifu, but he reacted by mounting an attack that was as much symbolic as it was designed to destroy the particular faction of his enemies against whom it was launched – the destruction of Mount Hiei. In both it was successful. The *sohei* of Mount Hiei, who had provided a refuge for rebels and Emperors for centuries, were destroyed forever as a military force as Nobunaga's samurai advanced up the holy mountain, hacking, burning and shooting to death any living thing that opposed them. As a symbol of his determination to crush all manifestations of the warrior monk the campaign send a shudder through the forts of the Ikko-ikki. Here was a warlord who meant every word he had used about them. Only one religious sect applauded. They were the Christian missionaries from Portugal, who saw in Nobunaga a destroyer of the 'enemies of God'.

90

The remarkable suicide of Miura Yoshimoto
The author has noted many unusual acts of suicide in the annals of the samurai, ranging from jumping headlong from a horse with a dagger half way down one's throat to being buried alive, but none are as bizarre as the act credited to a certain Miura Yoshimoto who, during a fierce battle at Arai Castle against the Hojo in 1516, cut off his own head! Japanese swords were renowned for their sharpness, and Yoshimoto used one by the famous Masamune, but it remains open to conjecture as to whether such a deed could be physically possible. It is recorded with much admiration in the *Hojo-Godaiki*, and this illustration is taken from a woodblock printed edition, which has modified the story slightly to show Yoshimoto dismounted when he performs the amazing act.

Nobunaga's campaign against the Ikko-ikki was conducted against a background of a growing estrangement between himself and the Shogun, whose position gave other *daimyo* an excuse to act against Nobunaga. Takeda Shingen in fact inflicted a defeat upon Nobunaga's ally Tokugawa Ieyasu at Mikata-ga-hara in 1572, and only the death of this redoubtable warlord in 1573 reduced the threat from the powerful Takeda war machine.

In 1573 Nobunaga sent Ashikaga Yoshiaki into exile, bringing the sorry history of the Ashikaga Shogunate to its end. The following month Nobunaga turned again towards Omi. As his army approached Asai Nagamasa's Odani castle, the latter appealed to Asakura Yoshikage for support. When Asakura began to lead his army towards his ally, Nobunaga intercepted him and chased the survivors back to Ichijo-ga-tani, where Yoshikage was forced to commit suicide. The Oda army turned back and easily overcame Asai Nagamasa, who also took his own life. Their heads were displayed in public in Kyoto, then lacquered and gilded to preserve for posterity Nobunaga's destruction of two samurai warriors. He awarded their lands to Hideyoshi, who built a castle at Nagahama, on the shores of Lake Biwa.

The time was ripe for Nobunaga to continue his military opposition to the Ikko-ikki. He began by isolating the Ishiyama Hongan-ji from its other satellites. Several times since 1570 he had suffered risings by a branch of the Ikko sect based in a fortress called Nagashima, on the estuary of the Kiso-gawa. In July 1574 Nobunaga attacked Nagashima, helped by a force of pirates from Ise, who bombarded the Ikko-ikki from the seaward side with heavy calibre muskets. By the end of August they were short of food and willing to treat, but Nobunaga was not inclined towards mercy. Instead he built a stockade around the two fortresses that still held out, Nakae and Nagashima itself, into which had crammed as many as 20,000 people. These fortresses were then set on fire, and anyone who attempted to escape through the palisade was shot down.

The Master of Musketry

The following year, 1575, Nobunaga's confidence was greatly increased by his classic victory of the Battle of Nagashino, where the late Takeda Shingen's son and heir Katsuyori was induced to use the legendary Takeda cavalry charge against Nobunaga's army, which had sheltered itself behind a loose palisade. Volley after volley of arquebus balls tore into the advancing Takeda samurai, until, confused and disorganised, they fell prey to the sharp swords of Nobunaga's army.

Nobunaga was by no means the first *daimyo* to use firearms. They had been known in Japan since 1542, when two arquebuses had been demonstrated to the local *daimyo* by some shipwrecked Portuguese sailors.

PLATE 20   *A retainer of the Tsuchiya, the last supporters of Takeda Katsuyori, in 1581*

The nemesis for the Takeda clan came in 1581. Takeda Katsuyori, defeated at Nagashino, was gradually abandoned by his father Shingen's old retainers as Oda Nobunaga and Tokugawa Ieyasu advanced into the mountains of Kai. Only the Tsuchiya were with him to the last. Tsuchiya Masatsugu had been one of the 'Takeda Twenty-four Generals' to be killed at Nagashino, and it was three brothers of the succeeding generation who were to die with him at Temmoku-zan.

This proud samurai, with the Tsuchiya *mon* on his *sashimono*, is wearing a *tatami-gusoku* (folding armour) – the simplest samurai armour of all. It consisted of a series of plates sewn on to a cloth backing and joined by links of mail. He has no *haidate*, or *sode*, but good *oda-kote*, the style of sleeve armour that had raised gourd-shaped plates. The *shikoro* of his helmet is made in the same way as his armour, but its bowl is of much stouter construction, being a typical *zunari-*, or *hineno-kabuto*. He is standing on the bridge leading to the entrance of one of Katsuyori's castles. Katsuyori was fond of castles, and many saw in his reliance upon passive defence a bad omen for the Takeda clan. The armour is based upon several extant specimens and drawings by Sasama.

The courtyard of the Honno-ji in Kyoto, the site of the assassination of Oda Nobunaga in 1582.

Two samurai armed with arquebuses. The introduction of firearms was the most decisive development in the whole of samurai warfare. At the Battle of Nagashino in 1575, Oda Nobunaga used hundreds of arquebuses to inflict a major defeat on the Takeda clan cavalry, an engagement commemorated every year on the site of Nagashino castle. The equipment of these two 'samurai' is authentic, with the addition of plastic bags to protect their weapons against the persistent rain that accompanied the 1986 celebrations!

Within months the swordsmiths of Japan, who were already highly skilled in metalwork, were turning out copies of the weapons and improving the design. There is little doubt that Nobunaga acquired a healthy respect for firearms when they were used against him. As early as 1560, during Imagawa's attempted march through his province, Tokugawa Ieyasu had made good use of concentrated arquebus fire in taking Nobunaga's fortress of Marune. The Ikko-ikki had their own large arsenal, and a ball from one of their arquebuses wounded Nobunaga in the leg during one of his attempts to take the Ishiyama Hongan-ji. But Nobunaga's decision to use arquebuses on a large scale, in a field battle, protected by field fortifications, and operating under such good discipline that some rudimentary form of rotational volley firing could take place, has the hallmark of an innovatory military genius.

The Ishiyama Hongan-ji was not quelled so easily. Its position on the watery delta of Osaka enabled the Mori clan to ferry supplies to it along the Inland Sea. In the summer of 1575 Nobunaga fought a sea battle during which many guns were used, in an attempt to prevent these supplies from getting through. The subsequent failure made him return to his original policy of isolating Ishiyama Hongan-ji by reducing its satellite fortresses. In 1577 he destroyed the Ikko strongholds at Saiga and the *sohei* of Negoro in Kii Province, and Ishiyama Hongan-ji stood alone. Only a combined attack on Nobunaga by Mori from the West and Uesugi Kenshin from the East could save it, but by 1578 Uesugi Kenshin was dead (perhaps the *ninja* in his lavatory was sent by Nobunaga?) and Mori, the warlord of the West, dared not move alone. Gradually the Ikko-ikki's resistance faded and in 1580, following the advice of the Emperor, the Ishiyama Hongan-ji, the last outpost of militant Buddhism, surrendered to Nobunaga.

In 1581 Nobunaga put on a splendid military parade through the streets of Kyoto, ostensibly for the pleasure of the Emperor, but in reality to impress upon the population Nobunaga's continuing triumph. It was almost his last flamboyant act. In 1582 Toyotomi Hideyoshi was besieging Takamatsu castle and sent an urgent plea to Nobunaga for reinforcements. Nobunaga responded rapidly, but thereby left himself perilously unguarded, and he was attacked in the Honno-ji temple in Kyoto by another of his generals, Akechi Mitsuhide. Nobunaga's bodyguard were taken by surprise as thoroughly as he had once ambushed Imagawa Yoshimoto. The Honno-ji was burned and, as the temple blazed around him, Nobunaga committed a defiant act of suicide. As word spread that he was dead the avaricious townspeople looted his glorious castle of Azuchi and burned it to the ground.

Momoyama Period
– Toyotomi Hideyoshi

The second of the trio whose military conquests unified Japan, and brought to an end the 'warring states' of the *daimyo*, was Toyotomi Hideyoshi (1539–1598), who is often referred to as the 'Napoleon of Japan'.

Toyotomi Hideyoshi

Akechi Mitsuhide, the destroyer of Nobunaga, bears the nickname of the 'Thirteen Day Shogun', which indicates approximately how long he lasted before being defeated by Nobunaga's protegé, Toyotomi Hideyoshi, at the Battle of Yamazaki. Hideyoshi, who managed to contrive for himself the inheritance of Nobunaga's *tenka*, in spite of opposition from practically all of Nobunaga's allies, enemies and surviving relatives, is one of the most fascinating characters in samurai history. He was the son of a woodcutter and joined Nobunaga's army as an *ashigaru*. He rose through the ranks on merit alone. Following Nobunaga's death he was able to turn the squabbles about inheritance and policy to his own considerable advantage, helped along by a number of profitable sieges and battles, such as Shizugatake in

PLATE 21   *Tokugawa Ieyasu at the Battle of Nagakute, 1584*

The Battle of Nagakute in 1584 was one of Tokugawa Ieyasu's finest victories. Here we see him in command wearing the actual armour which he is supposed to have worn there. It is preserved in the Kunozan Toshogu Shrine Treasure House in Shizuoka. It is a remarkably simple affair for such an important commander, but as such reflects Ieyasu's eminently practical approach to life.

The armour is a *nuinobe-do*, of solid horizontal plates joined by *sugake-odoshi*. The scalloped top edges are a feature often found on a *nuinobe-do*, whereby it differs from the *mogami-do* shown in Plate 17, which has flanged upper edges. This armour is also of *ni-mai*, two-piece, style, similar to the *okegawa-do*, and again differing from the *go-mai* five-sections, of the Hojo armour. (A *nuinobe-do* laced with cross knots would be called a *hishinui-do*.)

The *kote* are of very dense chain mail, which is far more 'European-looking' than many Japanese examples. His *haidate* and *suneate* are quite ordinary. The helmet is very splendid, being of an almost square cross section, and is set off with a delicate fern-leaf *maedate* crest with a devil's face. There is a second *shikoro*, the *shita-shikoro*, of mail on cloth, and a very fine *mempo* with moustache and beard. Ieyasu is pointing with his *saihai*, which has tassels of oiled paper.

The *maku* curtains bear the Tokugawa *mon*, and the banner of the Ii family can be seen going by behind.

1583. At the siege of Kameyama, Hideyoshi achieved the first victory in
samurai history by the use of mining. At Shizugatake he surprised his
enemy by a rapid advance by night. There seemed no end to his boldness.
Though he had the physical appearance, and to some extent the shape, of a
wizened monkey, as his contemporaries describe him, he is also admired as
'a veritable war-god on the field of battle'.

Only Tokugawa Ieyasu provided a counter to him at the indecisive Battle
of Nagakute in 1584. The two generals had glared at each other from extensive field fortifications near Komaki, which is today a suburb of Nagoya.
Defence was not a mode of warfare that appealed to the samurai spirit, so
Hideyoshi sent Ikeda on a secret raid into Ieyasu's Mikawa. The Tokugawa
observed his army and attacked them near Nagakute. It was a bloody
encounter and the unfortunate Ikeda lost his head, but Nagakute served, in
the short term at any rate, to gain him a valuable ally, as both recognised
the other's obvious merit. There was nothing to be gained from opposing
one another. Together they could conquer an Empire.

As Hideyoshi had risen from the peasant class to become a commander
of samurai, one of his first steps after achieving national control was to
ensure that no one could follow in his footsteps. By his edict of 1587,
known as the 'Great Sword Hunt', all non-samurai were forcibly disarmed.

The sword-collectors explained to the enraged populace that the weapons so gathered were to be melted down and made into nails and bolts for the huge statue of Buddha which Hideyoshi was building. Their compliance with the edict would therefore ensure their salvation in the next world, as well as benefiting the peace of the present life.

Hideyoshi the Castle-Builder

Hideyoshi's career becomes more remarkable once Nobunaga's domain has been secured and he is able to look further afield. One of his first steps was to build a mighty castle at Osaka, on the site of the Ishiyama Hongan-ji. Hideyoshi is known as a great castle-builder, and the huge white-walled fortress upon a sloping stone base is almost the symbol of the Momoyama Period, but he was also, like Nobunaga before him, a great destroyer of castles — other people's, of course! His overall plan was to reduce the number of fortresses throughout the country, leaving only the strategic provincial castles of the great *daimyo* whom he had subdued and who had sworn loyalty towards him, thus reducing the risk of rebellion against them or Hideyoshi himself. The castles that arose during the latter part of the sixteenth century were much larger and stronger than the more modest structures that had preceded them, as illustrated by documents referring to the Hojo family. The Hojo were great castle-builders, as evidenced by their central stronghold of Odawara and the various satellite fortresses that protected their domains. Birt's study of the Hojo comments:

Castle repair was a highly organised task in the Sengoku period and an important responsibility of the castellan. It was also highly detailed, as revealed in a 1563

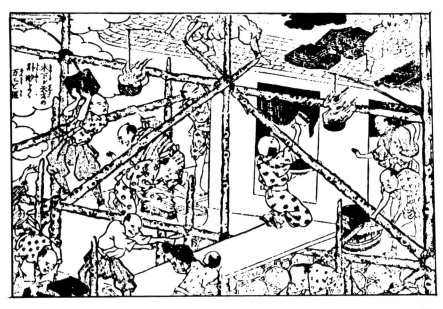

According to tradition, Toyotomi Hideyoshi not only built a fortress at Sunomata to oppose the mighty Inabayama, but built the whole structure in one night to impress his enemies! Here we see Hideyoshi's men furiously engaged on castle-building.

castle repair order to the residents of Tana village for work on Tamanawa castle. The order stated that if there were no typhoons, the walls were to be repaired every five years. The rate of work was set at four persons per ken *[6 feet] per day. The villagers were also ordered to bring the following materials:*

5 large posts	*10 bundles of Yamato bamboo*
5 smaller posts	*30 coils of rope*
10 bamboo poles	*20 bundles of reed*

The villagers were then given precise instructions for raising the palisade. They were ordered to: drive in the large wooden posts at intervals of one ken *in the earthworks; in between these posts, they spread sideways two bamboo sticks, and then arranged four bundles of Yamato bamboo; this was fastened by six coils of rope and then thatched with reed. The walls were eight* sun *[10 inches] thick, and were coated with a mixture of red clay and rock to make them durable. Given these materials and the method of construction, it is easy to see why the Sengoku castle required constant upkeep to maintain a battleworthy condition.*

Wood and earth were the main material for the Sengoku castles, but some stone was used for towers and gateways. It was the ill-fated Azuchi, and the colossal Osaka, which set the new standard for castle-building. Now stone was used for walls and parapets and the whole scale of castle-building became colossal. Nearly all the Japanese castles that remain to this day were completed at this time, though many have been much restored since.

PLATE 22   *Kato Kiyomasa collects a head during the Battle of Sendaigawa in 1587*

The Battle of Sendaigawa, the Sendai River, was the last major encounter fought by Hideyoshi's troops as they battled their way down the island of Kyushu to defeat the powerful Shimazu clan of Satsuma. (There is a full account of the campaign in *The Samurai – a Military History* by the present author.)

Kato Kiyomasa (1562–1611) was one of Toyotomi Hideyoshi's most renowned generals. He was born the son of the village blacksmith in Nakamura, which is now a suburb of Nagoya. Nakamura was also the home village of his mentor, Hideyoshi. At the Battle of Shizugatake in 1583 Kiyomasa was named as one of the *shichi hon yari*, the 'Seven Spears' who fought most valiantly that day.

In this plate we see him in a suit of armour which he is known to have worn, though it is not entirely certain if he wore it during the Kyushu campaign. It is preserved in the Tokyo National Museum in Ueno Park, Tokyo. Its strange design is supposed to represent the body of a monk. The *do* is an extreme version of a smooth-surfaced *hotoke-do*, which has been beaten to represent skin clinging to wasted ribs, and is finished in a most unusual pink lacquer. The left side of the *do* has been laced in *iro-iro odoshi* (multi-coloured lacing) to look like a monk's robe. The *kusazuri* are finished in the same way. The helmet is not Kiyomasa's favourite 'court-cap' style, but one designed to continue the theme of the human body. On the scalp is horse-hair combed back into a pigtail with a heavy peak.

Kiyomasa's unfortunate victim wears a *dangaie-do*, which is a *nuinobe-do* that has its upper plates laced in *sugake-odoshi* and its lower plates laced in *kebiki-odoshi*. As he has no doubt regarded himself as a person of some importance he has dispensed with a *sashimono*, and replaced the upper bracket for holding a *sashimono* by a small version of the old *agemaki* bow, which now serves no practical purpose.

In the background are samurai wearing the Shimazu *sashimono*, based on one dating from the time of Hideyoshi's adversary, Shimazu Yoshihiro, which is preserved in the museum of Shimazu memorabilia in Kagoshima City.

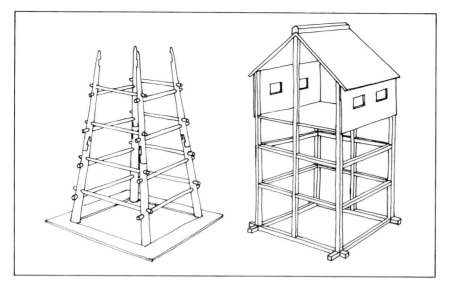

The siege tower
The author has been unable to find any contemporary reference for the use of the type of moveable siege towers familiar from Medieval Europe. Japanese siege towers tend to be immobile contructions designed to afford observation facilities rather than provide an assault platform. Some are of open construction, others solid-looking structures very similar to the permanent towers of the early sixteenth-century wooden castle such as seen in Plate 15.

The castles of Japan may be Hideyoshi's lasting monument, but his intangible legacy was a tradition of military excellence that sent highly-trained, well-equipped armies from one end of Japan to another, as he completed the work Nobunaga had begun. He became the first *daimyo* to overcome the two other main islands of Shikoku and Kyushu. His Kyushu campaign, in particular, was an outstanding achievement, as it involved controlling armies from a distance, forming alliances as well as fighting fierce samurai battles.

The Christian Samurai

Hideyoshi is also remembered for his persecution of the Christians, a trend which reversed Nobunaga's policy towards them. Nobunaga had sheltered the missionaries from Buddhist opposition, but as they rejoiced over the destruction of Mount Hiei, and applauded Nobunaga's quelling of the Ikko sect, little did his Jesuit friends suspect that they were seeing a pattern for the repression of religious movements that would be used against them before the century was out. The Jesuits had served Nobunaga's purposes as a lever against the Buddhist fanatics and a channel of goodwill that permitted the free flow of cannon and gunpowder into his castle storerooms. Hideyoshi soon came to see them in a very different light. Organised religion – any organised religion – posed a threat to loyalty, and that could not be tolerated. But what threat did Christianity pose?

From the point of view of samurai history any direct 'threat' was negligible. Never at any time was there an exclusively Christian army comparable to the fanatics of the Ikko-ikki or the *sohei* of Mount Hiei. *Daimyo* who had embraced Christianity saw to it that their followers received baptism, but although such men may have gone into battle with

102

A nineteenth-century painting on silk, copied from an original Western-style portrait of the Christian samurai, Takayama Ukon.

crosses on their banners and shouting Christian war-cries, they fought for the *daimyo*'s cause. It is at an individual level that we must look for illustration of the Christian samurai, and the Momoyama Period furnishes several suitable examples. One such was Takayama Ukon. He was born in either 1552 or 1553, and died in 1615, so his life encompasses exactly the time between St Francis Xavier's death, at the height of missionary activity, and Tokugawa Ieyasu's order expelling the missionaries from Japan.

He was baptised at the age of 11 and given the Christian name of Justo, at the same time as his father, Takayama 'Darie'. The Takayama were vassals of the Wada family, and when Wada Koremasa was killed in Nobunaga's service they found themselves under his successor, Wada Korenaga, who was the owner of Takatsuki castle, a fortress placed somewhat uncomfortably between Osaka and Kyoto, and entirely surrounded by the territory of the *daimyo*, Araki Muneshige. Wada Korenaga was jealous of the reputation the Takayama family enjoyed and contrived to have them murdered during a dinner party at his castle. The plot was discovered, and Ukon fought back so successfully that Korenaga fled wounded. Nobunaga, impressed by their reaction, transferred the castle to Ukon, who began to take a full part in his campaigns. We hear of him fighting against the Ishiyama Hongan-ji, but his greatest test came off the field of battle, when his overlord Araki Murashige revolted against Nobunaga in 1578.

Ukon had advised Araki not to side against Nobunaga, but as he was his vassal he was sworn to support him, and had sent his sister and her son as hostages to Araki for good behaviour. Nobunaga, however, realised Ukon's deep Christian commitment, and hoped to use it to persuade the young man into surrendering Takatsuki castle to him. He sent a Jesuit to Ukon, who bore a message from Nobunaga stating that he would execute the

PLATE 23 *Kato Kiyomasa's army creates havoc against the Koreans in 1592*

In this plate Kato Kiyomasa is seen engaging the Korean army during the Korean War of 1592–1598. In contrast to Plate 22 he is wearing one of the *naga-eboshi-kabuto* helmets for which he is famous. They were made by building up a false crown of wood and papier-mache on to a basic *zunari-kabuto*. The silver-lacquered one shown here is taken from a replica displayed in the museum of Hideyoshi and Kiyomasa in Nakamura Park, Nagoya, the birthplace of these heroes. The original is in the Tokugawa Art Museum in Nagoya, but is rarely displayed. Two different designs are in the Hommyoji

Museum, Kumamoto, and Kumamoto castle. He wears a red *jinbaori* and a *mogami-do*, with flanged upper edges.

His samurai and *ashigaru* are in 'battle dress' of *okegawa-do*. There is more variety among the samurai, as may be imagined, but the overall uniformity indicates the gradual separation of the warrior from the land that was going on during the Age of War. Soon even the lowliest *ashigaru* would become a samurai, and spend no more time tilling fields. They all wear the Kato *mon* on their *sashimono* and, in some cases, on their armour.

In the background flies

Kiyomasa's *uma-jirushi* standard, a long *hata-jirushi* bearing the motto and war-cry of the Nichiren sect of Buddhism, of which Kiyomasa was a member. It reads *Namu myoho renge kyo* ('Glory to the Holy Lotus'). Nichiren taught that salvation was to be found in the Lotus Sutra, hence these words.

The Korean costumes are based on trophies brought back to Japan after the Korean War, of which there are only a few examples, and on specimens displayed in the Central Historical Museum, P'yong-yang, North Korea, to whose staff the author expresses his gratitude.

Maeda Toshiie, Lord of Kaga
Maeda Toshiie was one of
Hideyoshi's most successful generals,
and acquired control over much of
the Hokurikudo Region of Japan.
This statue of him is in his capital of
Kanazawa, and behind the statue
may be seen the towers of the
Ishikawa Gate of Kanazawa Castle,
which is all that remains of his
fortress. Toshiie is wearing a gold-
lacquered armour, with a
spectacular gold-lacquered catfish-
tail helmet.

The defenders starve during a siege
Toyotomi Hideyoshi was a master of
siegecraft, and the extremes to
which the defenders could be
reduced is depicted sensationally in
this illustration from *Ehon Taikoki*,
an illustrated life of Hideyoshi, of
which several different versions
exist. In the bottom right a group
share a raw horse's leg, while others
appear to be preparing for
cannibalism.

Shibata Katsuie takes an enemy's head
Shibata Katsuie is best known for being the leader of the army defeated by Hideyoshi at the Battle of Shizugatake in 1583, when his general Sakuma Morimasa disobeyed his orders to remain in a fortified position. Katsuie was an accomplished leader of samurai, and this picture from the *Ehon Taikoki* shows him in happier days when he fought side by side with Hideyoshi in the service of Nobunaga. He is taking an enemy's head in grand style.

missionaries and destroy the churches in his domains unless Ukon handed over the castle. Takayama Ukon was placed in a frightful dilemma. His samurai honour, linked to the lives of his sister and nephew, had been placed as a counterbalance to his Christianity. After hours of agonised prayer he presented himself before Nobunaga as a supplicant, unarmed, and with a symbolically shaved head. Nobunaga was much impressed by Ukon's sincerity. Naturally, he took over the castle, but when the campaign was concluded he pardoned Ukon and increased his domains. Araki Murashige, too, had been impressed by Ukon's behaviour and did not harm any of the hostages.

Later Takayama Ukon took part in the Battle of Yamazaki at which Akechi Mitsuhide, Nobunaga's assassin, was defeated, and then came under the influence of Hideyoshi. At Nobunaga's funeral he declined to offer incense at the Buddhist altar, which may have offended Hideyoshi, but all was forgiven when Ukon took a valiant part in the Battle of Shizugatake in 1583. He was the commander of the frontier fortress of Iwasaki-yama, from which he was driven by an impetuous attack from Sakuma Morimasa. This was the attack that was to prove to be Sakuma's undoing when Hideyoshi brought over his rapid reinforcements. Although wounded in the encounter, and suffering the loss of many retainers, Takayama's defeat was instrumental in Hideyoshi's victory. He therefore gained greatly in standing with Hideyoshi, and went on to join in his expeditions to Shikoku and against the *sohei* of Negoro in Kii.

Those were the good years, but the conflict of loyalty remained and Takayama Ukon was but one of a number of Christian *daimyo* whose loyalty to the growing power of Hideyoshi could not be absolute. For Hideyoshi the key lay in a historical analogy. The Buddhist sect of Jodo-Shinshu, in its social and political manifestation of the Ikko-ikki, had brought great harm to the country until Nobunaga crushed it. Christianity, in his eyes, was no different. Thus began the unhappy times of persecution, which culminated in the martyrdom of the Twenty-Six Saints, who were crucified at Nagasaki on 5 February 1597. Hideyoshi also decreed that all the Christian fathers should leave the country, but his death in 1598 prevented him from carrying out this order.

For the next decade the Christian *daimyo* enjoyed a respite from persecution, until the Tokugawa regime became wary of them for the same reasons as Hideyoshi. Ukon was then living under the protection of Maeda Toshinaga, the *daimyo* of Kanazawa. In 1614 the Tokugawa Shogunate issued a decree expelling all missionaries and ordering the banishment of Takayama Ukon and other *daimyo*. Toshinaga's successor, Toshitsune,

PLATE 24 *Toyotomi Hideyoshi urges his troops to the siege of Odawara, 1590*

'In stature he resembled a wizened monkey, but on the field of battle he was a veritable war-god', wrote one contemporary of the 'Napoleon of Japan', Toyotomi Hideyoshi (1536–1598). This plate captures the dynamic presence of the leader who rose from being Nobunaga's sandal-bearer to become commander of tens of thousands. His armies conquered the island clans of Shikoku and Kyushu, gained an almost bloodless victory over the Hojo of Odawara and sent an invasion force to Korea.

It is the defeat of the Hojo that is illustrated here. Hideyoshi is wearing a black-lacquered helmet with a 'sunburst' crest at the rear. The original of this helmet has long since perished, but a faithful copy is on display in Osaka Castle Museum. He is pointing with his *warfan*, a delicate design of pearls on red silk, which still exists. He wears a *jinbaori*, or armour-surcoat, which was *de rigueur* for samurai generals, and was often richly embroidered.

Behind him stands his *uma-jirushi* (literally 'horse insignia') which was the name given to the commander's standard. Ieyasu used a large golden fan (see Plate 18) and Nobunaga had a huge red umbrella. Hideyoshi's was known as the 'golden gourd', the gourd being his original *mon*, and he is traditionally supposed to have added a gourd for every victory he won, until the final version shown here was known as the 'Thousand-gourd standard'. The Toyotomi *mon* of the paulownia is on the dangling black strips in front of the curtain of red tassels.

城中渇に臨ぐ
六角の使者を
欺く

110

Taking a bath
This illustration, taken from the *Ehon Taiko-ki*, probably depicts a scene during the siege of Chokoji in 1570, where Shibata Katsuie earned much praise. The defending warriors are bathing. The *fundoshi* or loincloth, and the characteristic samurai hairstyle may be clearly noted.

高松の城を水攻を大結搆さかへ成得る

The siege of Takamatsu Castle 1582
One of Hideyoshi's greatest achievements was the reduction of the Mori clan's fortress of Takamatsu. Noticing that it lay on low ground, Hideyoshi's engineers diverted a river, and with the help of a series of dykes the whole castle was flooded. It was during this siege that Hideyoshi received word of the murder of Nobunaga.

feared that Ukon would take up arms against him to defend himself against the expulsion order, but Ukon wrote to him saying, 'I do not strive for my salvation with weapons but with patience and humility, in accordance with the doctrine of Jesus Christ.'

On 8 November 1614 he sailed for Manila, together with the other expelled missionaries and native Christians. Forty days later he fell ill and died. He is honoured today in Japan as a man who combined within himself the two virtues of the noble samurai and the staunch Christian.

The Fall of the Hojo

By 1590 all of Japan had yielded to Hideyoshi except for the proud Hojo clan, who felt themselves to be safe behind the walls of Odawara and the outer, natural walls of the Hakone Mountains. We have seen earlier how the Hojo organised the repair of their minor castles. The main fortress of Odawara was in a much bigger league, built on the style of Osaka, with much use of stone in its construction. When Hideyoshi's intentions to destroy it became clear, orders went out for all samurai to pull back from the satellite castles into the safety of Odawara, and to bring their wives and children with them, a means of ensuring their safety and also encouraging a full participation in the fighting.

The castle almost burst with soldiers. Contemporary accounts describe how the roads between the duty stations were choked with troops, whose camps were so crowded that they resembled bamboo groves. Nevertheless the Hojo were hopelessly outnumbered. In all their forces cannot have been larger than 50,000 men, while Hideyoshi was able to mobilise as many as 200,000. He attacked the Hojo from three sides and, knowing how strongly defended the castle was, decided to starve them out. A small town grew up outside Odawara's walls, where Hideyoshi's samurai played *go* and grew vegetables. The only really fierce fighting occurred as a result of an attempt at treachery which backfired. A certain Natsuda Norihide, who was in charge of one of the gates, offered to betray the castle to Hideyoshi in return for a reward. His plot was discovered, and his troops replaced by reliable fighters, so that when Hideyoshi's men attacked they were met by a fierce resistance. Like other raids, however, it served to alleviate the boredom of the long siege. With the fall of Odawara the last of the independent *daimyo*, whose success had been a model for others, committed suicide. Their territory was given to Tokugawa Ieyasu, who established his headquarters not at Odawara but at the castle in a little fishing village nearby called Edo. It was a successful foundation, for this village of Edo is now the city of Tokyo.

PLATE 25   *Kuroda Nagamasa, bringing reinforcements to Korea in 1592, is attacked by the turtle ships.*

The Koreans may have been defeated by the Japanese on land but, once the Japanese were established on the peninsula, the Korean navy, under the command of Admiral Yi Sun Sin, began to cut their lines of communications. Admiral Yi is a national hero to both halves of Korea, and there are pictures of him and models of his 'turtle-ships' in Seoul and P'yong-yang. This plate is based on a splendid painting in the Central Historical Museum in P'yong-yang, and an excellent model of the ship. *The Samurai – a Military History* by the present author contains a full account of the naval battles of the Korean War and a discussion of the tactics of the turtle boat which are illustrated here. A sulphurous smokescreen was emitted from the dragon's head in the bow and cannon lined its sides.

The Japanese warship looks very primitive by comparison. Kuroda Nagamasa stands bravely in the stern and is instantly recognisable by his buffalo-horn helmet. It is similar to that shown in Plate 14, and is illustrated in colour in *The Book of the Samurai* by the present author.

The Korean War

Nobunaga's motto had been *tenka fubu*, 'the realm covered in military glory'. To Hideyoshi this 'realm' extended far beyond the shores of Japan itself. His invasion of Korea, which had as its goal the eventual conquest of China, is a unique episode in ṣamurai history. At no other time did the samurai attempt to conquer another country.

The first invasion sailed in 1592, and three columns under Konishi Yukinaga, a Christian *daimyo*, Kato Kiyomasa of the Nichiren Buddhist sect and Kuroda Nagamasa, marched up the Korean peninsula, carrying all before them. In almost every aspect of military behaviour the Japanese were superior. They were well supplied with firearms, had excellent field organisation, and the finest swords in the world. But the failure of the Korean army to stop them was not a failure shared by the Korean navy. Under the inspired command of Admiral Yi Sun Sin a fleet of heavily armed warships cut the Japanese lines of communication, and kept up relentless pressure on the supply of men and stores. Some of these ships, the famous 'turtle boats', were reinforced with iron plates. In time the pressure began to tell and, when China entered the war on the side of Korea, the Japanese became bogged down in a number of long sieges from which they had little hope of being relieved.

A second attempt was made in 1596, but this was brought to an end by Hideyoshi's death. The Korean War was therefore Hideyoshi's last campaign and ended a brilliant military career on a note of failure.

The *wakizashi*, the shorter of the pair of swords carried by samurai. This example, from a private collection, is of the Edo Period, and makes a *dai-sho* pair with the longer, but otherwise identical, *katana*.

Early Edo Period

The last of the traditional pre-modern historical eras of Japan is known as the Edo, or Tokugawa Period, Edo from the city that grew from the town Ieyasu chose as his home, and Tokugawa from Ieyasu's surname, as his family supplied a long line of Shoguns who ruled Japan for two and a half centuries.

The Triumph of Tokugawa Ieyasu

'Nobunaga piled the rice, Hideyoshi kneaded the dough, while Tokugawa Ieyasu ate the cake,' says the old Japanese summary of the relative contribution to samurai history of the three unifiers. Hideyoshi in fact left a cake much nearer to completion when he died in 1598, but he died in the way that all dictators dread, leaving an infant son to inherit.

The political situation that was finally to be resolved at the Battle of Sekigahara in 1600 had an eerie echo of 1582, and Nobunaga's sudden

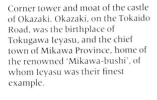

Corner tower and moat of the castle of Okazaki. Okazaki, on the Tokaido Road, was the birthplace of Tokugawa Ieyasu, and the chief town of Mikawa Province, home of the renowned 'Mikawa-bushi', of whom Ieyasu was their finest example.

Honda Heihachiro Tadakatsu, the companion of Tokugawa Ieyasu in all his battles, and a fine example of the spirit of the Mikawa-bushi. This statue of Tadakatsu wearing his famous stag's antler crest and huge wooden Buddhist rosary, stands in the grounds of Okazaki castle.

PLATE 26   *A Christian samurai, receives a blessing, ca 1596*

A Christian samurai, wearing a *namban-do*, an amalgam of European and Japanese armour, receives a blessing from a European priest before setting out for battle.

The enthusiasm for things European in the third quarter of the sixteenth century rarely extended beyond the acquisition of military equipment. This samurai has seen the quality of the stout European breastplate, and has had his armour-maker adapt it by drilling holes along its lower edge to take the suspensory cords for the skirt pieces, or *kusazuri*. He has also fitted a neckguard and 'browguard' to a morion-style helmet, which has been reversed for convenience in the operation.

The armour is based on several extant specimens in Japan of which the best known is the one preserved in the museum of the Toshogu Shrine at Nikko, which is supposed to have been worn by Tokugawa Ieyasu at the Battle of Sekigahara, and an almost identical suit in the Wakayama Toshogu Shrine. The priest is taken from one of the meticulously detailed figures of Europeans on the *'Namban Byobu'*, or 'Screen of the Southern Barbarians' in the museum at Kobe.

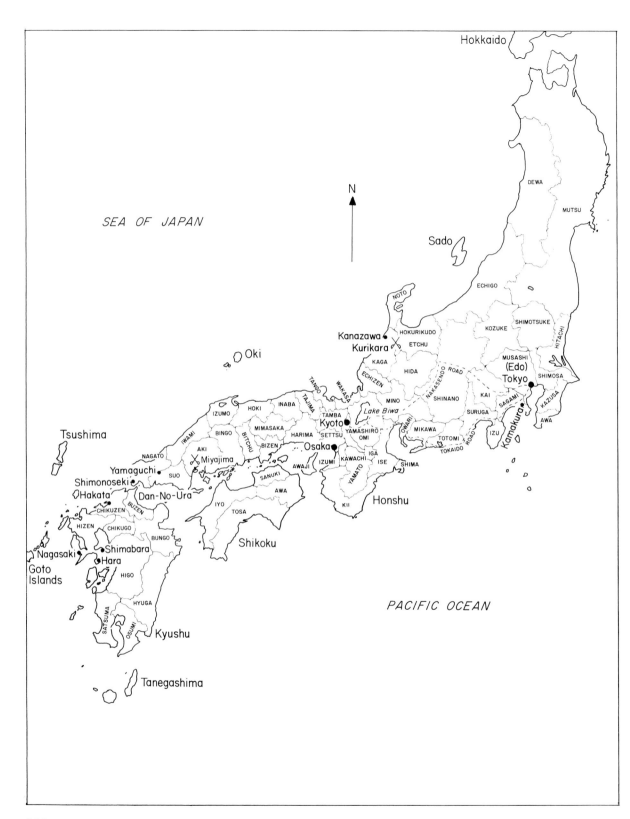

SEA OF JAPAN

Hokkaido

N

Sado

DEWA

MUTSU

ECHIGO

NOTO

Kanazawa
Kurikara

HOKURIKUDO

SHIMOTSUKE

KOZUKE

HITACHI

ETCHU

KAGA

HIDA

Oki

ECHIZEN

NAKASENDO ROAD

SHINANO

MUSASHI
(Edo)
Tokyo

SHIMOSA

TANGO

WAKASA

MINO

Lake Biwa

KAI

TAMBA

Kyoto

KAZUSA

Tsushima

IZUMO

HOKI

INABA

TAJIMA

YAMASHIRŌ
OMI

MIKAWA

SURUGA

SAGAMI

AWA

MIMASAKA

BINGO

BITCHU

HARIMA

SETTSU

OWARI

TOTOMI

IZU

Kamakura

BIZEN

Osaka

TOKAIDO ROAD

Yamaguchi

IWAMI

AKI

Miyajima

IGA

ISE

NAGATO

SUO

AWAJI

IZUMI

KAWACHI

SHIMA

Shimonoseki

Hakata

SANUKI

YAMATO

Honshu

Dan-No-Ura

CHIKUZEN

BUZEN

IYO

AWA

HIZEN

CHIKUGO

TOSA

KII

Nagasaki

BUNGO

Shikoku

Goto
Islands

Shimabara
Hara

HIGO

HYUGA

SATSUMA

OSUMI

Kyushu

PACIFIC OCEAN

Tanegashima

118

death at the hands of a rival. Once again there was a power vacuum, and once again the strong rushed to fill it. It soon became obvious that the fight was to be largely between Eastern and Western Japan – East in the person of Tokugawa Ieyasu and West represented by Ishida Mitsunari, who was allied to a number of very powerful clans, including the Mori of the Inland Sea.

Ieyasu was 58 years old in 1600. He had lived a samurai life since childhood. As a young man he had been very nearly killed in battle by an arquebus ball fired by a warrior monk. He had felt the impact of the shot, but did not discover what a narrow escape he had had until later, when he stripped off his armour and a bullet fell out of his shirt. He had been one of Imagawa Yoshimoto's followers prior to the Battle of Okehazama, and joined Nobunaga after it. It was Ieyasu who had taken Nobunaga's frontier fortress of Marune, making good use of concentrated arquebus fire. Since then he had matured from a spear-swinging, fanatical samurai to a calm, self-possessed leader of men, a veteran of Mikata-ga-Hara, Nagashino, Nagakute and Odawara. The fiasco of the Korean War was the only major engagement of Hideyoshi's reign in which he did not serve. Once the great man was gone it was time for Ieyasu to seize power. Unlike either Nobunaga or Hideyoshi he had no obligation to rule merely as Regent. He was a Minamoto, the Shogun family, and everyone knew it.

Sekigahara was his Waterloo. By cleverly threatening Ishida's lines of communication to the East, Ieyasu drew him into a pitched battle on ground of his own choosing, at the most strategically placed crossroads in Japan. Sekigahara divides Japan in two. This little village nestling beneath Mount Ibuki, where streams poured down from the hillsides, was the setting for the mighty confrontation one October morning, when the fog

---

PLATE 27 *The Tokugawa army assaults Osaka castle in 1615*

Following the spurious peace treaty that ended temporarily the 'Winter Campaign' of Osaka castle, Tokugawa Ieyasu's army redoubled their efforts to destroy this mighty fortress in the *Osaka natsu no jin*, the Summer Campaign of Osaka, the last pitched battle between samurai armies. Here the Tokugawa troops go into action against one sector of Osaka's massive walls that survived even the blitz of 1945. Several of the clans allied to, or subservient to, the Tokugawa, are seen here. The *ashigaru* of the Ii family, ever-loyal supporters of the Tokugawa, are instantly recognisable by their red-lacquered armour. Two *ashigaru* of the Date family, wearing

three little *sashimono* with one of Date Masamune's *mon* fire their arquebuses from behind the protection of a mobile shield. Its defence is a series of bundles of green bamboo, with gun slits cut through. They wear the now familiar *okegawa-do*.

The samurai dashing into the moat also wear the familiar battledress of *okegawa-do* and *zunari-kabuto*. Their *sashimono* have the *mon* of the Honda.

Also visible on the Tokugawa side are the troops of Uesugi Kagekatsu, whose submission to Tokugawa Ieyasu is now complete. They carry the red-rising-sun-on-blue flag that was the treasure of their house,

under which marched the samurai of the great Uesugi Kenshin. Their *sashimono* have a design of lovebirds in bamboo.

Inside the walls we see the banners of Sanada Yukimura, identical to those of his grandfather shown in Plate 15. Yukimura was the great hero of Osaka, and is personally credited with wounding Tokugawa Ieyasu during the siege. The yellow banners with the Oda *mon* provide a strange link with the past. They indicate the presence in the castle of Oda Yuraku, brother of Nobunaga and a noted master of the arts of the tea ceremony. The other *nobori* banners belong to Goto Mototsugu of Kyushu.

Cannon were never fully developed by the samurai. These examples at Sekigahara, with the author standing next to them to indicate the size of the barrels, are actually made of wood and bound with thick ropes of twisted bamboo. Such examples must have been little more than fireworks. It was left to the bronze and iron specimens imported from Europe to blast the stone castles of the Momoyama Period.

made it dark as night. The battle was fought through mud and rain by the largest armies then assembled in a field battle. The Tokugawa faction were ultimately victorious and Sekigahara marked the beginning of an immense upheaval for everyone.

It did not, however, mark the end of Hideyoshi's line. Although Ieyasu was proclaimed Shogun, Hideyoshi's son was still alive and, in 1614, Hideyori, now grown to manhood, packed his late father's masterpiece of Osaka castle with sympathisers ranging from embittered Christians to dispossessed *daimyo*. The castle held out until the following summer and was only then taken by means of a trick whereby the defenders were made to agree to a reduction in size of the moats. Even then it did not fall until a huge pitched battle had been fought outside its walls. This battle, the Battle of Tenno-ji, became what Sekigahara is often thought to be – the last field battle between armies of samurai. Ieyasu, now an old man, took part in the actual fighting and is believed to have been wounded by a spear thrust near the kidneys. The Tokugawa triumph was no pushover.

The New Shogun

So a new era began. Another generation learnt to use the word Shogun, and old people reminded their grandchildren of what the title meant. For the samurai it was an unexpected revolution. Even before the last body was carted from the dark valley of Sekigahara, Ieyasu was planning his future, drawing on all the lessons he had seen and experienced over 50 years of samurai warfare. First, there had to be no rebellions by the lower classes, and Hideyoshi's Sword Hunt, by which he had disarmed all the non-samurai classes, had all but ensured that.

Secondly, there had to be no rebellions by samurai, and this was not to be left to chance. As a rule of thumb he divided the *daimyo* into those who had supported him at Sekigahara and those who had opposed him. The strongest among the latter were given fiefs at the ends of Japan, if not the

Details of horse equipment
As noted in the text, basic horse furniture changed appreciably little throughout samurai history, but this illustration shows a horse of the early Edo Period with full 'campaign equipment' of fodder bags, supplies for the rider and a holster for a matchlock pistol.

ends of the earth. The former found themselves suddenly quite wealthy, and living in strategic provinces close to the main lines of communication. The waverers found themselves comfortably off and in possession of their own heads, which was a decided improvement on Nobunaga's treatment of any who did not rush to embrace him.

The third Tokugawa Shogun, Iemitsu, extended Ieyasu's principle by requiring all the *daimyo* also to maintain a residence in Edo, and actually live there, next to the Shogun's palace, one year in two, with their wives and children staying in Edo permanently. The *daimyo* were astounded, for even Nobunaga's bold innovations had not stretched to taking hostages from every samurai family in Japan. Yet everyone complied, for such was the power of the new Shogunate.

Ieyasu's earlier reforms set in motion a furious spate of castle-building and moving house. One Japanese historian likened Ieyasu's *daimyo* to potted plants, that were uprooted and taken to flourish elsewhere. But there was a positive side to it. Ieyasu consciously strove to maintain and preserve the best features of *daimyo* rule as his system of local government, in the form of the *baku-han* system, whereby government was shared between the *bakufu* and the *daimyo* territories or *han*. Many of the *han* had been well administered, and it was a mark of Ieyasu's wise statesmanship that such a system could be allowed to continue.

In fact the control of the other *daimyo* by the Tokugawa family was so successful that it lasted for two and a half centuries, with little of the attendant rebellion that had plagued the Ashikaga or the Hojo *shikken*. One extraordinary feature of the Tokugawa *bakufu*'s relations with the *daimyo* is that never during the whole of the Edo Period were the *daimyo* subject to taxation by the central government. Instead the *bakufu* contrived

PLATE 28   *Tachibana Muneshige in camp, 1600*

Tachibana Muneshige (1567–1642) lived, and largely prospered, through some of the most tumultuous years of the Azuchi-Momoyama and Edo Periods. In 1587 he helped Hideyoshi in his defeat of the Shimazu clan of Kyushu and received a large grant of lands. He took part in the expedition to Korea and, together with Kobayakawa Takakage, gained a victory over a Chinese army. Later he was one of the *daimyo* who rescued Kato Kiyomasa from the siege of Uru-san. On his return to Japan his fortunes changed. He backed the wrong horse at Sekigahara and was dispossessed, but was restored to favour with the Tokugawa in 1611 and took part in the suppression of the Shimabara revolt at the ripe old age of 71.

He is seen here peering over the top the *maku*, the curtains that customarily surrounded a general's field headquarters, which bear his ornate *mon*. A retainer holds the even more ornate banner of Tachibana Muneshige, which bears the discs of the sun and the moon on either side of a *bonji*, a Sanskrit character. The inscription reads 'Tenshoko Daijin', i.e. the Goddess of the Sun, Amaterasu Omikami, divine ancestress of the Emperors of Japan.

His helmet is a simple *zunari-kabuto* with a *shikoro* laced in blue *sugake-odoshi*. Once again, this simple design has been given some ornamentation, in his case in the form of a 'halo', and a plume of cock's feathers.

Next to him stands a young page. The boy has not yet performed his *gembuku*, or 'manhood ceremony', which would be accompanied by the shaving of the long forelock of hair which he has fastened back with his pigtail. The unshaven forelock was regarded as being very attractive on a youth. Nevertheless the boy is in full armour, and is prepared to play his part on the field of battle.

All the details are based on actual specimens, and the Tachibana family records.

124

to keep the *daimyo* in a constant state of genteel poverty. They were obliged to make generous donations towards the building and upkeep of the Shogun's fortresses of Edo, Osaka, Nagoya and Nijo (in Kyoto), which included the supplying and transportation of men and materials. Much of these materials consisted of huge blocks of stone, so castle-building became a constant drain on finance and manpower.

Communication in Edo Japan

It is also not generally realised just how difficult transport was in Japan until comparatively modern times, a factor that has considerable bearing on samurai history. Accounts of journeys made during the Edo Period make the 'horror stories' of stagecoach driving in eighteenth-century England, with its muddy, potholed roads and lurking highwaymen, seem positively luxurious. Transport along the Shogun's highways followed routes determined almost totally by accidents of geography. Such roads that existed were far from continuous, being cut many times along their length by rivers, of which few were bridged. In fact during the Edo Period the number of bridges across Japanese rivers actually decreased as difficulty in communication was seen as a hindrance to potential rebellion.

Examples of the simple wheeled carts used for transportation purposes in the towns and in the countryside. The example on the right is laden with bales made of rice-straw. (Toei-Uzumasa Film Studios, Kyoto)

So, once peace was established by Ieyasu, bridges were allowed to fall into disrepair and the accepted means of crossing a swollen river was to be carried on the shoulders of the burly tattooed porters, whose livelihood was this unusual form of ferry service. When on the roads, personal transport was either a horse, a *kago*, or palanquin, ranging from a simple litter to an elaborately shuttered, lacquered version, or one's own two feet. Wheeled traffic was completely banned from the Tokaido, the Great East Sea Road that linked Kyoto and Edo, because of the damage it would do to the surface. In fact the only wheeled vehicles to be seen anywhere were the traditional ox-carriages used by the Imperial Court for their short journeys in Kyoto, various farm carts and the decorated wagons for shrine festivals.

Such considerations give one a greater respect for the achievements of men like Hideyoshi in actually moving their colossal armies from place to place. We must remember, however, that the decline in transportation systems only set in once wars had ceased. In Hideyoshi's call-to-arms, addressed to Tokugawa Ieyasu prior to the siege of Odawara, he commands his ally to repair all bridges along the Tokaido and build new ones.

With such apparent difficulties it is astonishing to learn that the major highways of Japan were always teeming with people moving from place to place. The major reason for this was the Shogun Tokugawa Iemitsu's

The most welcome sight for a samurai travelling along one of the main highways of Japan on a *daimyo*'s procession to or from the Shogun's capital at Edo was a post-station, where lodgings could be obtained for the night. This is the Magome Honjin, the official post-station in the village of Magome, an important stop on the old road through the central mountains that linked Kyoto and Edo.

The Taiko-mon, or Drum Gate, of Hikone Castle
Hikone is a good example of the castles that were built during the Early Edo Period. This old photograph shows the *Taiko-mon*, with its guard house built over the stout wooden doors.

sankin-kotai, or Alternate Attendance System. Reference has been made above to the dual residence requirement forced upon the *daimyo*. The other feature of the *sankin-kotai* was that, when the *daimyo* changed their residence from Edo to provincial capital or back again, they did so accompanied by a splendid retinue of samurai, gorgeously dressed and fully equipped for the Shogun's service. As most of the *daimyo* had to do this trip in one direction or another every single year it ensured a continual financial commitment, an infallible hostage system, and an opportunity for the Shogun's staff to keep themselves fully informed on any gossip from the provinces.

An alternative to road transport were journeys by river or sea, a need which grew with the expanding economy of the Edo Period. A pack horse could only carry two bales of rice and, as the years went by, *daimyo* had an

PLATE 29 *Hosokawa Tadaoki (1564–1645) has his sword tested during a lull in the fighting in the siege of Osaka*

Tadaoki was the grandson of a certain Mibuchi Harusada, whose surname he used until the time of Sekigahara. Mibuchi Harusada had been adopted into the Hosokawa family, whose earlier illustrious members are illustrated in Plate 13. Tadaoki served under the three unifiers of Japan. Nobunaga gave him Tango Province in 1580, and he remained loyal to Nobunaga in spite of being married to Akechi Mitsuhide's daughter. In 1590 he took part in the Odawara campaign and besieged Nirayama castle on Hideyoshi's behalf. At the time of Sekigahara Ishida Mitsunari took many daimyo's families as hostages in Osaka castle, hoping thereby to force them to support him against Ieyasu. Among them was Tadaoki's Christian wife, Gracia, who had been baptised in 1587. Tadaoki stood firm against Ishida's threats, but it cost his wife her life. He took part in the Battle of Sekigahara and the siege of Osaka castle.

Tadaoki had a fondness for ornamenting his helmets with feathers. He is described as having a pheasant's tail in his helmet at Sekigahara. Here he sports peacock's plumes out of a straightforward *zunari-kabuto*. The armour, and the swords, are modelled on the actual specimens.

The testing of his sword on the corpse of an executed criminal has been done by a *hinin*, a person of outcast status, forced to work in the execution grounds. Around him are the remains of those defeated by the Tokugawa armies. The *nobori* banner bears the *mon* of the Hosokawa.

increasing need to ship vast quantities of their crop to the cities of Edo and Osaka to convert it into cash. River transport had been used for centuries, but few river journeys could be accomplished without considerable stretches overland. For example, in 1638 an experiment was undertaken whereby rice from Kaga Province was taken by land to the Northern shore of Lake Biwa. It was then ferried by boat to Otsu and on down the Yodo River to Osaka. By the end of the seventeenth century a 'shuttle service' of rice-ships had been established between the rice-growing areas of Northern Japan and the cities of Edo and Osaka. One voyage sailed along the Pacific Coast to Edo. The other went South-West through the Sea of Japan, passed through the Straits of Shimonoseki, and sailed up the Inland Sea to Osaka.

A youth of the samurai class
This actor from the Toei-Uzumasa studios in Kyoto is dressed in typical fashion for the period. He wears *hakama*, and has a short *haori* over his *kimono*. He carries a bamboo and paper umbrella.

The Shimabara Rebellion

Reference was made in the previous chapter to the virtual suppression of Christianity under the Tokugawa *bakufu*. The expulsion of Christian samurai such as Takayama Ukon was merely one stage in the process. The final hardening of the Tokugawa attitude came after an insurrection in 1638 known as the Shimabara Rebellion, a rising small in itself, but one that produced repercussions at a national and international level.

Tokugawa Ieyasu

First of the Tokugawa Shoguns and the victor of Sekigahara, Tokugawa Teyasu is a vital figure in Japanese history. This fine statue of him is in the grounds of Okazaki Castle, where Ieyasu was born in 1542. His suit of armour is very similar to the one he is supposed to have worn at Nagakute.

A samurai wearing a haori

An actor from the Toei-Uzumasa film studios wearing a very unpretensious *haori*.

The *daimyo* of the Shimabara peninsula was Matsukura Shigeharu, whose methods of dealing with people who were suspected of being Christians were among the cruellest in the savage history of the persecutions. A favourite torture of his was to lower his prisoners into the boiling, sulphurous hot springs of Unzen until they were scalded to death. The revolt against him broke out in Shimabara on 17 December 1637 and was led by a group of *shoya*, village headmen, who had formerly served under Christian *daimyo* such as Konishi Yukinaga. One outstanding feature of the rebellion is that, from very early on, it became a decidedly Christian affair, even though the motives may have been as much economic as religious. The nominal commander was a youth called Amakusa Shiro, who comes over as something of a 'Joan of Arc' character, acting as an inspiration for the cause and playing the part of a figurehead for the army.

What is more surprising is the sluggishness of the *bakufu's* response. Part was due no doubt to the communication difficulties discussed above, which were particularly severe in the case of journeys to Kyushu. The trip from Edo took 6 days overland to Osaka followed by 10 days on board ship, so a rapid response from Edo was physically impossible. Local help was ruled out because of the Tokugawa regulations forbidding intercourse between neighbouring *han*, even to the extent of preventing them from assisting one another in this sort of circumstance. So two neighbouring armies sat idly by as the revolt spread around the peninsula while the regulatory mechanisms which the *bakufu* had proudly set up to contain such rebellions prevented any action from being taken.

The rebels thus began well and took everything in their stride. Soon they controlled half the Shimabara peninsula, but their attempt to take the mighty Shimabara castle failed, and, faced with the approach of a *bakufu* army, their leadership decided to fortify the abandoned castle of Hara at the Southern end of the peninsula. Here they withstood a long siege against a veteran warrior called Itakura Shigemasa, who had been generously rewarded for his actions during the great siege of Osaka in 1615. His conduct of this siege was, however, so inept that the *bakufu* were forced to send considerable reinforcements, which mortified him. Itakura then launched an ill-prepared attack designed to capture Hara castle before the

PLATE 30   *A townsman defeats a samurai in unarmed combat, ca 1630*

A townsman uses unarmed combat techniques to defeat an armed samurai. Although the wearing of the two swords was restricted to the samurai class these swaggering warriors did not always have it their own way. Many stories tell of bands of *chonin* (townspeople) in cities such as Edo or Osaka who joined together in gangs to defeat unscrupulous samurai.

Both parties in this tussle are wearing *kimono*, a long garment like a dressing gown, underneath a pair of wide *hakama* (trousers). *Hakama* fastened first with a pair of straps from front to back, which were concealed by the stiffened flap at the back, and a pair of tying cords secured neatly at the front. The swords were thrust into these belts.

others arrived, but it was beaten off to the jeers of the defenders.

On Lunar New Year's Day 1638, Itakura tried again, and led the first charge himself until he was killed by an arrow. The loss of the commander shocked the *bakufu*. If a band of peasants and Christians could do this to the mighty Tokugawa war machine, what might an experienced *daimyo*, with a samurai army, hope to achieve? So far the siege was acting just like Kusunoki Masashige's famous defence of Chihaya. It showed their weakness, and invited imitation.

The Tokugawa troops were in an embarrassing state, and at one stage got so desperate that they asked a Dutch ship to bombard the castle for them, but the moral disgrace of having to depend upon foreigners negated any military advantage. All the besiegers could hope for was to starve the defenders out before any one else joined their rebellion, or any similar actions started elsewhere in Japan. Such a siege required patience, but as the weeks went by the strategy began to pay off. The capture of some rebels out on a sortie confirmed that food supplies were running very low. Soon came the final assault. It was carefully planned, but began prematurely when a signal fire was lit by mistake. Soon thousands of samurai poured into the attack in a disorganised charge, each trying to gain as much personal glory as possible by being the first into the attack. The castle fell, but not without considerable loss to the attackers.

Shimabara was a portent of the samurai decline. The all-conquering Tokugawa army had been shown to be susceptible to rebellion. Ieyasu thought he had controlled the *daimyo*, but the biggest challenge to his successors had come from a different direction. Shimabara also hastened the end of Christianity in Japan, and was followed within a few years by the closing of Japan to the outside world, which was to have such an effect on the country's later history. No foreign ship was allowed to land, except for a few Dutch who were confined to the island of Deshima in Nagasaki. No Japanese were allowed to leave, and any who did, and were foolish enough to return, were executed. From being an outgoing, adventurous nation whose samurai had visited and traded with the Philippines and Siam, Japan became deliberately isolated and turned its back on the world.

Later Edo Period

The Shimabara Rebellion marked the last serious attempt to defy the *bakufu* by force, and is an appropriate incident from which to continue our discussion of the role of the samurai in Tokugawa society during the period of seclusion.

The Urban Samurai

The need, discussed above, for supplying cities with rice arose out of the fact that the samurai of the Edo Period was essentially an urban creature. Nobunaga had begun the trend of separating the samurai from the soil when he disciplined his *ashigaru* and treated them as regular soldiers with smart uniforms and the opportunity for promotion. Hideyoshi, who had begun his glorious career as a humble *ashigaru*, accelerated the trend by encouraging the growth of castle towns and disarming the peasantry by his Sword Hunt, until in the Edo Period there was a very clear distinction between samurai and farmer. The samurai class, of whom the *ashigaru* were now the lowest ranks, lived in the castle towns alongside the merchants and craftsmen, and fought for their *daimyo* on the Shogun's behalf, when there was anything to fight about.

PLATE 31   *A samurai leads his contingent to serve the Shogun, ca 1650*

Throughout the period under discussion the wealth of a samurai, assessed in *koku*, (one *koku* was about 180 litres) provided the basis whereby the feudal service he was required to provide to his overlord might be assessed. The most important set of such regulations were set out by the Tokugawa Shogun in 1629 and remained in force, with little modification, until the end of the Tokugawa Period. Using the requirements for a samurai whose wealth was valued at 200 *koku* (theoretically enough rice to feed 200 men for 1 year), we have therefore invented this imaginary samurai, who is making his unhurried way along the Tokaido Road to serve the Shogun. Besides his personal service, mounted, he supplies for the Shogun's use one samurai on foot, who has just returned from a successful foraging expedition, one armour-bearer (who carries a large lacquered box on his back, containing the lord's helmet, and perhaps a spare suit of armour), one spearman, one groom and one baggage-carrier.

In the space of a very few years, such processions across Japan were to lose all martial connotations and become the biennial journey to pay respects to the Shogun, under Tokugawa Iemitsu's *sankin-kotai*, or 'Alternate Attendance System'.

Note the *hachimaki*, or headbands worn by the two samurai, augmented with a portion of chain mail. The armour is *okegawa-do*.

Within these towns and cities the samurai class constituted the majority of the population. In Sendai, the castle town of the *daimyo* Date Masamune, samurai formed 70 per cent of the inhabitants, while in Kagoshima the proportion was the largest – about 80 per cent. By contrast, in the country as a whole, the samurai were always the minority, probably no more than 7 per cent of the population, but a minority that wielded enormous power.

While the samurai lived in towns the farmers lived in the countryside and grew the food. That at any rate was the theory, though there was a 'grey area' between the two classes, where one finds the *shoya*, the village headmen, who could possess enormous local power, and various 'country samurai'. There were also the notorious *ronin*. A *ronin* (the name means 'man of the waves') was a samurai who had become dispossessed owing to the death or disgrace of his master. Some *ronin* could find employment with other *daimyo*, but as their trade was warfare such opportunities decreased with the establishment of the Tokugawa Shogunate, apart from their roles as 'hired swords' so beloved of the Japanese movie industry. But the poverty which the *ronin* experienced was to some extent shared by all low-ranking samurai. They were paid a fixed stipend in a world of rising prices, but were required to maintain themselves and their followers in true samurai style, fully equipped and armed, and always ready for battle muster. Detailed regulations existed which laid down the number of men and their equipment which samurai of a certain rank would be required to supply in times of war. Promotion was limited once battles had ceased, so many samurai turned to trade and handicrafts to make ends meet. Farming

A swordsman
This illustration by the artist Hokusai depicts a samurai drawing his sword, perhaps to take part in a street brawl. He may well be a *ronin*, a samurai without a master to serve.

A cart laden with rice bales
A photo from the Toei-Uzumasa film studios depicting one variety of cart used during the Edo Period.

138

and umbrella-making are among the occupations of the 'black economy' listed for samurai.

At the same time the world of the castle town was one that put endless temptations in their way, all of which cost money. The growing wealth of the merchant classes encouraged various forms of entertainment to flourish, including the *kabuki* theatre, which was officially banned to the samurai class, but much patronised by them. *Kabuki* was to the vulgar townsmen what the stately *noh* plays were to the noble samurai: a form of theatrical art that mirrored the lives they led. While the sons of *daimyo* sat motionless through the stylised re-telling of the deeds of their tragic and honourable ancestors, the citizens screamed, shouted and rolled in the

A prominent sight in any town in the Edo Period was the watchtower, from which fires could be readily spotted and attended to. This reconstruction is part of the Toei-Uzumasa Film Studios in Kyoto.

aisles as a *kabuki* troup re-enacted a fight between townsmen and samurai, a love-suicide of a merchant's daughter, or a farmer outwitting his superior. It was brash, gaudy, emotionally unrestrained, and blatantly counter to the moral standards of the Shogun, all of which attracted the samurai in droves. *Kabuki* was banned several times, but all attempts at curtailing it proved ineffective.

The gradual neglect of the martial arts in favour of office work, the need for supplementary trades, and the lure of townsmen's pleasures produced an economic effect far beyond the official boundaries of the samurai class. If the suppliers of credit, prostitutes and theatres were the new profiteers, the older craftsmen, such as swordsmiths, suffered with their former patrons. A poignant example is recorded for the swordsmiths of Kanazawa. At the time of the foundation of the Kaga *han* there had been a great demand for their skills. Maeda Toshitsune (1593–1658) once placed an order for five *katana* and 650 *yari* (spears), the order being fulfilled by seven sword-smiths. One good sword by the leading Kaga swordsmith, Kiyomitsu Shichiemon, could cost the equivalent of one *koku* in wages, plus materials (The *koku* was the amount of rice considered necessary to feed one man for 1 year) and Kiyomitsu was used to receiving orders for up to twenty *katana* at any one time. Yet, within two generations, his grandson Chobei was forced by poverty to the poorhouse, where he continued to make one or two swords.

An actor at the Toei-Uzumasa Film Studios in Kyoto showing the typical samurai hairstyle, whereby the front half of the head was shaved bare and the rest of the hair was gathered into a pigtail which was oiled and tied up.

In 1720 the *daimyo* of Kanazawa placed an order for swords, but the swordsmith chosen had to look up old records to find out what price to ask. Many of the swordsmiths by then made more money from making pots and pans, and petitioned the City Magistrates to allow them to gather firewood. 'There have been no orders for swords from the *han* or from the samurai...', they wrote. 'We are starving and our business prospects are poor.'

Swordsmiths were only one of the many tradesmen who came under the heading of *chonin*, or townspeople, whose lives were regulated by the samurai. There were rules for practically everything and some of the following, a selection from regulations published in Kanazawa in 1642, show an admirable, if somewhat paternalistic concern for public health and safety:

PLATE 32   *A ninja prepares to kill a victim, ca 1640*

A *ninja* assassin, dressed in black, prepares to leap down through the gap he has made in the ceiling onto his terrified victim. *Ninja* dressed almost all in black for night work and in a khaki-brown garment during daylight hours. The costume is based on exhibits in the Ninja Museum at Iga-Ueno. As the art of the assassin was one of secrecy it is questionable how much of 'ninja-lore' is authentic, but no book on samurai would be complete without them!

Chonin, regardless of who they are, will be held responsible if they are slovenly or commit improprieties towards samurai.

It is forbidden to keep dogs as pets or to walk along the street next to samurai.

Chonin are not to gather in shops and gossip loudly about others, nor are chonin in shops to sit around in rude positions.

Persons who urinate from the second floor of houses in the city, regardless of whether it is night or day, shall certainly be punished. If a traveller at an inn commits such an act the innkeeper shall be held responsible. This is to be explained to all children, travellers, and persons of low status. Spitting from the second floor, throwing waste water from the second floor, and opening the second floor windows and staring at passers-by or calling out rude comments to them are also prohibited . . . .

This was the Tokugawa Peace, a world based on the Confucian ideals of order and benevolent authority, where everyone knew his place and was in his place.

An actor at the Toei-Uzumasa Studios in the role of a samurai. He is wearing an ornate long-sleeved *haori*.

The Loyal Retainers

'Great Peace Throughout the Realm' was the aim and motto of the Tokugawa and, by and large, that peace was maintained for 250 years. In 1702 there occurred an incident which, in its own way, shocked the *bakufu* as much by its evidence of the continued existence of samurai values as the Shimabara Rebellion had shocked it by their apparent absence. The story is a classic of revenge and spawned hundreds of plays, prints and, more recently, films depicting the tale of the Forty-Seven Ronin.

Secret signs of the ninja
This wax dummy in the Ninja Museum in Iga-Ueno shows a samurai making the secret signs associated with the "invisible men", the famous *ninja*, that were supposed to confer great powers.

A daimyo's procession
This illustration depicts a daimyo's procession from the mid-nineteenth century, as may be inferred from the fixed bayonets carried by the samurai. Note the townsmen with their heads pressed tightly to the ground.

The *daimyo* whose death made his retainers into *ronin* was Asano Naganori (1667–1701), who owned a *han* worth 50,000 *koku* in Harima Province. He was one of two *daimyo*, then on their periodic visit to Edo, who had been selected to entertain representatives of the Emperor at the Shogun's Court – a very great honour. The other *daimyo*, Kira Yoshinaka, was charged with instructing Asano in the correct behaviour, but when his pupil failed to present him with the customary gifts he became abusive and scornful. On one occasion he criticised Asano in public, causing the other to lose his temper, and wounded Kira on the forehead with his *wakizashi*. Even to draw a weapon in the Shogun's presence was a serious offence, and Asano was made to commit *hara-kiri*. His forty-seven samurai, who had now been made *ronin*, plotted Kira's death as revenge. What is extraordinary about the story is the fantastic lengths to which they went in order to make Kira think that they had all split up, had no communication with each other, and had all abandoned the profession of samurai. Their leader, Oishi Yoshio, even divorced his wife, and kept up a facade of drunken, dissolute pleasure-seeking. One snowy night in December 1702 the *ronin*, dressed in home-made armour, struck at Kira's mansion in Edo.

The attack was a masterpiece of military organisation which would have done credit to a modern-day SAS. operation. Twenty-three attacked from the rear, while the rest approached from the front. A small group climbed the wall with rope ladders, but being unable to obtain any keys from the terrified guards they smashed the gate down with a mallet. While some of the *ronin* stationed themselves outside with bows, to cut down anyone fleeing, the others broke into the house itself and started searching for Kira. He and his followers are often depicted as craven cowards to contrast them with the gallant *ronin*, but in fact he was well defended by samurai as loyal as the forty-seven. Three of his samurai held the *ronin* off from Kira's quarters for some considerable time.

Kira Yoshinaka was eventually found hiding in an outhouse. He was first invited to commit *hara-kiri*, but as there was a danger of a counter-attack

PLATE 33 *The Shogun Tokugawa Yoshimune leads manoeuvres in 1720*

The energetic Shogun Tokugawa Yoshimune (reigned from 1716 to 1745) produced many reforms in the Shogunate, and made a valiant attempt to revive the martial accomplishments of his ancestors. Mock battles and manoeuvres were conducted on the plains below Mount Fuji, and in this picture we see the Shogun himself, wearing the elaborate armour that is preserved in the Kunozan Toshogu Shrine

Museum in Shizuoka.

The armour is a classic of its kind. It is basically a revival *yoroi* – but what a revival! No expense has been spared in ornamenting it to a standard even more exquisite than the old *yoroi* shown in Plates 1 to 8, with which it is instructive to compare this specimen. It has a sixteenth-century *mempo*, with a handlebar moustache, and an enormous *yodarekake*. The helmet is

a graceful *sujibachi*. The *haidate* are of a later model, but the *suneate* are big and heavy. His *tachi* sword is bejewelled and very ornate. The samurai behind him wear the style of *jingasa* helmets with steeper conical bowls than those that are found in earlier times. Their 'battledress' stands in marked contrast to their leader, whose armour was not made for real fighting.

Front, side and rear views of the formal samurai dress known as the *kami-shimo* ('upper and lower'), which consisted of the more usual *kimono* and *hakama* (wide trousers), but instead of the *haori*, as shown on page 142, a jacket called the *kataginu* was worn. The *kataginu* had stiffened shoulders, giving the costume its characteristic appearance, and would normally be of the same material as the *hakama*, as in the case of the dress of this actor at the Toei-Uzumasa Film Studios in Kyoto.

by Kira's supporters, Oishi cut off his head with the very dagger with which Asano had committed suicide and the raiders departed. By now all Edo was awake and the people crowded the streets to see the bizarre procession go by: forty-six bloodstained men (one had died during the raid) carrying a wooden bucket in which was Kira's head, making for the Sengaku-ji where Asano was buried, there to place the head on their master's tomb.

Their action placed the *bakufu* in a nice dilemma. Should they condemn the *ronin* for murder, and punish them, or reward them for their fidelity to the ideals of the samurai life? In the end the laws of the land had to take precedence and the remaining *ronin* committed suicide at Sengaku-ji, where they are buried, leaving behind them a noble legacy of samurai virtue that was never to be equalled.

The Fall of the Tokugawa

The forces that eventually overthrew the Tokugawa *bakufu* and laid the foundations of modern Japan did so in the name of an institution that was far older than that of the Shogun, and with a potential far greater for inspiring loyalty and nationalist feelings. The opposition to the Tokugawa came from men who rediscovered the magic in the name of the Emperor.

The impetus for their actions came from a very different direction than the simple loyalty that had inspired Kusunoki Masashige to die for the Emperor, or the promise of personal gain that had motivated some of his contemporaries. From the beginning of the nineteenth century there were frequent incursions into Japanese waters by foreign vessels and, when Commodore Perry's black ships sailed majestically into Tokyo Bay in 1854, it was seen that the power of the Western World was not something that could be ignored. The foreigners had either to be accepted or defied. The factor in this political turmoil that is so fascinating is that the Shogunate was overthrown by men who opposed opening up Japan to Western nations and saw the Shogun as a traitor in that he was signing treaties and entertaining embassies. At the same time, however, these men also saw, more clearly than the Shogun, that unless they absorbed the military

PLATE 34   *A Samurai guard kills an intruder in 1750*

In this plate a samurai uses his *wakizashi*, the shorter of the pair of swords normally carried, to kill a *ronin* (literally 'a man of the waves' – a samurai who has no master, and no income).

The samurai is wearing the *kami-shimo*, the formal attire of a *daimyo's* retainers. On top of the *kimono* shown in Plate 30 he wears a winged jacket with stiffened shoulders. He has probably left the longer of his swords in a sword rack, but sees the danger, and acts.

The *ronin* is a scruffy character, with untidy hair and rough-and-ready clothes. He too, has only a *wakizashi*, probably owing to poverty. His trousers are *ko-bakama*, the shorter form of *hakama*, tucked into gaiters.

148

lessons of the Western nations they could never hope to defeat them. Thus began a period of time which appears to a cursory glance to be an unbridled enthusiasm for anything Western. In fact a careful examination reveals that it was nothing of the sort. All the new materials, techniques and methods that the Japanese adopted had sound utilitarian considerations behind them, the most important of which was a desire eventually to use them against their providers. Thus the Japanese noted the use of military music on board ship following the British bombardment of Kagoshima in 1863. It was seen to be useful for morale – it would be useful for them.

But a feudal institution like the Shogunate was no longer appropriate. It had to be removed, and the name of the Emperor provided the focus around which such opposition could be organised, by appealing to something that was even more 'Japanese' than the Shogunate. The two most powerful *daimyo* at the time not related to the Tokugawa were those whose territories comprised Satsuma, at the Southern tip of Kyushu, and Choshu, at the Western end of Honshu. Both were *tozama*, the 'Outer Lords' of Ieyasu's reckoning, who had been placed under the watchful eye of pro-Tokugawa men. Both were equally opposed to foreign intercourse, and both were equally against the continuation of the Shogunate. Various outrages against foreigners by these *daimyo* complicated the Shogun's relations with foreigners in the capital and gave rise to claims for reparation which the Shogun could not refuse, but which lowered his prestige with his fellow countrymen. In 1863 Satsuma and Choshu prevailed upon the Emperor officially to expel the foreigners and forbid Japan's ports to them, a decree which both clans rushed to obey. We have noted one result of this action above – the bombardment of Kagoshima by British ships. A year later a combined fleet forced the Straits of Shimonoseki, between Kyushu and Choshu, and bombarded the Japanese forts. It was a harsh lesson for Satsuma and Choshu.

In 1866 the incumbent Shogun died, and was followed within a few months by the Emperor Komei. Their successors, Tokugawa Keiki and Emperor Mutsuhito (soon to be known as Meiji) were now new men at the helm, who realised that a nation divided against itself could not stand. The

---

PLATE 35   *The murder of Ii Naosuke by Imperial loyalists in 1860*

'Sonno-joi!' – 'Honour the Emperor and expel the barbarians!' – was the rallying cry of the factions opposed to the increased intercourse with Western nations that led to the opening of Japan to the world in the 1850s and 1860s. Ii Naosuke (1815–1860) the Shogun's chief minister, was the noblest victim to

die at the hands of those who wished to resist the Western alliances by force.

He was murdered early one morning in March 1860. He had been travelling in a shuttered palanquin and was stopped by *ronin* from the Mito *daimyo*.

This plate is based on numerous

contemporary illustrations of the shocking deed. The bearers have been depicted with the traditional tattoos sported by such men. The assassins run off in triumph with Naosuke's severed head, leaving his headless corpse behind. The guards wear the Ii *mon* on their *haori* jackets.

movement for the restoration of the ancient system of government by the Emperor grew in force until it was literally irresistible. In November 1867 the Shogun formally handed over to the Emperor the commission of Shogun which Minamoto Yoritomo had first received in 1192. For a while it seemed that the final step in the great revolution would be accomplished peacefully and that, once the Shogun had yielded, his followers would loyally copy his example. But it was not to be. Kyoto at the time was guarded by samurai from Aizu, in the North of Japan, tough, fanatical samurai whose fidelity to the Tokugawa Shoguns was legendary. They were ordered to surrender by the allied clans of Satsuma and Choshu, but refused to give in, and withdrew with the Shogun to Osaka. There the remaining adherents of the Tokugawa gathered, all bitter at the downfall of the Shogun and all determined not to give up without a final struggle. Their immediate anger turned against the Satsuma headquarters in Osaka, which consisted of a palace for the *daimyo* and barracks for the samurai. This was taken and burned, and then the whole Tokugawa force turned towards the capital. They were met by the Imperial forces near Fushimi, 7 miles to the South of Kyoto.

The Battle of Fushimi which ensued is often treated as a footnote in Japanese history, a minor inconvenience. In fact it was one of the most decisive battles in Japanese history and lasted longer than many of the great encounters of the Momoyama Period. It actually lasted for 3 days, from the 28 to the 30 of January 1868, and the Tokugawa troops were only

The Battle of Ueno on 4 July 1868 was the last encounter between the Imperial Troops and the last remnants of the Shogun's army. This contemporary print is preserved in the Memorial Shrine at Ueno.

The statue in Ueno Park of Saigo Takamori, whose doomed Satsuma Rebellion of 1877 made him the last of the samurai warriors.

154

defeated when one of their number, stationed on the left flank, deserted them for the Emperor. As they fled before the victors, the Shogun took a ship from Osaka to Edo, and his erstwhile supporters, as a last gesture of defiance, set fire to the palace built by Hideyoshi, the man whose family the Tokugawa had supplanted, within the walls of Osaka castle. Perhaps they had originally wished to suffer the fate of Hideyoshi's son and conduct a siege from Osaka itself? But they were broken. The Shogun, as we noted above, had been taken to Edo, where he formally surrendered the Eastern capital to the Emperor. Some stubborn Tokugawa loyalists retired to the North, where they held out for another 6 months. One small band made a last stand at Ueno, which is now part of Tokyo, and on 4 July 1868 were attacked by an overwhelming force of Imperial troops. The stubborn Tokugawa samurai fought to the last man.

With their collapse the Tokugawa resistance faded and the history of the samurai moved swiftly towards its close. One by one the edicts came. In 1871 the wearing of swords was made optional, and in 1876 it was banned altogether to everyone except members of the armed forces. One Satsuma samurai, Saigo Takamori, found it too much to stand and, in his native province, raised a rebellion against the new order. He was faced with, and destroyed by, the conscript army of the new Japan, whose modern rifles cut down Saigo's swordsmen. His inevitable defeat, and his heroic last stand which ended with his suicide, were no more than fitting for that final flowering of the spirit of the samurai which Saigo Takamori represents. With his death the samurai of real life passed away, to be replaced by the samurai warriors of myth and story, who have grown in stature as the years have gone by, always the heroes, ever noble and ever brave.

PLATE 36   *A komuso uses his flute against an assassin, ca 1790*

Amongst the strangest sights on the streets of Japan in the Edo Period were the wandering, flute-playing monks called *komuso,* a word that literally means 'monks of emptiness'. Their origin is something of a mystery, though members of the sect itself, the Fuke-shu, which is a branch of Zen, invented several spurious claims to ancestry, including descent from the Kusunoki clan. Their traditional wear consisted of a dark blue or black *kimono,* and a special sort of *kesa* worn over the left shoulder, but the most noticeable feature of dress is the remarkable *tengai,* the basket hat that entirely covered the head. The reeds were woven tightly everywhere except in front of the eyes, so that the wearer could not be identified, yet could view the world outside. A short sword was carried in a cloth bag tied with two cords that represented the principles of *yin* and *yang.* There were certain rituals about drawing the sword, and how combat might be conducted, though our example in this plate (as in so many Japanese movies) has not waited to draw his sword but has used his *shakuhachi* as a club. One recent commentator on the *komuso* noted that such practice 'would have led to a slight mistuning'!

The anonymity afforded by *komuso* garb led many *ronin* to adopt the *komuso* life unofficially, which probably gained the sect a bad name on several occasions.

The assailant in this picture has prepared for action. He has pulled up the skirts of his *hakama* and tucked them under his belt. His flowing sleeves have been tied back with the *tasuki* sash.

The traditions of the Fukeshu have been revived in the last century at the Myoan-ji in Kyoto, a sub-temple of the Tofuku-ji. The author visited the Myoan-ji in 1986, and it is on materials kindly supplied by the monks that this picture is based. The author also had the unusual privilege of meeting a present-day *komuso,* in full traditional costume, on a bus in Hiroshima.

Readers who are interested in learning more about the Fukeshu are referred to the excellent article by James H. Sanford in *Monumenta Nipponica,* volume 32, pp. 411–440.

蒲生

右兵衛

大夫

藤原

賢秀之像

The Noble Samurai. This warrior is
dressed in contemporary style for the
Gempei Wars. His quiver of arrows is
at his side, and he is about to fire an
arrow with a broad U-shaped head.
These were used for hunting, but
may also have served to cut through
the suspensory cords on a suit of
armour.

Nasu no Yoichi hits the mark.
One of the most celebrated demonstrations of skill given by a mounted archer occurred at the Battle of Yashima in 1184. The Taira fastened a fan to the mast of one of their ships and challenged the Minamoto to bring it down. This drawing by Hokusai shows the young Nasu no Yoichi earning great glory for himself by hitting the fan with his first arrow, which added considerably to the morale of the Minamoto.

那須の與市宗高

159

Left: Sword versus warfan. One of the most notable single combats during the sixteenth century occurred between the two rival commanders at the Fourth Battle of Kawanakajima in 1561. Uesugi Kenshin led a surprise dawn attack on the field headquarters of Takeda Shingen. The raid was so sudden that Shingen was initially forced to defend himself with the warfan with which he had been directing his troops. The illustration is by Hokusai.

Right: Miyamoto Musashi. A rather crude ink drawing of this illustrious but greatly feared swordsman. This simple caricature of him sums up the forbidding aspect he presented to many of his contemporaries.

Yamabushi. See pages 296–7 for a colour reproduction of this plate, together with full caption on
page 295.

Overleaf: A swordfight. The *Ehon Taikō-ki* shows us
a fierce contest between non-armoured swordsmen
and samurai.

166

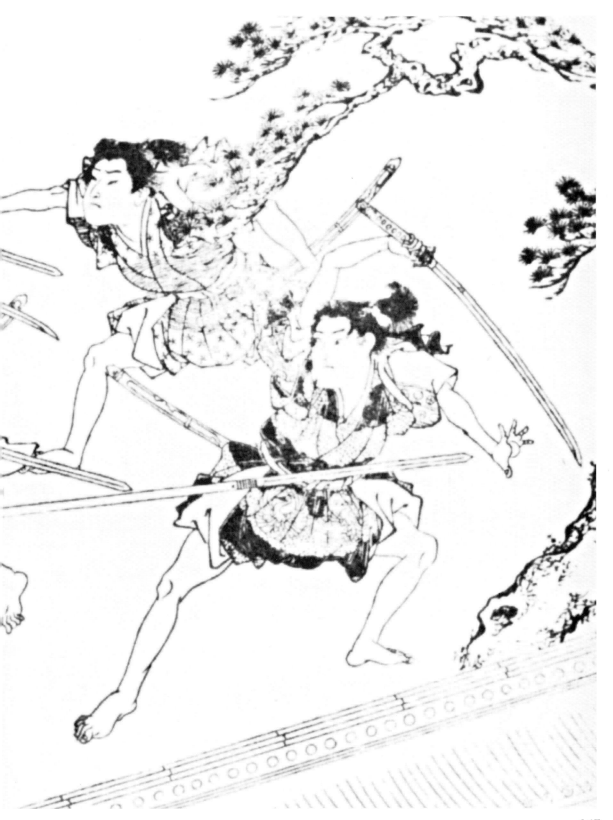

上臈強く
館て敷るの
拙指却く
駛卒と
煩らむ

Overleaf: A fight with *tampo-yari*. An illustration from the *Ehon Taikō-ki* showing a contest between spearmen using practice spears.

Left: The deer kills the wolf. The sixteenth century is not noted for the number of individual challenges to combat. One exception is the fight between Yamanaka Shika-no-suke and Shinagawa Okami-no-suke. Here the victorious Yamanaka takes his opponent's head using his *tantō*.

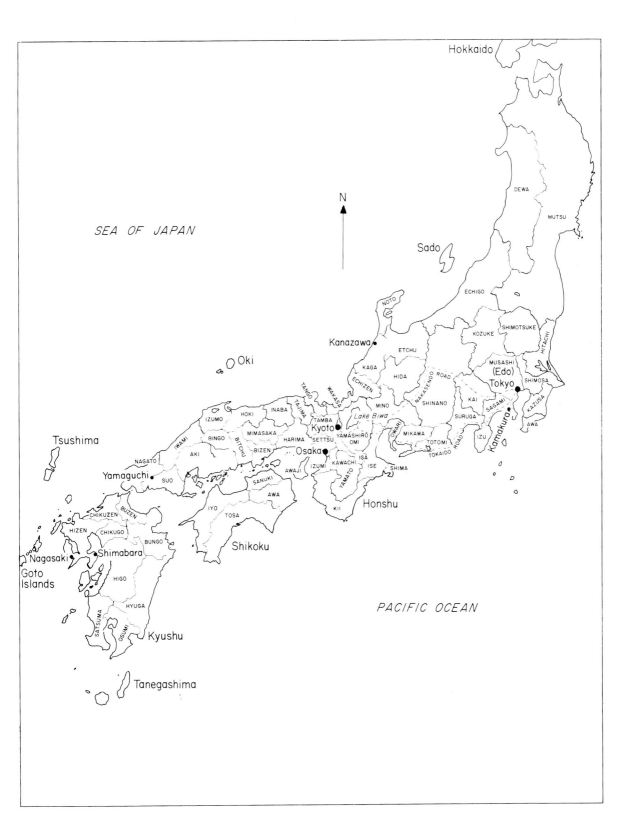

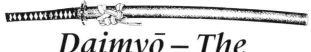

Daimyō – The Warlords of Japan

Hōjō Sōun leads his followers into Izu

Hōjō Sōun's most decisive move was his invasion of Izu, an operation nominally carried out to avenge the murder of the former *shugo* of the province. It resulted in the allegiance to Sōun of the former retainers of Izu, and Sōun's establishment as a daimyō. In this illustration, taken from an eighteenth-century wood-block-printed edition of the *Hōjō Godai-ki*, Sōun used his war-fan to signal to his men in a charge. One of his samurai lunges at an enemy with a barbed rake.

In 1491 a 60-year-old samurai, who, the chronicles tell us, had 'clear eye-sight, good hearing and all his own teeth', invaded the province of Izu and started a revolution.

The man's name was Ise Shinkuro Nagauji, better known to posterity as Hōjō Sōun, and known to the eastern provinces as the first 'Samurai War-lord'. The eventual success of his conquests, and his ability to control them and pass them on to his descendants, marked him out as a new breed of samurai leader, and he was to become famous for his military skill, his po-litical cunning, and his religious faith. He was also to become legendary for his longevity. He was certainly no wild young samurai warrior when he invaded Izu, and he still had another 27 years of active life ahead of him.

Hōjō Sōun called himself a *daimyō*, a word which, when literally trans-

lated means 'great name'. 'Warlord' is an English word which conveniently encompasses in its associations everything that made the daimyō what they were. The revolution Hōjō Sōun caused in Izu, which gave him the territory for his own, brought to that particular area of Japan the notion of *gekokujō*, 'the low overcome the high', the savage principle of opportunistic rebellion sweeping away the old order, which was to characterise sixteenth-century Japan, and set the pattern whereby other 'great names' could be made in other parts of Japan, until by the third quarter of the sixteenth century these daimyō warlords controlled huge territories as independent princes.

The Hōjō family, whom we shall examine in some detail in this chapter, are prime examples of the daimyō of the Sengoku Period, the 'Age of War', which is roughly coterminous with the sixteenth century AD. In the chapters which follow, we shall note various aspects of the role of the daimyō of the 'Age of War', and compare them with those of the 'Age of Peace' which followed.

The rise of the samurai

The part of Japan where the Hōjō established themselves was known as the Kantō, a word which means 'east of the barrier'. The barrier in question was an ancient toll-barrier in the Hakone Mountains, although the mountains themselves were as secure and forbidding a barrier as any that the hand of man could provide. The deeply wooded Hakone Mountains, which

The Hakone Mountains
The proud Hōjō family, the archetypal daimyō of the Sengoku Period, relied as much on the natural defences provided by the Hakone Mountains as on their numerous castles. This view is taken looking across terraced rice fields at the time of the transplanting of rice seedlings in May.

The Samurai

The samurai were the élite of old Japan, and the daimyō were the élite of the samurai. This actor from the Toei-Uzumasa Film Studios in Kyōto is dressed in the costume of the samurai retainer of a daimyō of the Edo Period, with the characteristic two swords. He wears a loose jacket, called a *haori*, and on his feet are wooden *geta*.

are foothills to the crowning glory of the gigantic Mount Fuji, provided an obstacle to east–west communications until the present century, allowing the inhabitants of the fertile Kantō plain, with its ready access to the sea, to develop relatively unhindered by political and military changes in the more sophisticated western provinces. Civilisation came from the west, from the capital city of Nara, until AD 794 when it was replaced by Kyōto, also in the west.

The Kantō, by contrast, bred warriors. From the Kantō had come the samurai warriors of the Minamoto clan in the twelfth century, who had fought the western Taira clan in a fierce civil war from 1180 to 1185, which had ended with the Taira destroyed in a naval battle so bloody that the seas had turned red. The Taira had ruled from Kyōto, marrying successive daughters into the imperial family and making their own family the dominant line of government. The victorious Minamoto needed no political chicanery. It was military force that had put them in a position of power, so it was by military force that they would rule. The Emperor was condemned to being a shadowy living god. Real power lay with the possessor of the title of *Shōgun* which the Minamoto leader was granted by the powerless Emperor – 'commander-in-chief for the suppression of barbarians'.

The first Shōgun, Minamoto Yoritomo, chose to base himself at Kamakura, in the heart of the Kantō, past the barrier and far from Kyōto. But even the mighty Minamoto were not to last forever, and in 1333 the old imperial capital became also the Shōgun's capital when the founder of a new dynasty, the Ashikaga, moved his seat of government westwards. The Ashikaga dynasty, too, began its own curve of triumph and decline, frustrated by the problems of controlling a disparate country where communications were difficult and centuries of warfare had bred distrust and resilience among their subjects.

The Ashikaga Shōgun's rule in the provinces was devolved through men called the *shugo* and the *jitō*. The *jitō* were the civil arm of local government, and the *shugo* the military. The Nambokuchō civil wars of 1330 to 1392 greatly weakened the authority of the *jitō* until, by the beginning of the fifteenth century, the *shugo* stood alone as the Shōgun's deputy and military governor. Many were related by blood to the Ashikaga. Others were appointed for no better reason than that they were the strongest samurai in the province and thus more likely to command respect. It was useful for the Ashikaga Shōgun to have someone they could rely on, and gradually the *shugo* acquired more devolved powers.

The centre collapses

As long as the Ashikaga stayed in control there was no problem of stability, and when the fifteenth century began the Ashikaga were at the height of their powers. Ashikaga Yoshimitsu had built a pavilion coated with gold, and had entertained princes and ambassadors, and now his successors looked as if they would lift the dynasty to greater heights. Then one by one, the blows came. In 1441 the sixth Ashikaga Shōgun, Yoshinori, was murdered. He was succeeded by an 8-year-old son, who died two years later, to be followed by his younger brother Yoshimasa. Yoshimasa, in fact, reigned as Shōgun for 30 years, and witnessed the gradual seeping away of all Shōgunal authority. Power passed into the hands of the *shugo*; but theirs

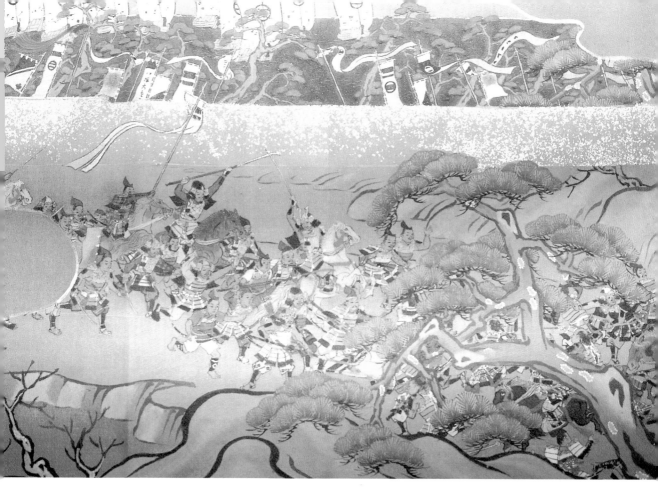

The Battle of Minatogawa
This section of a painted scroll at the Nampian Kannon-ji at Kawachi-Nagano (reproduced here by kind permission of the Chief Priest) depicts the last battle fought by the hero, Kusunoki Masashige. In the background, troops of the Hosokawa clan are landed from boats, an action which cut Kusunoki off from assistance, and led to his death by suicide. It was the defeat of the Kusunoki that paved the way for the establishment of the Ashikaga dynasty of Shōguns.

was an ordered world, traditionally controlled from the centre, and the centre, in the shape of Kyōto and the artistic and sensitive Shōgun, kept pulling them in. So they clung to Kyōto, to their mansions and their gardens, and to the Ashikaga grandees who made a great show of 'carrying on as normal'. Meanwhile their own authority in the provinces began to slip away, until in 1467, in an act of reckless disregard for political reality, the *shugo* once more gathered in Kyōto, but this time it was to fight a war amongst their own kind.

The Ōnin War, which had Kyōto as its first battlefield, dragged on for ten years, during which the fighting spread to the provinces and the *shugo* families fought each other to extinction. Others rushed to fill the gaps their deaths had caused, persons who knew nothing of the Shōgun's commissions and poetry parties in Kyōto. These 'new men' were peasant farmers, or oil sellers, or blacksmiths, men who realised that only military force was now needed. They would gather round them a handful of like-minded souls who were good fighters, and build a secure stockade on a hill, from where they could defend their rice fields. No tax-collector would be coming from Kyōto. No message would arrive from the Shōgun requesting them to chastise rebels on his behalf. Now was the time to build one's own kingdom and make a name for oneself, to make oneself a 'big name' – a daimyō.

That was where most of the daimyō came from. Some *shugo* families did survive and themselves became daimyō, but they tended either to be remote from Kyōto, or to have received the commission of *shugo* as an act of desperation on the part of the Shōgun. In the majority of cases, daimyō were created by *gekokujō*-style usurpation. Existing *shugo* were murdered by their subjects. Brothers, fathers even, were deposed. Daughters were traded like horses to secure alliances, as the territories grew from one hilltop fortress to two, then three, surrounding a fertile valley. Then a neighbour's lands were seized, and the area doubled, and so it grew. The map of Japan began to resemble the playing-board for a game of *go*, where the protagonists begin with an empty board. One by one spaces are surrounded and captured, then themselves are swallowed within another growing territory, until at the end of the game there are no spaces left to occupy, and there is only one winner.

Hōjō – the exemplary daimyō

The end of the game was over a century away when Hōjō Sōun led his samurai into Izu. Over the next four generations of the family, the Hōjō illustrated all of the aspects of daimyō rule which are discussed in the following chapters, the foremost of which was the ability to wage war.

The first point to note about the Hōjō was their comparatively humble origin. The Hōjō did not originate in the Kantō. Hōjō Sōun was very probably the son of a minor official of the Ashikaga Shōgun, based in Kyōto. He was born in 1432 and was educated by the monks of the Daitoku-ji, and was therefore 35 years old when the old capital was torn apart by the long and terrible Ōnin War. Sōun managed to leave Kyōto and the devastation the Ōnin War had caused sometime around 1469. He had with him a band of six loyal samurai, and took up a position with Imagawa Yoshitada, who had married Sōun's sister, and held the post of *shugo* of Suruga province. In 1476 Imagawa Yoshitada was killed in battle, and a succession dispute arose among the Imagawa retainers. Sōun, who was perceived as a well-educated and disinterested party, acted as chief mediator between the factions, and secured the succession for his nephew, Imagawa Ujichika. The grateful Ujichika rewarded his uncle with the castle of Kōkokuji, and Sōun's band of loyal samurai started to grow.

The need to build a retainer band was a vital characteristic of the daimyō. The small band of followers which Sōun had brought with him from Kyōto grew into an army as Sōun developed the means to feed them, and the success to attract them to him. These were the men he led into Izu, the most important turning-point in his career. It is also a classic illustration of *gekokujō*. Sooner or later every successful daimyō had to strike, and strike hard to establish himself as somehow superior to the competition, and to intervene in a succession dispute in a neighbouring family was an ideal technique. The *shugo* of Izu was of the Ashikaga family, one Masatomo, and when he died his son, known only by his boy's name of Chachamaru, succeeded to the post by murdering his mother and his elder brother. The old retainers of Izu were horrified at the act and turned against him. Hōjō Sōun, watching from the neighbouring province, resolved to avenge the father. He crossed the provincial border and attacked, forcing the treacherous Chachamaru to commit suicide. All the retainers of the former *shugo* gladly submitted to the honourable Sōun, and by their acclamation Izu was his.

Odawara castle
Odawara castle became the capital of the Hōjō territories when it was captured by Hōjō Sōun in 1518, and stayed in their possession until 1590, in spite of numerous attacks by the Takeda and the Uesugi. The present keep is a modern reconstruction.

Sōun had therefore moved on from the ownership of one castle, given by the Imagawa, to controlling a whole province, with no grant from a Shōgun, or commission from the emperor. It is about this time that he changed his name to Hōjō. There had been a famous Hōjō family centuries before. Sōun had no connection with them, of course, but the name had a certain ring to it, and in the climate that was developing in Japan at the time, surnames, like provinces, were there for the taking.

Four years later, he cast his eyes eastwards along the sea coast and sided with one of the quarrelsome branches of the doomed Uesugi family. This further piece of opportunism won him the strategic castle of Odawara, soon to become the Hōjō capital, and gave him a secure base in western Sagami. In 1512 he captured the old Shōgunal capital of Kamakura, and then completed the conquest of Sagami province in 1518 with the defeat

Building a Castle

This scene represents the building of a castle round about the year 1600. Two officials examine the plans, while a surveyor checks the line of building. In the background a final stone is levered into place around the massive earth core, while the wooden beams that will form the skeleton of the keep begin to take on the shape of the finished building.

The building of castles was one of the most important steps in

establishing the *daimyō* of the Sengoku Period as the most important powers in their particular areas. Whereas earlier castles had been fortresses made of wood and earth that clung to the natural topography of mountains, or were concealed among meandering watercourses, the new castles had all their defences built in to their design, and much stone was used in their construction. Their location was chosen on the basis of the control it offered over lines of

communication through their provinces, regardless of any natural defensive aspect. Toyotomi Hideyoshi appreciated the power of a large and well-garrisoned castle, and took steps to restrict their proliferation among potential rivals. Castle-building was further controlled under the Tokugawa.

Many of the Japanese castles that have survived to this day, such as Himeji and Hikone, were started during the Sengoku Period.

of the Miura family at Arai in 1518 – a battle famous for the defiant act of suicide by the Miura family's heir, who is supposed to have cut his own head off.

Ujitsuna and Ujiyasu carry the flag

The following year Hōjō Sōun died at the age of 87, a man who had sprung from nowhere, who had witnessed the Ōnin War and its destruction of the *shugo*, and had gone on to become daimyō of two provinces. He had, in fact, retired from the position of daimyō the previous year to allow his son Ujitsuna to begin his rule while he still had his father to help him. The succession of a series of eldest sons was one of the Hōjō dynasty's great strengths, which stands in marked contrast to the unhappy experience of

Hōjō Ujitsuna
Ujitsuna was Sōun's son and heir, and continued the process of conquest of the Kantō which his father had begun. He defeated the Uesugi at Edo, the Satomi at Kōnodai, and established the temple of Sōun-ji in his father's memory.

182

other families we shall discuss in a later chapter. Although less colourful a character than his father, Ujitsuna was to continue the process of conquest and consolidation that Sōun had begun.

The vital factor in the continuity of the operation was the loyalty of the family retainers. Soon after his father's death, Ujitsuna founded the temple of Sōun-ji in Sōun's memory, which impressed the old retainers considerably, and they showed their faith in Sōun's heir by fighting valiantly for him when he expanded the Hōjō domain further into the Kantō by defeating the Uesugi at their castle of Edo in 1524. This village at the mouth of the Sumida River, which is now the city of Tōkyō, was the key to Musashi province, which Ujitsuna confirmed by defeating the combined forces of Satomi Yoshitaka and Ashikaga Yoshiaki at the Battle of Kōnodai in 1538.

To some extent, Ujitsuna had a much more difficult task than his father. Sōun, admittedly, had had the uphill job of establishing himself from nowhere; but by the time Ujitsuna was in command, there was much less opportunity for *gekokujō*. Ujitsuna's enemies were daimyō like himself, not decaying *shugo*. Apart from the odd opportunistic assassination and the dubious activities of *ninja*, issues had to be settled by warfare. Ujitsuna, therefore, concentrated heavily on building up his army, and establishing an efficient system of military obligation, which is discussed in detail in the following chapter. He also established laws, and made sure that within the Hōjō domain it was Hōjō law that mattered. But the daimyō was still first and foremost a military leader, and Ujitsuna saw it as his duty to lead his samurai personally into battle.

The Sōun-ji
It was vitally important for Hōjō Ujitsuna to retain the loyal service of his late father's old followers, and one way in which he did it was to found this temple, the Sōun-ji, at Yumoto, near Odawara. It lies at the foot of the Hakone Mountains, on the course of the old Tōkaidō road, and has recently been re-roofed.

Like his father before him, Ujitsuna groomed his son Ujiyasu for his eventual succession. Also like Sōun, Ujitsuna left behind a set of House Laws to guide future generations. In one section he warns: 'After winning a great victory, a haughty heart, disdain for the enemy, and incautious actions often follow. Avoid this. There have been many families in the past destroyed in this manner.'

Ujitsuna died in 1541. The third daimyō, Hōjō Ujiyasu, continued the conquests of his predecessors until, by 1560, when he retired in favour of his son Ujimasa, the Hōjō controlled most of the Kantō region.

Ujiyasu was Sōun reborn. To defend the Kantō from the north, his father had established a series of forts along the Sumidagawa, and in defending one of these, Kawagoe, Ujiyasu won his most celebrated victory in 1545. The Battle of Kawagoe has a special place in samurai history in that it was fought at night, which alone pays tribute to Ujiyasu's skills in handling troops. In 1564 Ujiyasu again demonstrated his skills as a general in a remarkable 're-run' of his father's battle at Kōnodai in 1538. In the second Battle of Kōnodai, Hōjō Ujiyasu, son of the previous victor, defeated Satomi Yoshihiro, son of the daimyō formerly vanquished.

The territories meet

At this point a new dimension entered into the Hōjō's plans. The smaller daimyō of the Kantō had now been squeezed into extinction, or had submitted as vassals of the Hōjō. Ujiyasu now had to face the threat from other

Hōjō Ujiyasu
Hōjō Ujiyasu (1515–70) was the grandson of the founder of the family, Hōjō Sōun, and the descendant most like his illustrious predecessor. He led the celebrated night attack on the besieging forces of the Uesugi at Kawagoe in 1545, which was held for the Hōjō by his adopted brother Hōjō Tsunanari, and won the second Battle of Kōnodai in 1564. It was Ujiyasu who led the family to its greatest heights of achievement, in spite of competition from other powerful daimyō, such as Takeda Shingen.

The second Battle of Kōnodai (1564)
Kōnodai, on the edge of what is now Tōkyō Bay, saw two battles between two generations of the Hōjō family and the Satomi. In both, the Hōjō were victorious. In this vigorous illustration from the *Hōjō Godai-ki*, the Hōjō samurai use their swords and spear to deadly effect against the Satomi soldiers.

Takeda Shingen
The greatest rival to the Hōjō's
domination of the Kantō was Takeda
Shingen, who had built his own
territory in much the same way as
they had. The collision between the
Hōjō and the Takeda marks a new
phase in the history of daimyō
confrontation. Smaller daimyō had
been squeezed out, and rivalry
became a contest between large-
scale daimyō who controlled huge
armies. This contemporary painting
of Shingen is in the Preservation
Hall of Nagashino castle, and is
reproduced here by kind permission
of the Horai-cho local government
office. He is wearing a red *jinbaori*
(surcoat), a monk's *kesa* (scarf), and
his helmet is covered by a horsehair
plume.

successful families whose own territories bordered the Kantō, and who had built their own multi-provincial domains in much the same way as the Hōjō. The history of the next two decades became one of a series of fights, alliances and treaties between the three power-blocs of Hōjō Ujiyasu, Takeda Shingen and Uesugi Kenshin.

The latter two names were every bit as formidable as the Hōjō, but fortunately spent a great deal of time fighting each other at five successive 'Battles of Kawanakajima', so that their incursions against the Hōjō took the form of minor raids. We will refer to the Takeda and Uesugi many times in the pages to come. Both were innovative in their strategy and tactics, and the fact that they were so evenly balanced made most of their contests indecisive, leading a later generation of historians to dub their Kawanakajima encounters 'mock battles'. In fact they were no more mock battles than any of the encounters of the Sengoku Period, and the fourth Battle of Kawanakajima in 1561 (described by the present author in '*Battles of the Samurai*') had one of the highest percentage casualties of any battle in which samurai engaged.

Consequently, grand strategy became the most important martial art. It was strategy that took into account all the military necessities of knowing when to attack, where and with what, as well as less glamorous considerations, such as the making and breaking of alliances and treaties. There was still territory to be won by the giving of battle, but the prize changed from the winning of one castle, or even half a province, to securing control of two or three provinces at one stroke. The skilled strategist thus took a long-term view of warfare, conducting operations by outstretching the enemy

The daimyō's castle
The symbol of the daimyō's power was the castle. It acted as a centre of the economic life of his territory, and provided defence in times of war. In this photograph, we are looking from within the castle walls to the battlements of Kanazawa castle.

army and then cutting his lines of supply and communication. Thus the mark of a good daimyō was that he could field an army of well-trained samurai, who had received a reasonable amount of military training, without denuding his fields of agricultural workers. So prolonged, and so intense, were these 'little wars' that every available man was needed. It is at this stage of Japanese history that *ashigaru* (foot-soldiers) began to emerge as an important factor, but still only as a separate unit under well-disciplined samurai, as illustrated by the Takeda army in the *Kōyō Gunkan*:

Ashigaru taishō shū *(units):*
Yokota Juro'e 30 horsemen, 100 ashigaru
Hara Yozaemon 10 horsemen 50 ashigaru

Different areas of Japan called for their own tactical skills. The Takeda, for instance, carried out most of their offensive campaigns on the flatlands of Echigo and the Kantō, and accordingly developed a powerful cavalry arm, able to strike swiftly and heavily. They used cavalry as mounted spearmen, and the days of the élite mounted archer were seen no more. The spears could be carried as lances, or used for cutting from the saddle, the horseman leaning forward in his stirrups. A long-bladed *naginata* (glaive) could also be very effective in a charge.

186

Leading into battle
This illustration from an eighteenth-century, wood-block-printed edition of the *Ehon Taikō-ki*, or 'Illustrated life of Hideyoshi', reminds us that a daimyō of the Sengoku Period was expected to set an example by leading his army into battle. The *mon*, or badge, identifies this daimyō for us as a minor family called Miyake.

The armour of the samurai also changed. No longer was it carried to the battlefield in a box and donned for combat; with long-drawn-out battles ranging over a wide area, the samurai had now to live and sleep in their armour. Thus, for example, whereas earlier armour had numerous silk cords holding it together, in the new conditions of warfare these collected lice, sweat and dirt, and complicated designs were abandoned. Samurai were still encouraged to emulate their ancestors, but the successful general in these warlike times thought not in terms of samurai but of samurai armies, and no individual glory, no noble deed, was to come in the way of the serious business of winning battles. Needless to say, old traditions died hard, and there are numerous instances of glory-seeking samurai all but ruining a carefully planned campaign in their pursuit of honour. The invasion of Korea in 1592 developed into a race between two rivals to see whose army could enter the capital first, and the preliminary campaign to the great Battle of Sekigahara in 1600 nearly collapsed when two generals each insisted on leading the assault on a vital castle.

The nemesis of Nobunaga

The bow, the original samurai prestige weapon, was relegated to specially trained *ashigaru*, who were most useful as sharpshooters. As for the majority of lower-rank soldiers, they acted as foot spearmen, or formed the numerous corps armed with the most devastating addition to the samurai arsenal – firearms. Firearms were introduced to Japan by the Portuguese in 1542, and were eagerly adopted. While supplies were still limited, they were prized as samurai weaponry; but as the nimbler swordsmiths converted their trade to that of a gunsmith, vast quantities were produced, and squadrons of *ashigaru* trained in their use. It was the ideal *ashigaru* weapon, as the minimum of training was needed to enable it to be fired with all the accuracy of which it was capable.

There were, no doubt, some daimyō to whom this comparatively crude weapon came to be looked on as inappropriate for a samurai. The gun, after all, equalised the lowest and the highest by demanding no greater strength, control or daring than it took to pull the firing mechanism or load a bullet. To a noble samurai it represented the encroachment of barbarian culture into that most traditional of all Japanese social arenas: the battlefield. It defiled both the possesser and the victim, who was thereby deprived of an honourable death. But daimyō who believed in these views tended to be either very rare, or dead. In practice, wars had to be won, and no major daimyō would dare to be without large numbers of firearms.

All that divided the daimyō on the question of firearms was the way in which they were used, and Hōjō Ujiyasu did not live to see the ultimate proof of their worth. He died in 1571, and four years later some sound military thinking, rather than social considerations, led Oda Nobunaga to his famous decision to line up three ranks of matchlockmen at Nagashino. The Takeda and the Hōjō had kept the *ashigaru* to the rear, or in small units under individual commanders, where their guns were less effective. Nobunaga's volley firing, on a large enough scale, tended to ensure that someone would at least hit something. The result was the destruction of the Takeda cavalry on a colossal scale, and a revolution in daimyō thinking.

It also established Oda Nobunaga as the first of the 'super-daimyō', who had begun to acquire some of the former Shōgun's notional powers. But for the Hōjō, the visible result of the lessons of Nagashino was an investment in the defensive architecture of their castles and the natural walls of the surrounding mountains. The destruction of the Takeda, which took until 1582, and the unexpected death of Uesugi Kenshin in 1578, which was followed by a succession dispute, both served to give the Hōjō tranquil borders. Following the family tradition, Ujimasa retired in 1577, leaving his son Ujinao with a false sense of security. From within their kingdom

Hōjō Ujimasa (1538–1590)
Ujimasa was the eldest son of Hōjō Ujiyasu and took part in all his father's campaigns. The turmoil in the rival families of Uesugi and Takeda gave Ujimasa a false sense of security, which was to be totally eclipsed in 1590 when Odawara fell to Hideyoshi's army.

of the Kantō they heard of Nobunaga's murder in 1582, and the take-over by one of his former *ashigaru*, Toyotomi Hideyoshi. Then they began to hear of Hideyoshi's conquest of western Honshū, his taking of Shikoku island, the astounding conquest of the vast southern island of Kyūshū, and by the time they had grown used to the idea that Japan had a new Shōgun in everything but name, an army of 200,000 men was encamped around Odawara castle.

The new daimyō

Here, in 1590, the story of the Hōjō as daimyō came to an end. The siege was long, but largely bloodless, and ended with Hideyoshi ordering the suicide of Ujimasa and the exile of Ujinao. The Hōjō territories were given to Hideyoshi's ally, Tokugawa Ieyasu, but within ten years their vanquisher was to die, leaving an infant to inherit, and with the Battle of Sekigahara in 1600 the great game of *go* was won, and Japan was covered with the playing-pieces of one daimyō – the Tokugawa.

All the existing daimyō had already submitted to Hideyoshi. Now they were forced to submit to the Tokugawa, and to their relief were allowed to keep their heads on their shoulders. In his wisdom, Tokugawa Ieyasu recognised the skills and systems by which these warlords had built up and governed their territories. Their petty kingdoms had been managed well, as we shall see in the chapters that follow, and Ieyasu saw the possibility of using the existing structures as part of his new domain, which was the whole of Japan. So the former warlords became the 'local government' of the dynasty he founded. The Japanese expression is the *baku-han* system,

A daimyō's procession
One of the subtler ways by which the Tokugawa Shōguns sought to control the daimyō was by the *sankin-kōtai*, or 'Alternate Attendance' system. This required the daimyō to leave their families in Edo, the Shōgun's capital, and alternate their own residence between Edo and their own *han* each year. The roads of Japan, therefore, witnessed a succession of gorgeous parades. These daimyō followers are from a scroll depicting such a procession, in the Hōsei-Nikō Kenshōkan, at Nagoya, and are reproduced here by kind permission of the curator.

which combined within it the best of centralised government through the Shōgun's *bakufu*, and the local duties of the daimyō's territory, or *han*. The price the daimyō had to pay was to be severed from their traditional provinces and to be settled elsewhere in Japan, where they had no local loyalties that could spark a rebellion. The first few years of the seventeenth century thus saw a colossal act of moving house. The *fudai-daimyō*, the traditional supporters of the Tokugawa, were given the provinces that controlled the most vital lines of communication. The *tozama-daimyō*, the 'outer lords' who had submitted after Sekigahara, or whose loyalty was felt to be less than total, were given domains far from their roots and far from one another.

The *baku-han* was a successful system that lasted until the Meiji Restoration and the establishment of modern Japan in the mid-nineteenth century. The Tokugawa family supplied a dynasty of fifteen Shōguns over two and a half centuries, supported by the descendants of the original daimyō warlords. We shall see in the pages that follow how they coped with the various demands made on them by peace and war to maintain the continued benevolent rule, under the Shōgun, of the daimyō, the 'Samurai Warlords'.

Focus of Loyalty

Throughout samurai history, whether in peace or in war, the daimyō had one outstanding role to play – to be the leader, to act as focus for loyalty, as through him the family, the clan and the domain were personified. A writer of the Edo Period put it succinctly: 'The relation of parent and child is limited to this life on earth; that between husband and wife continues into the after-life; that between lord and retainer continues into the life after that again.'

This vital loyalty took various expressions, many of which we will examine in the chapters that follow: self-sacrifice in battle, thorough and unspectacular management of a *han's* finances, following-in-death by the bizarre and wasteful act of suicide known as *junshi*, revenge for a beloved dead master, or total loyalty to a family in spite of a dishonourable heir whose conduct betrays the good name of his ancestors. But many of these expressions belonged solely to times of peace. In the Sengoku Period, loyalty required a mixture of the unspectacular and the dramatic, none more so than the total commitment to a defeated daimyō to restore the family fortunes. There is no better illustration of this than the 'Samurai of the Crescent Moon' – Yamanaka Shika-no-suke Yukimori.

The Samurai of the Crescent Moon

The name of Yamanaka Shika-no-suke Yukimori is one almost totally unknown outside Japan, and as the personification of samurai loyalty to a daimyō he deserves to be better known. Yamanaka Shika-no-suke risked his life for the restoration of the Amako family of Izumo Province, to whom the Yamanaka were related. He fought his first battle at the age of 13, when he took an enemy head, and met a tragic death at the age of 34, but by far the most famous episode occurred at the time of the destruction of the Amako family, when he is said to have prayed to the new moon (the 'three-day' crescent moon as the Japanese call it). He had been born on the fifteenth day of the eighth lunar month of 1545, the day of the most brilliant harvest moon, and believed himself to be a heavenly child of the moon. 'Burden me with the seven troubles and eight pains,' he prayed, a Buddhist prayer inviting the gods to place the suffering of the Amako family upon his shoulders.

The Amako had claimed hegemony over the Chūgoku, the southwestern extremity of the main Japanese island of Honshū, at the time of Tsunehisa (1458–1541), but their sway declined over subsequent generations, until they were opposed by the up-and-coming Mōri Motonari (1497–1571) during the rule as daimyō of Amako Yoshihisa. There were many battles with the Mōri in which Yamanaka took part, and at the Battle of Shiraga Yamanaka Shika-no-suke led 200 mounted samurai, and carried out daring tactics of withdrawing calmly then returning to the fray up to

A samurai in formal dress
A daimyō's loyal retainer served him in times of peace as well as war. Here we see a samurai in his formal attire of *kami-shimo*, which consisted of a winged jacket (the *kataginu*) with matching *hakama* (trousers) over a *kimono*, as depicted by an actor at the Toei-Uzumasa Film Studios in Kyōto.

Yamanaka Shika-no-suke
This print by Kuniyoshi depicts Yamanaka Shika-no-suke praying before the crescent moon when he made his vow to restore the fortunes of the Amako family: a vow that ended with his own death. For this reason, Shika-no-suke is one of the paragons of samurai fidelity, though, sadly, he is little known outside Japan.

seven times, against a large army that was running them hard. His military fame was utterly without question, but was not enough to prevent the Amako's castle of Toda-Gassan being captured by Mōri Motonari. The defeated daimyō Yoshihisa retired from the life of a samurai to become a monk, and lived until about 1610, but his loyal retainer was not giving up so easily. He gave his famous prayer to the crescent moon, and from this moment on, in exile, Shika-no-suke's fight began to complete the restoration of the honourable family.

As Yamanaka was only a clan vassal, it was vital for him to work through existing members of the Amako family. The most senior member of the family was a certain Katsuhisa (Yoshihisa's father's first cousin), who had long since been a monk at the Tōfukuji in Kyōto. Yamanaka contacted him and persuaded him to return to lay-life and bring together the remnants of the Amako. With Yamanaka as his military commander, they could now plan the restoration of the Amako territory. Yamanaka sensibly realised that it would be a mistake to attempt the recapture of Toda-Gassan castle. Instead he conducted guerrilla operations against the Mōri in various places. On one raid he was captured by Kikkawa Motoharu, but managed to trick his way out of the trap. In 1578 he went to Kyōto to seek alliance with the most powerful daimyō in Japan, Oda Nobunaga, and appealed to him for the restoration of the Amako.

At that time the Mōri and the Oda clans were in a head-on collision. The Mōri had been supporting the fanatical monks of the Ikkō-ikki against Nobunaga, ferrying in guns to their fortress at Ōsaka. To take on the Mōri on their home ground was a difficult proposition for Nobunaga, as they controlled most of the shipping in the Inland Sea, which could cut off any army advancing overland. To have an ally in the Mōri heartland was an attractive proposition, and Oda Nobunaga's general, Toyotomi Hideyoshi, was already in the process of capturing Kōzuki castle in Harima province. Once it was secured, Nobunaga allotted it to Amako Katsuhisa and Yamanaka Shika-no-suke, who were immediately besieged by the Mōri with a great army of 30,000 men.

Detail from the Ōsaka Screen
In this detail from a painted screen, in the Hōsei-Nikō Kenshōkan in Nagoya, depicting the siege of Ōsaka castle in 1615, we see a mounted samurai advancing into the attack. He is wearing a white *horō* on his back.

Takeda Katsuyori was less well served than the Amako in terms of the loyalty paid to him by his retainers when the family was facing destruction. One by one, the old retainers of his father, Shingen, abandoned him to his fate. Castle gates were shut in his face, and common soldiers deserted, until only a handful of companions was left to face death with him at Temmoku-zan. Here Katsuyori prepares to write a farewell message as the news of the Tokugawa advance is brought to him. In the far distance is the graceful cone of Mount Fuji.

At the time Hideyoshi had a Mōri general confined in his castle of Miki, and, hearing of the danger to the Amako, detached half his army to relieve them. But he was overridden, and received an order from Nobunaga to abandon Kōzuki castle to its fate. There were, apparently, more important strategic considerations than the fate of the Amako. Hideyoshi brought back the troops as they were. The Amako army was isolated and surrendered without the least resistance to the Mōri general, and Katsuhisa committed suicide. By this final act, the Amako were destroyed and obliterated. The loyal Shika-no-suke was taken prisoner and murdered in cold blood while under escort on the road at Takahashi in Bitchū province.

What are we to make of the story of Yamanaka? It is a strange tale of a daimyō's retainer having faith in the fortunes of a doomed family even when the daimyō himself had renounced the struggle. That Yamanaka eventually failed makes his efforts even more tragic, and so much more like the classic heroic failure, whose pattern we find throughout samurai history. There is a marked contrast here between Yamanaka and, say, the retainers of Takeda Katsuyori, hundreds of whom pledged service to Tokugawa Ieyasu when he was defeated in 1582. Yamanaka Shika-no-suke, with his stubborn adherence to samurai honour and the demands of loyalty, has a special place in the history of Japan.

The practical obligations of loyalty

Samurai history is dotted with similar examples of loyalty to a daimyō to the point of death, where a warlord's wishes were carried out in spite of extreme personal suffering. The above account shows this side of the nature of loyalty – the behaviour of the loyal retainer acting essentially as an individual; but the daimyō could not command a kingdom of individuals. There was more to being a samurai than fighting fiercely and loyally in battle. There had to be organisation, delegation of command, and discipline on the battlefield. In times of peace there had to be efficient administration, and a means for converting peace-time samurai into soldiers. The umbrella under which this happened was the *kashindan*, or retainer band, which was mentioned in the context of Hōjō Sōun. The samurai who served a daimyō in a *kashindan* were vassals in a highly developed feudal system. They held lands granted to them by the daimyō, in return for which they would fight his wars. As war was mercifully not a continual process, their services were 'retained', hence the word 'retainer' (in Japanese *kashin* or *kerai*).

Although the definition of a retainer could be made with precision, during the sixteenth century there was a considerable ambiguity and diversity about what constituted samurai status. The popular use of the term today, which usually embraces all Japanese warriors, was truer in the sixteenth century than it was at any other time in Japanese history, before or after. The overriding factor was the enormous increase in the numbers of men who called themselves samurai because they bore arms. Even though there was a great social difference between, say, the son of a daimyō, who had a horse, splendid armour and servants, and a minor part-time samurai from a village, each was part of the same system, which had as its primary function the aim of delineating the military obligation of each and every retainer. So, when war came, each retainer not only supplied devoted individual service, as in the example of Yamanaka above, but also supplied other men and equipment in proportion to the amount of income he received from his landholdings. There were two ways of expressing this in-

Rice fields and mountains
The basis of any daimyō's wealth was the yield of his rice fields, and this view, taken from the summit of Shizu-ga-dake in Shiga prefecture, shows how every bit of available flat land can be pressed into service.

Cooking rice for the army
We are reminded of the mundanities of command by this fascinating illustration from the *Ehon Taikō-ki*. A huge cauldron bubbles away, cooking rice for Hideyoshi's army, while sweating foot-soldiers poke the fire and unload straw bales.

come. The first was in terms of *koku*, which was the rice yield of the fields (one *koku* was 180.4 litres of dry measure, the amount that would theoretically feed one man for one year). Alternatively, as in the case of the Hōjō retainers, in *kanmon*, which was the cash equivalent. The resulting obligation was called the retainer's *yakudaka*.

The daimyō compiled registers of *yakudaka*. In the Hōjō's 1559 register (see Appendix I), the *Odawara-shū shoryō yakuchō*, the units (*shū*), which would make up the army in wartime, are delineated either geographically (for example, Izu-*shū* and Edo-*shū*) or according to a very broad functional definition (for example, *go-umawari-shū*, 'bodyguard', and *ashigaru-shū*, 'foot-soldiers'). There were also separate categories for the Hōjō relatives (*gokamon*) and allies (*takoku-shu*). There are several very good examples of the ratios of obligation used for *yakudaka*, which are missing from the Hōjō example. Asakawa's study of the Iriki family of Kyūshū quotes the muster of troops by the Shimazu daimyō when they attacked Takabaru castle in 1576. A 30 *koku* samurai had to supply personal service, plus one other; a 60 *koku* man added another follower, and so on up to 300 *koku*, who served personally, attended by ten other samurai. When Hideyoshi invaded Korea in 1592, the daimyō nearest to the embarkation port in Kyūshū had to supply six men per 100 *koku*, with lesser proportions from more distant supporters. The Jesuit François Caron, writing at the end of the Sengoku Period, noted that:

each of them must, proportionably, entertain a select company of Souldiers, always in readiness for the Emperor; so that he who hath a thousand koku *yearly, must bring into the field, when ever he is in command, twenty Souldiers & two Horse-Men.*

Thus the Lord of Hirado, who hath 60,000 koku *a year, must entertain, as he easily may, one thousand two hundred Foot, and one hundred and twenty Horse, besides Servants, Slaves, and what more is necessary for the Train.*

197

(The 'Lord of Hirado' at the time was the daimyō Matsuura Shigenobu 1549–1614.)

Such mobilisation orders could only work if the daimyō had the ability to survey his retainers' lands accurately and assess their value of income. As the sixteenth century progressed, the means for doing this became more sophisticated, and a daimyō acquired a very detailed knowledge of the location and extent of his retainers' holdings. It also gave the daimyō two additional powerful tools in ruling his domain. First, the *kandaka* meant that the retainer's relationship to the daimyō could be expressed in terms of income, rather than the mere possession of land. Great income meant great responsibilities, and the appointment to prestigious positions, such as *jōshu*, keepers of castles, and *bugyō*, magistrates.

Second, it made it much easier for a daimyō to transfer retainers from

Samurai resting in the castle
This unusual illustration from the *Hōjō Godai-ki* shows samurai polishing swords, playing *go*, and *sugoroku* (backgammon). One man is inspecting an arrow, while in the background sit their suits of armour and various weapons.

Hamamatsu castle
Hamamatsu castle covered a strategic section of the Tōkaidō road, and was owned by a succession of daimyō through the Edo Period as the Tokugawa Shōguns moved them from one fief to another. It had its most celebrated taste of action in 1572, when Takeda Shingen advanced on Hamamatsu and fought the Tokugawa at the Battle of Mikata-ga-Hara.

one set of lands to another. In particular it meant that a retainer's holdings could be split up geographically while still ensuring the same income. This reduced the risks of rebellion by retainers, as the lands, and therefore the people who worked them, were not a contiguous whole. It is also worth noting that retainers who were granted castles were given ones far away from their traditional territories. This, of course, was more pronouncedly so in the case of conquered enemies who had grudgingly pledged service.

To some extent, this anticipated the physical separation of the samurai from the land which was to be the hallmark of the Tokugawa class system. The retainers of all classes now identified themselves more and more with the daimyō, and less and less with the land they farmed. A relationship of dependancy developed as the retainer came to rely on daimyō authority to help him collect taxes from his lands. The relationship between a retainer and a daimyō thus gradually changed from one of independence and local identification to one of dependence and association with a great name. This was fine as long as the daimyō kept winning, but as the Takeda were to show dramatically in 1582, when a daimyō sneezed, the retainers caught a cold.

The élite retainers

Within every *kashindan* were an élite, a select group of senior retainers, called usually *karō* (elders). There are many surviving records of retainer bands in the sixteenth century, most of which are arranged in similar ways under these élite persons. Our source for the Takeda is the list of retainers in the *Kōyō Gunkan*, which is itself based upon two earlier registers of Takeda retainers, one of 1567, which contains 235 names, and the other of 1582, which lists 895 surviving members of the Takeda *kashindan* who pledged service to Tokugawa Ieyasu following the destruction of Takeda Katsuyori by the combined armies of Oda and Tokugawa.

The Takeda *kashindan* consisted largely of three parts:

1 In the first place we have the *jikishindan*, or direct retainer band, who were divided into the *go-shinrui-shū* (relatives), the *go-fudai karō-shū*, the 'elders', and the leaders of the separate *ashigaru-shū*, the *ashigaru-taishō*.
2 The second main grouping was the *sempo-shū*, the unit for the surviving retainers of the many daimyō conquered by the Takeda, such as the Sanada family of Shinano.
3 The final section was the *kuni-shū*, the regional *bushi-dan* from the Takeda lands, who ranged down to village samurai.

Takeda Shingen was the leader of this 'Ever-victorious, invincible, Kōshu Warband', as he called it, of which the élite core were the hand-picked leaders, magnificent in action, of whom 24 brave and fierce individuals became well known as the 'Twenty-Four Generals'. The *Kōyō Gunkan* records Shingen's criteria for a good general, which laid as much stress on peace-time work as on the field of battle: 'Concerning honouring the exploits of great generals, first, (they must be) persons of judgement, second, (they carry out) punishments in the province, third, they achieve great victories in battle, we honour their fame in these three.'

The 'Twenty-Four Generals' is, in fact, not a contemporary term, but one invented later. The Japanese as a race seem peculiarly fond of numerical categories, and the 'Takeda Twenty-Four Generals' is a popular concept from stories and illustrations. The selection of the 24 relates to their popu-

The Takeda 'Twenty-Four Generals' Every daimyō had an élite corps of senior retainers. In the case of the Takeda family, the élite were the so-called 'Twenty-Four Generals'. The term is not contemporary, and different illustrations depict different individuals. This scroll is in the Memorial Hall on the site of Nagashino castle.

larity with the masses in the Edo Period, and we see them in the portraits included in three painted scrolls of the Twenty-Four Generals, on which there are various faces of generals. The commander-in-chief Shingen is painted in the top centre, and 24 individuals are arranged to left and right in two rows. The 24 generals join Shingen and Katsuyori, and Shingen's younger brothers Nobukado and Nobushige are shown in various ways.

I have examined these scrolls carefully, and discovered that there are, in fact, 33 individuals represented. Furthermore, some of the greatest names in the Takeda hierarchy are not included at all. One example is Hajikano Dene'mon Masatsugu, an *ashigaru-taishō*, or general of *ashigaru*, a demanding post, who added his own unique chapter to the Takeda legend, when in 1569 Takeda Shingen led his army against the Hōjō. On approaching Odawara, the Takeda army was met by a swollen river. Shingen ordered his army to stop while the depth was tested, and Hajikano volunteered for this dangerous task. He drove his horse into the angry waters and began to swim it across. So deep was the river that at one time all that could be seen of Hajikano was the *sashimono* banner on his back, which bore a design of a playing piece from the Japanese board game of *shōgi*. Hajikano's piece was the spear, which in *shōgi* can only move forwards, a reason he put forward to Shingen for his confidence in advancing!

Another strange omission is Morozumi Bungo-no-kami Masakiyo. Masakiyo is said to have been the youngest son of Takeda Nobumasa, and was therefore Shingen's great-uncle. He is believed to have been 81 years old at the time of his death at the fourth Battle of Kawanakajima, and held the rank of *ashigaru-taishō*. Shingen had, in fact, made this old general *honjin-hatamoto*, 'headquarters-samurai', for the battle, a comparatively safe position, but the headquarters was attacked in a surprise charge by Uesugi Kenshin. The old general drew his sword, plunged into the enemy and was killed. Shingen bitterly regretted his death, and Morozumi is one of only three Takeda generals to be buried at Kawanakajima.

Other names surprise one by their inclusion. Anayama Baisetsu and Oyamada Nobushige are included but, after years of service to Shingen, these two later betrayed his son Takeda Katsuyori. Nevertheless, the concept of the 'Twenty-Four Generals' remains a popular one, and they can

---

A daimyō in command

The great warlord Uesugi Kenshin sits with his generals to receive a message from a wounded scout. As Kenshin was a Buddhist monk he wears the traditional white headcowl. Behind him fly the three banners that always indicated his presence: the red rising sun on blue which was the treasure of the Uesugi house; the elaborate version of the character for 'dragon', which was always raised on the battlefield as his army went into an attack; and on the viewer's right the character *bi*, the first syllable in the name of Bishamon-ten, under whose divine protection Kenshin lived, which was flown at his headquarters on a battlefield.

His generals, accompanied by retainers carrying their personal banners, sit beside him. From left to right, they are as follows: Shimojō Saneyori (white ring on red), who was in the forward division at the fourth Battle of Kawanakajima in 1561; Takanashi Masayori (chequerboard); Nakajō Fujikashi, who received a personal commendation from Kenshin for his action at Kawanakajima, has the red flag with white designs; Honjō Shigenaga has the bold character *jō*; and Suda Chikamitsu, also of the forward division, has the gold swastika.

The wounded samurai bears the Uesugi *mon* of love-birds on his *sashimono*, which identifies him as a retainer of a member of Uesugi Kenshin's family, or of someone regarded as equivalent to a family member.

be found represented at the festivals held every year in the area around Kōfu, Shingen's old capital. Many others of the famous daimyō of the age had their 'number of generals'. Tokugawa Ieyasu had 16, Uesugi Kenshin either 14, 17 or 28, depending on which version you read.

One factor that was common to the generals on both sides, as indeed it was to many powerful daimyō retainers of the period, was the giving of honorific titles. In addition to their surname and given name, they tended to be known as 'Feudal Lord of...'. The surprising thing about these titles, which appear in Japanese as '...no kami' is that they frequently refer to territories not actually owned by the clan in question, and often hundreds of miles away. Shingen's great-uncle, Morozumi Masakiyo, was 'Bungo no kami', the nominal feudal lord of Bungo province on the island of Kyūshū, over a thousand miles to the west, and which probably none of the Takeda had ever visited. Other titles reflect nearby territories controlled by other daimyō which the retainer's overlord coveted. Baba Nobuharu, one of the most skilled to the 'Twenty-Four Generals', was Mino no kami, Mino province being a possible future gain for the Takeda as part of an advance on Kyōto. At one time, there were living no less than three prominent samurai all bearing the identical title of 'Suruga no kami'. One was Katō Nobukuni, a general of the Takeda who had responsibility for the teaching of archery; another was an Uesugi general, Usa Sadayuki, the truce-bearer

The 'Twenty-Four Generals' at Shimobe
Every May, the Takeda 'Twenty-Four Generals' are brought to life in the *Shingen-kō* Festival at Shimobe, in Yamanashi prefecture. The character on the far end of the line is Yamamoto Kansuke, easily recognisable by his buffalo-horn helmet. The 'generals'' names are painted on their *sashimono* banners, which would not have been done in the sixteenth century.

after Kawanakajima, and the third was a retainer of the Mōri daimyō in the west of Japan – Kikkawa Motoharu. None had any direct connection with Suruga province, which was actually owned by the Hōjō.

In spite of all the honorific titles, feudal obligation and rewards, not all lord-vassal arrangements succeeded, even among the élite. There were, in fact, some spectacular failures, such as Sasa Narimasa (1539–88). He was one of Hideyoshi's most senior retainers, granted a fief of 100,000 *koku* in Etchu province, but when Hideyoshi was opposed by Oda Nobuo in 1584, Narimasa backed Nobuo, and was chastised by his former comrade, Maeda Toshiie. Hideyoshi dealt with Narimasa with the great generosity that was his hallmark, and transferred him to a new fief in far-off Higo province in Kyūshū in 1587, giving Narimasa then following warning as he did so:

1 *To the 53 local magnates the same fief as before is to be granted.*
2 *No land survey shall be made for three years.*
3 *Due precaution is to be taken never to embarrass farmers.*
4 *Due precaution is always to be taken that no insurrection shall take place.*
5 *No charge shall be made upon farmers for the contribution to the public works to be carried out at Ōsaka.*

The above are strictly and carefully to be observed.

Unfortunately Sasa Narimasa betrayed the trust Hideyoshi put in him, and was 'invited' to commit suicide.

The lord's horse
Two samurai attendants wait with the lord's horse outside the *maku*, the curtained enclosure used to screen the field headquarters of a daimyō. The *mon* on the *maku* is the chrysanthemum-on-the-water design of Kusunoki Masashige. This is a further section from the scroll of Kusunoki's career owned by the Nampian Kannon-ji at Kawachi-Nagano, and is reproduced here by kind permission of the Chief Priest.

The call to arms

With a call to arms, the *kashindan*, with its detailed records of obligation, was transformed from a paper army into a fighting force. An example relating to the year 1557 has been preserved in the archives of the Uesugi family. It is in the form of a highly detailed letter, which is not surprising considering that the man who is being summoned is Irobe Katsunaga, Kenshin's *gun-bugyō*, a rank equivalent to Chief of Staff. He lists the disturbances attributed to Takeda Harunobu (Takeda Shingen) and warns Katsunaga of the dangers to the province of Shingen's belligerence:

Concerning the disturbances among the various families of Shinano and the Takeda of Kai in the year before last, it is the honourable opinion of Imagawa Yoshimoto of Sumpu that things must have calmed down. However, since this time, Takeda Harunobu's example of government has been corrupt and bad. However, through the will of the gods and from the kind offices of Yoshimoto, I, Kagetora have very patiently avoided any interference. Now, Harunobu has recently set out for war and it is a fact that he has torn to pieces the retainers of the Ochiai family of Shinano and Katsurayama castle has fallen. Accordingly, he has moved into the so-called Shimazu and Ogura territories for the time being. . . . My army will be turned in this direction and I, Kagetora will set out for war and meet them half way. In spite of snowstorms or any sort of difficulty we will set out for war by day or night. I have waited fervently. If our family's allies in Shinano can be destroyed then even the defences of Echigo will not be safe. Now that things have come to such a pass, assemble your pre-eminent army and be diligent in loyalty, there is honourable work to be done at this time.

With respects
Kenshin,
1557, 2nd month, 16th day

A celebratory banquet
In this page from the *Ehon Taikō-ki*, a group of senior retainers feast after a victory. Their food is served to them on lacquered trays, and the *saké* is flowing freely!

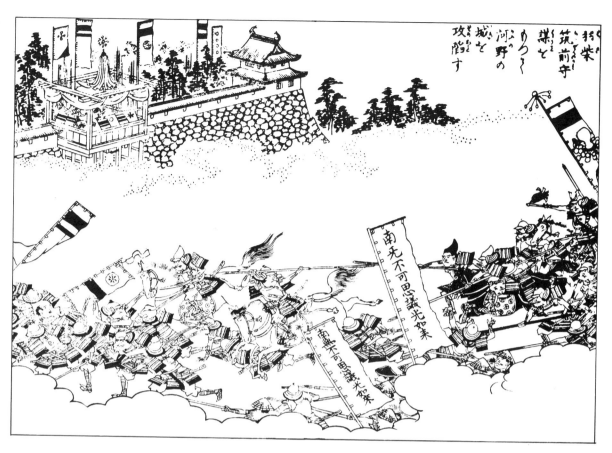

将柴筑前守
築を
もりて
河野の
城を
攻略す

Hideyoshi attacks a castle
Here the *Ehon Taikō-ki* shows Hideyoshi's troops neutralising an opportunistic attack by the defenders of a castle, identified by the caption as Kawano.

Needless to say, less important retainers received a less imposing call to arms and, in the case of the part-time samurai of the countryside, a general proclamation would suffice. The well-known example from about 1560 of the call to arms against Uesugi Kenshin by Hōjō Ujimasa (though sealed by his retired father Ujiyasu as the young daimyō was off campaigning) has sometimes been ridiculed as evidence of his lack of concern for the quality of his troops. In contrast, it shows the universality of the definition of samurai referred to above, and his willingness to reward any who serve him well:

1 All men, including those of the samurai class in this country district, are ordered to come and be registered on the 20th day of this month. They are to bring with them a gun, spear, or any kind of weapon, if they happen to possess one, without fearing to get into trouble.
2 If it is known afterwards that even one man in this district concealed himself and did not respond to the call, such man, no matter whether he is a bugyō *or a peasant, is to be beheaded.*
3 All men from 15 to 70 years of age are ordered to come; not even a monkey tamer will be let off.
4 Men to be permitted to remain in the village are those whose ages are above 70 years, or under 15 years, and too young to be used as messengers, but the others are all ordered to come.
5 It will be good for the men to prepare for the call by polishing their spears

and preparing small paper flags to be taken with them. Those who are fitted to be messengers, and desire to do that service, will be so permitted.

6   All the men covered by this order are to come to Katsukui on the 4th day and register before the lord's deputy and then return home...if the appointed day happens to be rainy they are to come the first day the weather is settled. Men must arrive at the appointed place properly armed with anything they happen to possess, and those who do not possess a bow, a spear or any sort of regular weapon are to bring even hoes or sickles.

7   This regulation is generally applicable, and even Buddhist priests who desire to do their duty for their native province are ordered to come.

It is ordered to pay strict attention to the implications of the above seven articles, and if there be anyone who disregards this ordinance and neglects his duty, such a one is to be severely punished; while the man who is careful and eager to be loyal to his lord will be rewarded with the grant that is reasonable and suitable to him.

By such means, the sixteenth-century warlord assembled his army. The obligation of loyalty was fulfilled in part. It could now be tested on the battlefield.

Commander-in-Chief

When the samurai clan went to war, the daimyō's role became that of transforming this retainer band with its patterns of loyalty into an efficient fighting unit on the battlefield. The daimyō thereupon assumed the demanding role of commander-in-chief of the domainal army.

Setting off to war

Setting out for war
This picture from the *Ehon Taikō-ki* shows the meticulous preparations made when an army set out for war. Armour is removed from boxes, bamboo flagpoles are threaded through the banners and, in the left foreground, an attendant fixes a samurai's *sashimono* into place on the back of his armour.

Once the troops had been assembled, the actual process of setting out for war was attended by much ceremony, whether it was for a long campaign, or as a farewell ritual immediately prior to the start of a battle. There are copious records of the form these rituals took, which have provided the basis for the re-enactments of such ceremonies in the former castle towns of noted daimyō. I am well acquainted with two of these – the Uesugi *Butei shiki* at Yonezawa, which re-enacts the departure ceremony of Uesugi Kenshin, and the *Shingen-kō matsuri* at Kōfu, which is part of a number of

Four Generals at the Nagashino Festival
A general's military costume was often embellished by the wearing of a surcoat, called a *jinbaori*. The four men here are taking part in the annual Nagashino Festival.

commemorative events for Takeda Shingen. (I have also had the unique privilege of being invited to play the part of Shingen's general, Baba Nobuharu, at the latter celebration in 1986.)

In ancient times, according to Japanese legend, a battle would customarily begin with a blood-offering to the gods of war in the form of a human sacrifice, either a captured prisoner or a condemned criminal, though there does not appear to be any written evidence for such practices continuing beyond the eighth century AD, and certainly during the time of the samurai the blood-sacrifice is confined to the offering of severed heads after the battle, rather than an actual sacrifice beforehand. Nevertheless, the need for prayers to the gods of war, of whom the most important was Hachiman-dai-Bosatsu, the deified spirit of the Emperor Ōjin (201–312) and tutelary deity of the Minamoto clan, permeates much of the ritual surrounding departure for war and victory ceremonies.

The ceremony of departure was centred around the practical need for a review of troops. With his army drawn up ready to march off, the daimyō would sit, surrounded by his generals in a semicircle, against the backdrop of the *maku*, the large curtains used to screen the headquarters position from view. In the case of Uesugi Kenshin, who was a Buddhist monk, this would have been preceded by his praying for victory within the shrine of the Buddhist deity Bishamon-ten inside Kasuga-yama castle. Only then would Kenshin go out into the courtyard to take his seat with his generals.

There he would partake of the traditional farewell meal, served to him with great dignity. There were three dishes, *kachi-guri* (dried chestnuts – probably included for no reason other than the literal translation of the characters used is 'victory chestnuts'), *kombu* (kelp – a basic ingredient in Japanese cooking) and prepared *awabi* (abalone), all three of which were regarded as bringing good fortune. He would also drink *saké* (rice wine), served within three cups, one inside the other. The number three was also regarded as bringing good luck from the divinations of yin and yang geomancy, and the three cups represented heaven, earth and man.

When the army was ready to move off, an attendant would tie the commander's sword round his waist, then his quiver of arrows (rarely encountered in the Sengoku Period) after which the daimyō would stand up, take his signalling fan and receive the shouts of his assembled troops. There were various ways of doing this, but there are two shouts in common – the first being 'Ei!' (Glory!), to which there is given the response 'Ō!' (Yes!). In the *Shingen-kō-matsuri*, the man playing the part of Shingen's *gun-bugyō*, Yamamoto Kansuke, orders the other generals to raise their swords, and calls, 'Ei! Ei! Ō!', to which the generals reply, 'Ei! Ei! Ō!'. In the Uesugi version, it is 'Kenshin' himself who calls 'Ei! Ei!', and his generals reply, 'Ō! Ō!' repeated twice. This shout was also given at the end of a successful battle. (There is a splendid example in Kurosawa's film *Ran*.)

Traditionally, the general would then mount his horse, put on his helmet, and the flags would be raised. Just before the procession moved off, a Shinto priest would bless the army with the chanting of *sutras*. Uesugi Kenshin would also re-dedicate to Hachiman the 'Hachiman-bow' which was a treasure of the Uesugi. After this, Kenshin would mount his horse, surrounded by his three banners: the Bishamon-ten, a red rising sun on blue (a gift from an emperor), and the 'warring dragon' flag, which led a charge by the Uesugi samurai.

Organisation on a battlefield

Armies were controlled on the battlefield using a range of visible and audible signalling methods. Of the latter, the most important were the *taiko*, the big war-drums and the *horagai*, the conch-shell trumpet. War-drums varied in size from the very large specimens mounted in the open-work towers of castles, to ones carried in a frame on a man's back. In the eighth chapter of the *Hōjō Go-dai ki*, we read: 'The *horagai* was blown when a battle plan was put into disorder. Similarly on hearing the voice of the *taiko* the soldiers would regroup...'

In another section of the *Hōjō Go-dai ki*, we hear of the use Hōjō Sōun made of a *yamabushi* who was adept at playing the *horagai*:

The soldiers obeyed the commands of the horagai, *and those proclaimed by the* taiko. *There was a* yamabushi *called Gakuzenbo of Ōyama in Sagami [province]. He took the Buddhist name of Satsuma, and possessed a large* horagai. *This* yamabushi *was especially skilled in blowing the* horagai. *It could be heard for a distance of 50 chō [about six miles!]. When Hōjō Sōun set out to war this* yamabushi *came from the Ōyama temple. He was [made] a* hatamoto *and blew the* horagai. *It is said that his descendants blow the* horagai *to this day.*

Horagai were also used for time-keeping.

The use of flags to identify and control units of troops was based on a very sophisticated use of heraldry. Prior to the sixteenth century, heraldry in Japan had not gone much further than the straightforward identification of an army. Now it became the means for subdividing and controlling an army, made necessary by the need to control large bodies of troops. My study of the army of the Shimazu shows how the troops fielded by the Shimazu grew from 3,000 in 1411 through 5,000 in 1484, to an estimate of possibly 115,000 at the siege of Minamata in 1576. Even during the straightened circumstances forced upon them by Hideyoshi's defeat of them in 1578, they were still able to supply 10,600 warriors for the Winter Campaign of Ōsaka in 1614. Complex manoeuvring of such numbers, such as the early morning clash during the fourth Battle of Kawanakajima (1561) between the Takeda (16,000) and the Uesugi (13,000) also presupposes quite sophisticated methods of troop recognition and signalling, in addition to well-rehearsed drill and discipline. Also, armour was becoming uniform in style, and the gradual introduction of armour protection for the face, which within the century was to develop into a complete mask, made the need for quick identification more pressing than ever. The response to this was a considerable development of the use and design of flags, notably in three forms: the *nobori*, the *uma-jirushi*, and the *sashimono*.

The *nobori* is the familiar form of long vertical flag, supported along the top edge, which can be seen everywhere in Japan today, from shops to temples. Its military use seems to be well established by the third quarter of the sixteenth century, and several contemporary painted screens show a great profusion of *nobori*, many of which have *mon* (family badges).

The *uma-jirushi*, literally 'horse insignia', was introduced to distinguish the person of a general, which was the function of the European 'standard'. According to regulations introduced early in the Edo Period, a daimyō with an income of 1,300 *koku* or over was entitled to a *ko-* (small) *uma-jirushi*, held by one man, while those with 6,000 *koku* and over could have an *ō-uma-jirushi*, which required two or three people to hold it. A samurai 'standard-bearer' would either have the *uma-jirushi* seated in a leather pocket at the front of his belt, or strapped into a frame on his back. In the case of the *ō-uma jirushi* the other two men would hold on to separate tethering cords.

The *uma-jirushi* did not always take the form of a flag. Several three-dimensional objects were used, such as a large red umbrella by Oda Nobunaga, and the *sen nari hisago* or 'thousand gourd standard' of Toyotomi Hideyoshi. Of the flag versions, one well-known example is Uesugi Kenshin's red sun disc on dark blue. The flowing *hata-jirushi*, popular in earlier centuries, continued to be used in armies, and in the case of Katō Kiyomasa (1562–1611) served as his *uma-jirushi* in the form of a long white banner with the Nichiren motto *Namu myōhō renge kyō*, which is preserved in the Hommyō-ji in Kumamoto.

The sashimono

The real innovation in heraldic display in the sixteenth century was not in the use of large flags but in the introduction of a personal banner for the

The sashimono *of Tadano Samon*
See overleaf for the account of how this particular *sashimono* inspired a comrade in the heat of battle.

Detail from the Ōsaka Screen, showing **sashimono**
The *sashimono* was the most important addition to Japanese heraldry during the sixteenth century. It consisted of an identifying device, usually a flag, fixed to the back of a suit of armour. This picture is from the painted screen of the siege of Ōsaka in the Hōsei-Nikō Kenshōkan at Nagoya.

individual called the *sashimono*, and worn on the back, its shaft slotting into a specially constructed carrier. Two cords ran under the armpits from the *sashimono* shaft to two rings on the front of the armour, to help hold the flag in place. *Sashimono* sometimes bore the *mon* of the commander, though there were many exceptions, as we shall see, and some cases where the *sashimono* was not actually a flag at all but a three-dimensional object.

Two examples of the use of *sashimono* appear in the chronicle *Meiryō Kohan*: 'At the time of the Ōsaka campaign there was a retainer of Kii Raisen called Yabe Tora no suke, of great strength with a *sashimono* of length two *ken* [12 feet!], and a long sword over three *shaku* [3 feet].'

The second extract shows how a striking *sashimono* could inspire a comrade:

There was a retainer of Satake Yoshinobu called Tadano Samon. He was expert in the ways of horse and bow, spear and sword, and furthermore became a samurai of great bravery and strength. . . . At the time when this Samon went to the battlefield he wore a large sashimono. *The* sashimono *was a* nobori *of white cotton cloth on which was written in large characters, 'hitoashi-fu ko Tadano Samon' [Tadano Samon who will not take one step backwards]. There was once a time when the Sasaki army were defeated in battle. One of their common soldiers had lost heart and retreated, but when he was about to drink water from a stream by the road-side, he saw the great* sashimono *where it had fallen into the water. He saw the characters on it, and regretted that he had retreated. This mere footsoldier hurried back and charged into the midst of the great army of the enemy. He fought with*

Battle across a river
At the signal given by a bursting rocket, samurai ford a river into battle, under the covering fire of their arquebusiers. (From the *Ehon Taikō-ki*.)

214

Smashing an aqueduct
A reliable water supply was vital to the defenders of a castle. In this illustration from the *Ehon Taikō-ki*, the besiegers of Chōko-ji castle are attempting to smash the aqueduct, having driven off the guards. It was the destruction of the aqueduct that led to Shibata Katsuie's final, desperate charge into the midst of the enemy. (See *Battles of the Samurai* by this author.)

great desperation and took three helmeted heads. . . . He ended his career with 200 koku.

The best evidence of the role heraldry could play on a battlefield is the Hōjō army under Hōjō Ujiyasu in about the year 1559. The *shū* units in the 1559 register, referred to in the previous chapter, are largely preserved on the field of battle, with great use being made of the heraldic *sashimono*.

Ujiyasu's army consisted of two major parts, the first being the troops supplied by his well-established and loyal family retainers, the 28 *roshō*. Of these the 20 *shōshō*, 'captains', formed the first rank, while behind them were the 8 *karō*, 'elders', five units of which were identified by the use of different coloured *sashimono*, and therefore called the *go-shiki sonae*, or 'five colour regiments'. Thus Hōjō Tsunanari (1515–87), the victor of the Night Battle of Kawagoe, led men with yellow flags on their backs; Hōjō Tsunataka wore red; Tominaga Masaie (who is recorded as the keeper of Edo castle in 1564) wore blue; Kasawara was white; and Tame, black.

It is almost certain that each of these coloured flags would bear in addition the Hōjō *mon* of the *mitsu uroku*, the fish-scale design, which is depicted on a red *sashimono* preserved in the Kanagawa Prefectural Art Museum in Yokohama. There is also a reference to black *sashimono* ('*sashimono* should be black and new') in a military ordinance issued by Hōjō Ujikuni (1541–97) in 1574.

The most fascinating use of heraldry in the Hōjō army is, however, found in the core of the army, the *go-hatamoto* 48 *banshō*. The 48 *banshō*, 'captains', were under Ujiyasu's direct command, and were divided into 6 companies of 7 *banshō*, and one of 6. Each *banshō* commanded 20 men, and every unit was distinguished by a single *kana* on his *sashimono*. The interesting point about this arrangement is that the seven units were grouped in accordance with the *i-ro-ha* syllabary. The *i-ro-ha* is a poem which contains every one of the phonetic *hiragana*, and is traditionally used as a way of teaching Japanese children their alphabet, so that the order was:

– *i, ro, ha, ni, ho, he, to*
– *chi, ri, nu, ru, o, wa, ka,*
– *yo, ta, re, so, tsu, ne, na*
– *ra, mu, u, i, no, o, ku,*
– *ya, ma, ke, fu, ko, e, te*
– *a, sa, ki, yu, me, n,*
– *mi, shi, e, hi, mo, se, su*

This meant that the *sashimono* of Ujiyasu's army spelled out a poem, which roughly translated, means 'Colours are fragrant, but they fade away. In this world of ours none lasts forever. Today cross the high mountain of life's illusion, and there will be no more shallow dreaming, no more drunkenness.' Among this group we know that a certain retainer called Nanjō Gemba-no-suke, along with his own men, wore the character 'u' on his *sashimono*.

There are few details regarding the heraldry of the other units, though one may assume that the allies (the *takoku-shū*) displayed their own *mon*. The *ashigaru-shū*, who were little regarded at this time, were kept in a homogeneous unit under reliable command, probably with little identification.

Heraldry and the Takeda

Hōjō Ujiyasu frequently found himself in arms against his belligerent neighbour Takeda Shingen, and there is considerable evidence of the use of heraldry by this renowned commander. The most important flag was a large *nobori*, preserved today in the Takeda Museum at the Erin-ji at Enzan (Yamanashi-ken), bearing in gold characters on blue the motto 'Swift as the wind, silent as the forest, fierce as a fire, steady as a mountain'. Other flags included what is now the oldest surviving 'rising sun' flag in Japan. He also had two long red *nobori* bearing Buddhist prayers, and a personal flag with three Takeda *mon* with 'flowery' edges.

Shingen also used heraldic devices to differentiate the various units of his army in a similar fashion to that of the Hōjō. Instead of the Hōjō use of colour and *kana*, the various units of the Takeda are distinguished by the flags of their commanders. There is little use of the Takeda *mon*, or indeed of any device resembling a *mon*. Instead there is a predominant use of bold design and colour. Two examples from the *go-shinrui-shu* are Takeda Nobutoyo, who used a black flag bearing a white sun's disc (Nobutoyo was the son of Shingen's younger brother Nobushige, who was killed during the fourth Battle of Kawanakajima in 1561, where it is believed he used the same flag), and Ichijō Nobutatsu, another of Shingen's brothers,

216

The flags of the Hōjō army, 1559
These are the *hiragana* characters
used on the *sashimono* of the Hōjō
army. (See text for full description.)

いろはにほへと
ちりぬるをわか
よたれそつねな
らむうゐのおく
やまけふこえて
あさきゆめみし
みしゑひもせす

who had a flag divided horizontally into two halves, white on top and red underneath. From the *go-fudai karō-shū*, we find Baba Nobuharu, killed during the pursuit from Nagashino in 1575, whose flag was a black zigzag on white. All are displayed at the Takeda festivals (see pages 154–5).

Takeda Shingen's arch-rival, Uesugi Kenshin, is less fortunate in his present-day commemoration. Of his 'Twenty-Eight Generals' who are personified at the annual re-enactment, nine of the families died out during the Edo Period, and are therefore not recorded in the illustrated register of 1841, which the organisers of the *Butei-shiki* have used to reconstruct the

Kakizaki leads the charge of the Uesugi samurai

This plate illustrates the pivotal moment during the fourth Battle of Kawanakajima in 1561. The Takeda army had crossed the river in secret during the night, expecting the Uesugi army to come fleeing across their front after a dawn raid by a Takeda unit on their camp. In fact, the reverse happened. Guessing Takeda Shingen's plan, his rival Uesugi Kenshin had similarly transferred his army by night. As dawn broke, the Uesugi samurai pounced upon the Takeda flanks in a devastating charge.

The Uesugi vanguard was led by Kakizaki Kageie, whose *uma-jirushi* (personal standard) bore a large golden grasshopper, and whose samurai wore a *sashimono* charged with the unlikely sounding device of a giant radish! To their rear are the flags of Shimazu Norihisa (the same black cross as the better-known family of Shimazu in Kyushu), whose samurai accompanied Kakizaki in the charge, and in the distance appear the flags of two minor Uesugi retainers, Ōishi (star pattern) and Nozokito.

To the rear of the Takeda lines is the flag of Hara Toratane, whose position close to Shingen's headquarters meant that his soldiers received the brunt of the charge. The *ashigaru* in the foreground bear the Takeda *mon* on black, indicating that they follow a family member, namely Takeda Nobushige, Shingen's brother, who was killed during the battle. Note how the spearman carries his sword blade downwards, it being the only practical way for it to be carried if it is thrust through the belt and the wearer has to use a spear. (The author is indebted to Messrs. Bottomley and Hopson for this point of detail.)

flags used in the re-enactment of the departure for war of their favourite son. The 1841 register is extrapolated backwards to a register of 1575, which, unlike the Takeda list, gives no indication itself of flags, but has the additional advantage that it lists the weapon types to be supplied by each unit (see Appendix II). As they are heterogeneous collections, it is reasonable to assume that the Uesugi army, like the Takeda, fought in units under the banner of the commander. This is supported by the notes and illustrations which the festival committee kindly supplied to me. Once again, there is a minimal use of actual *mon*. Two of the most remarkable designs are recorded for Kakizaki Izumi-no-kami Kageie, leader of the Uesugi vanguard at the fourth Battle of Kawanakajima in 1561, who used a personal *uma-jirushi* of a golden grasshopper on a blue field, while his followers had red *sashimono* charged with a white *daikon*, the giant radish!

Heraldry and specialised units

In the three examples above, there seems to have been little use made of heraldry to indicate differing functions, other than the broad categories of *ashigaru*, *go-umawari-shū*, etc.; not that this is surprising, because the battle-field organisation of the time, being based on registers such as the Hōjō 1559 survey, relied on retainers supplying their own troops and fighting loyally for the daimyō. The one exception is the use of *sashimono* to distinguish the *tsukai-ban*, or messengers, whose role was a vital one in warfare. The Tokugawa *tsukai-ban* used a *sashimono* bearing the character *go* (the figure 5), and the Takeda *tsukai-ban* bore a centipede. The colours are variously described as being black on white, white on black, black on red, gold on black and gold on blue. The chronicle *Musha Monogatari* tells us a good story about the Takeda *tsukai-ban* which is interesting in that it illustrates the meticulous regulations in a daimyō's army, and also the refreshing discovery that samurai could have a sense of humour!

Takeda Shingen instructs one of his tsukai-ban
The *tsukai-ban*, or messengers, were a vital arm of any daimyō's army. Here Takeda Shingen instructs one of his messengers, who has a centipede on his *sashimono*, at the second Battle of Kawanakajima, also known as the Battle of the Saigawa. (See *Battles of the Samurai* by this author.) This version is from a woodblock print in the author's collection.

Among the honourable [followers] of Takeda Shingen-kō, were the twelve o-tsukai ban. Their sashimono were white flags with a black centipede. However, among them was a person called Hajikano Den'emon who wore a white flag without a centipede. Shingen-kō inspected them and questioned him why he did not have the same white flag sashimono as everybody else in the tsukai-ban. Shingen-kō got angry when someone disobeyed orders, and Den'emon had disobeyed military regulations. Den'emon showed a one sun [2.5 cm/1 in long] centipede that had attached itself to the loop of the sashimono under his armpit. Said Den'emon, if I attach it in place of the other centipede, I shall mingle with the other warriors, as it is like the others. Shingen-kō began to laugh.'

This is the same Hajikano Den'emon Masatsugu whose use of a different *sashimono* design was described in the previous chapter.

The use of messengers and scouts was the most reliable way in which orders were transmitted and the units of an army controlled from the daimyō's headquarters. In the *Kōyō Gunkan*, we read that 'Sixty horsemen and one on foot from the samurai retainers of Itagaki were sent out as *o-mono miso* [scouts], but seeing no enemy approaching in the vicinity they returned. . . .' Membership of a *tsukai-ban* was highly regarded, as is indicated in the chronicle *Tosenkigyō*:

There was a retainer of the Echizen-Shōshō Tadanao called Hara Hayato Sadatane. He was originally a retainer of Takeda Shingen, but following the downfall of Takeda Katsuyori the Shōshō Tadanao, hearing at second hand of the fame of his

Warrior wearing a horō
The *horō* is surely the most impractical addition to a suit of armour ever devised. It consisted of a cloak on a bamboo frame, which took the place of the *sashimono* on the back of armour. It was often worn as an identifying device by messengers.

military exploits, engaged him [as a member of] the kuro-horō shu *[the 'black horō unit']. He served diligently as an army messenger.*

Note how the brave samurai is appointed to a responsible position, and that Tadanao's messengers were distinguished by wearing a black *horō*. The *horō* was a cloak-like bag, worn on the back of the armour, which was often stiffened with a basketwork cage, surely the most impractical item of military equipment ever devised, though even *sashimono* must have been a hindrance in the heat of battle. In fact, the painted screen in Hikone castle, depicting the Summer Campaign of Ōsaka, shows an *ashigaru* patiently holding a samurai's *sashimono* while the latter delivers the *coup de grâce*. Oda Nobunaga's retainer band included his own *go-umawari-shū*, which was divided into two parts: the red *aka horo-shū* and the *kuro horo-shū*.

The use of heraldry to distinguish such units presupposes a growing specialism of weaponry or tactics within a samurai army, and this was indeed slowly happening. The change from organisation based on feudal service to a more 'professional' army was a gradual development during the final quarter of the sixteenth century. Great impetus was given by Oda Nobunaga's victory of Nagashino in 1575, which owed a great deal to his use of *ashigaru* firing arquebuses against the advancing Takeda cavalry. This implies a considerable degree of discipline and shows how the use of *ashigaru* had developed. Their position at the very front of Nobunaga's army, rather than at the rear as in the case of Hōjō Ujiyasu's standard battle plan, is a striking difference. As his career progressed, Nobunaga became one of the first daimyō to issue his *ashigaru* with a simple, standard suit of armour, and there are many illustrations showing these *okegawa-dō*, and the lampshade-like *jingasa* helmets, emblazoned with *mon*, which became the typical *ashigaru* armour of the period.

One of the Takeda generals, Obu Toramasa, somewhat anticipated this future development in heraldry by dressing all his soldiers in uniformly coloured armour: a bright-red lacquer. Records tell us that this was common to all ranks, and included horse-harness and the *sashimono*, which bore a white crescent moon. Obu Toramasa's troops were known as the 'red regiment', thereby providing circumstantial evidence that the troops provided by such a retainer fought as one group under that general. They 'exploded on the enemy like a ball of fire', according to the *Kōyō Gunkan*. This was later adopted by his younger brother, Yamagata Masakage, and subsequently copied at the suggestion of Tokugawa Ieyasu by one of his chief retainers, Ii Naomasa (1561–1602). His 'red-devils', as they came to be known, are depicted on the painted screen of the Summer Campaign of Ōsaka, which is in the Ii Art Museum in Hikone. Incidentally, Yamagata Masakage was killed at Nagashino in 1575, and his troops wore a black *sashimono*.

The rituals of victory

Even more ceremony surrounded the celebration of victory than attended the setting out to war. After a battle, the victorious daimyō would reward his loyal followers. Great honour was attached to having taken the first head, though as mounted troops were able to return their trophies more quickly than foot-soldiers, the claims often had to be revised at a later

Samurai with arquebus
The introduction, by the Portuguese, of firearms in 1542, was a major turning-point in the history of Japanese warfare. All daimyō used firearms, but few realised how effective they could be if employed in large quantities. This was demonstrated at the Battle of Nagashino in 1575, which is commemorated every year by the festival shown here, where reproduction arquebuses are fired from the site of the keep of Nagashino castle. The gunner is wearing full samurai armour.

The Hōjō take Fukane
The taking of Fukane castle by the Hōjō army was attended by appalling savagery. The heads were cut off all the defending garrison, and displayed. This illustration from the *Hōjō Godai-ki* reminds us of the often savage and bitter nature of samurai warfare.

stage. There is, therefore, no shortage of written source material relating to brave exploits and head-taking in particular. One *kanjō* (letter of commendation) from Uesugi Kenshin and dated 1561, is addressed to Nakajō Echizen-no-kami Fujikashi, who died in 1568, praising his behaviour at the fourth Battle of Kawanakajima.

We departed on the tenth day of the ninth month, and at the time when we gave battle to Takeda Harunobu at Kawanakajima in Shinano, he was a person unparalleled in the earnestness of his efforts. It is a fact that relatives, retainers and even reserve troops, a large number of whom were killed in battle, were inspired to loyal military service. Even thought the rebels sent a thousand horsemen into the attack we won a great victory, an event that will give us satisfaction for many years to come. Futhermore, there was also much glory gained. These loyal exploits will certainly never be forgotten by the descendants of Uesugi Kagetora. We admire

Climbing a castle wall
The stone walls of a Japanese castle
had a natural slope, owing to the fact
that they were built around an earth
core. This acted as a protection
against the shock of an earthquake,
but provided an easy ascent, up
which an attacking army could
climb, as in this illustration from the
Ehon Taikō-ki.

his military exploits all the more set beside the great importance of his loyalty, which is not surpassed by anyone.

A general account of the army's exploits was also valuable, as in the following fragment from the *Kōyō Gunkan*:

Concerning the exploits of the samurai retainers of Takeda Shingen, in the first place the spearmen met, [earning] fame for their lances, and renown when the same ones grappled with and pulled down horsemen. We also praise the second rank of spearmen.

Most of the ritual surrounding a victory celebration concerned the bizarre practice of head inspection, which we will discuss later, but for a retainer,

or an ally, alive and victorious, there were other more welcome privileges, as we read in the chronicle *Yamamoto Toyohisa-shiki*, which refers to the Ōsaka Campaign:

That night twenty-three heads were taken. At dawn on the seventeenth day twenty-four men were summoned before Hideyori . . . and received rewards of gold. One man called Kimura Kizaemon who had suffered a wound was given surgery.

Most daimyō appreciated the effects of hot-spring bathing for treating wounds, and general recuperation after a battle. The actual location of these hot springs was kept secret, as a wounded daimyō would be at his most vulnerable to an assassin. Takeda Shingen had three secret springs, one of which, at Shimobe in the mountains of Yamanashi prefecture, celebrates Shingen's use of its healing waters in an annual festival. The care Shingen took of his wounded is confirmed by the records of the Erin-ji. Four months before one of his five battles at Kawanakajima, he requested the monks to be ready to provide rest and recuperation facilities for the wounded.

The battle having been fought and won, the trophies taken and examined, the part-time samurai of the territory could now return to their fields, until by the end of the sixteenth century even this would stop, and even these lowly samurai would be warriors and nothing else, having no function in life other than to serve their warlord with loyalty and devotion in peace and war.

The wounded general at the healing spring
The beneficial effects of hot springs have long been known to the Japanese, and every daimyō had his own 'secret springs' where he could recuperate safely from wounds. Takeda Shingen had a secret spring at Shimobe, and his use of the healing waters is commemorated annually by a festival, where local people dress up as Shingen and his 'Twenty-Four Generals'. The man in the foreground represents Shingen himself, and wears a mock bandage.

The Cultured Warlord

It is sometimes difficult, when scanning the pages of the war chronicles of the sixteenth century, to appreciate that the samurai, and a daimyō in particular, was regarded as the supreme aesthete and the arbiter of good taste. How could the hand that wielded the bloody sword so readily caress the delicate surface of a tea bowl? This apparent dichotomy between the utterly barbarous and the utterly beautiful is one of the most difficult concepts to understand in the life of the samurai.

It is tempting to discern a certain national trait, an innate ability that comes simply with being Japanese, to translate the most functional of objects into works of art, even to weaponry and instruments of death. That most deadly of weapons, the Japanese sword, is well recognised as having an outstanding beauty of its own. Somehow the samurai appreciated that perfection of form and perfection of function went hand in hand, and that perfection of form required a commensurate elegance of behaviour that complemented the elegance of the surroundings. There is no doubt that the families of daimyō, if not all samurai, were trained as extensively

A musical interlude
Seated on an improbably dramatic crag, the great general Toyotomi Hideyoshi listens to music while contemplating the siege of a castle. As well as a drum and flute, he is entertained by two men playing the *shō*, an ancient Japanese form of 'Pan's Pipes'.

in matters of literature and aesthetics as they were in the arts of war. More than one daimyō likened the literary and the martial arts as being the two wheels of a carriage.

Patronage of the arts was one aspect of the daimyō life that we were not able to identify in the turbulent world of the Hōjō family, but the 'super-daimyō' of the latter part of the sixteenth century, of whom Oda Nobunaga and Toyotomi Hideyoshi are the outstanding examples, were also considerable patrons of the arts. They employed artists to paint the screens that divided room from room in their palaces, and commissioned potters to produce vessels for the tea ceremony. Their tastes reflected their wealth, enabling them to share in peaceful luxury when not fighting. It is to Hideyoshi that we owe the elevation of the tea ceremony to an art form. The tea ceremony consists of an aesthetic exercise performed around the simple pleasure of sharing tea with friends. It is at once ritualistic and artistic. It involves the aesthetic appreciation of the tea bowl from which the tea is drunk, the flower arrangement and the vase which complement it, and the overall design of the tea house and the garden. A rare tea bowl could be more welcome to a daimyō than a fine sword, and was frequently much more difficult to acquire.

Nobunaga was also a patron of the *Nō* theatre, and is recorded as having chanted some choruses from the *Nō* play *Atsumori* before setting off to the Battle of Okehazama. *Nō*, like tea and the contemplation of a cleverly designed garden, brought serenity in much the same way as did the practices of the meditative Zen sect of Buddhism, to which many samurai were attracted because of its inner tranquility. But the appreciation of taste gave

Tea house of the Gyokusen-En, Kanazawa
The performance of the tea ceremony was one of the highest expressions of taste enjoyed by the cultivated warlord. This is a side view of the exquisite tea house of the Gyokusen-En, a garden in Kanazawa.

the cultivated warrior more than a serene and a composed mind, however useful that may have proved on the battlefield or in conference. It was also the means that sorted the accomplished man from the common, that proclaimed a subtle ostentation that may sometimes have teetered on the edge of vulgarity, but never quite managed to slip off. This cultivation, this refinement, was the mark of true aristocracy, and was part and parcel of being a daimyō, of being an élite among the élite.

The fortress of beauty

All the wealth of Japanese art and architecture that has survived to our day – and there is a great deal of it – points to the fierce warrior as patron of the arts, exercising the remarkable skill, noted above, of being able to transform the functional into the beautiful. Take, for example, the development of the Japanese castle. There is no more beautiful example of military structure in the entire world, and yet these graceful buildings, which soar above sweeping stone walls, evolved largely through savage military necessity. A castle of the early sixteenth century, such as would have been known to an early daimyō like Hōjō Sōun, was either a *yamashiro*, 'mountain castle' or a *hirajiro*, 'castle on the plain'. In each case, the style of architecture, if such a term is applicable, was entirely subservient to the need for defence, and the construction of the means of defence depended entirely upon the fortress's location, and would follow the lines of strength. A *hirajiro* would make use of a river or a swamp. A *yamashiro* would make use of rocky crags, concealing trees, and the slope of the ground. I have visited the recently excavated site of Odani, the *yamashiro* of the Asai family, burnt by Nobunaga in 1573. The buildings of Odani were spread across two hills joined in a saddle, and there is good visibility from every level. Only on the top is there an expanse of level ground, where Asai Nagamasa had his great hall.

One influence of Nobunaga's victory at Nagashino in 1575 was the beginning of what was almost a defensive mentality among the daimyō,

The site of Odani castle
This overgrown patch of land on the top of the wooded hill of Odani was the site of the main hall of the *yamashiro* of the Asai family. A few stones are all that is left of the fortifications, which were burned down by Oda Nobunaga in 1573. Odani has recently been excavated.

leading to the establishment of the huge fortresses we see today. For the first time stone was used in their construction, the labour being assessed by and supplied to the daimyō in much the same way as he obtained military service from among his subjects. But the spate of castle building, which Japan witnessed from 1580 to about 1615, was only partly connected to the introduction and effective use of firearms. As domains grew, the careful balance between agricultural and military needs could be solved by a strict division of labour between military men and farmers, and it was the achievement of very powerful daimyō, such as Oda Nobunaga, to produce a corps of professional soldiers. The new castles, many of which survive to this day, were built as the economic centre of the territory. They were also built very large, so that, if necessary, the entire standing army of the daimyō could be sheltered within the vast encircling walls.

Nobunaga's own castle of Azuchi was the first, and the greatest, of this new trend. It was built to control Kyōto, but it was not built there, but on a rocky plateau overlooking Lake Biwa. Where Nobunaga's creation differed, even from its contemporaries, was in the lavish decoration that was applied to it, so that this great step forward in castle design intimidated as much by its appearance inside and out, as by its strong walls and its armaments. Sadly, Azuchi castle is no longer with us. When Nobunaga was murdered in 1582, Azuchi proved no more impregnable to excited looters and arsonists than any other castle that had suddenly lost its leader, and it was burned to the ground.

Several other castles have survived and, if one disregards those that have been rebuilt in ferroconcrete in the last 20 years, there is a wealth of material for study. Inuyama, which floats on a wooded hill above the

Inuyama castle
Inuyama castle, which seems to float over the Kisogawa, enjoys one of the loveliest settings of all Japanese castles. It is also one of the best preserved, and is unique in being the sole remaining Japanese castle still under private ownership.

Kisogawa, is a very fine example. It is the only castle in Japan still in private hands, and its owners, the Naruse family, have cared for it since it was given to their ancestor, the daimyō Naruse Masanari, whose father Naruse Masakazu (1538–1620) had fought for Ieyasu. The site received its first defences in 1440 as a *yamashiro*, for which it was ideally suited, and the present tower-keep dates from 1600, replacing an earlier one which suffered when Inuyama was taken during Ieyasu's Komaki campaign in 1584.

Although from the outside the keep appears to have three storeys, in reality there are four. The uppermost storey commands an extensive view from the balcony that surrounds it, but the first storey holds the most interest. The daimyō's 'audience chamber' is built into the centre of the room. It is of modest dimensions, and fitted with sliding doors at the rear, through which samurai could come to the lord's aid at speed. The wooden floor which entirely surrounds it is 3 m (10 ft) wide and called the *musha-bashiri*, the 'warriors' run'. The other floors share the same austere design of plain, dark wood; the floors being connected one to another via alarmingly steep staircases.

Interior of Inuyama castle
The daimyō's private quarters at Inuyama are surrounded by a highly polished wooden corridor, called the *musha-bashiri*, or 'warrior's run'. To the rear of the room are sliding doors, behind which armed guards could be concealed.

The castle town – a world in miniature

As the sixteenth century gave way to the seventeenth, the castle, standing alone, surrounded by bare ground, itself gave way to the castle town, the *jōkamachi*. The castle towns symbolised in their design the feudal hierarchy which the daimyō had created for themselves and their retainers. They

were ordered places which, by their physical layout, made a statement about the classes within society, and the nature of the cultivated daimyō.

Edo castle, the seat of the Shōgun, was surrounded by the residences occupied by the daimyō on their annual visits, the *yashiki*, which we shall study in more detail later. The daimyō's own castle towns back in the provinces were simply miniature versions of Edo. Around their castles, where the family, and some senior retainers lived, were the homes of the other retainers, their distance from the castle walls being in roughly indirect proportion to their rank. The higher retainers, the *karō*, were placed just outside the keep, within the castle walls proper; the lower were outside the walls, protected perhaps by a moat, or an earthen wall. Completely walled cities on the European model were unknown. Between the two groups of samurai retainers lay the quarters of the favoured merchants

A home of a retainer in Nagamachi, Kanazawa
The narrow streets of the Nagamachi quarter of Kanazawa disclose the tiny courtyard of a former samurai's dwelling. Stepping stones lead to the door from the more formal granite paving.

Garden of the Toyokawa Inari Shrine

This charming garden, within the extensive grounds of the Inari Shrine at Toyokawa, shows many of the classic features of the Japanese garden, a miniature landscape with which every warlord would be familiar. *Koi* swim in the pond, which has its edge set off with tightly clipped box bushes. An ornamental pagoda balances the background.

and artisans, most, if not all, of whom would be engaged in trading and producing the goods that were in demand from the samurai class. Outside the ring of lower samurai lay a quarter of temples and shrines, whose buildings acted as an outer defence cordon, and from where the roads could be sealed off and guarded. From the edge of the castle town began the fields of the farmers, who grew the rice to support those within the jōkamachi's boundaries.

The city of Kanazawa is one of the best examples of such a layout. Owing to its position far from the Pacific coast, Kanazawa was spared the bombing of the last war which destroyed the layout of nearly every other city of comparable size, and it is possible to walk round Kanazawa today, as I did in 1986, and appreciate at first hand the effort of town planning that went into its original design. Kanazawa was the territory of the Maeda family, whose founder was Hideyoshi's general, Maeda Toshiie (1538–99).

Their castle town is built on a high plain between the Sai and the Asano Rivers. At its centre are the remains of the old castle, whose outer walls now house the university. Only the huge Ishikawa gate and tower remind one of its martial past, but even these remains are considerable. Across the road from the gate is the Kenrokuen, which is now a public park but which until 1871 was the private garden of the Maeda daimyō. The Kenrokuen is one of the best examples in Japan of the formal landscaped garden, but its most eloquent tribute to the civil engineering skills of the day lie in the way in which its lakes and waterfalls are fed with water. Water is in fact channelled from a distance of 10 km (6 miles) away, where the Saigawa is tapped, a system that was built in 1632 and is still functioning perfectly.

The best surviving examples of the retainers' residences are found in the quarter called Nagamachi. Here are quiet courtyards and tiny gardens surrounded by mud and plaster walls roofed with tiles. Of the merchants' quarters, little remains except the names, such as Ishibikichō, 'stone-cutters' quarter' and Daikumachi, 'carpenters' quarter'. To reach the temple areas, you have to cross one of the rivers – a forceful reminder of how the religious buildings were deliberately situated as the outer lines of defence.

It is possible, having seen Kanazawa, to imagine how Edo must have looked to the early European visitors before fire, earthquake and war took their toll of the Shōgun's capital, the bustling city that became Tōkyō. How fascinating it must have been to have looked with the eyes of someone such as Thomas McClatchie, who recorded his impressions of the soon-to-be-destroyed daimyō mansions of Edo for the members of the Asiatic Society of Japan in December 1878:

In passing through the streets of the city of Yedo, and most especially in what is commonly termed the 'official quarter' lying inside the Castle moats, the attention of the visitor is particularly attracted by long continuous buildings lining the roadway on either side. These present towards the street an almost unbroken frontage, save where a few large gateways, composed of heavy timbers strengthened with iron clamps, interpose to relieve the monotony of the general style of architecture. The buildings mostly stand upon low stone foundations, surrounded by small ditches; the windows are barred, and the general aspect gloomy in the extreme. They often differ widely as regards size, shape, mode of ornamentation etc.; but there is yet manifest a general likeness, there are still noticeable many common attributes which at once serve to stamp them, to the observant eye, as structures of one and the same type. These are the nagaya, *or barracks, for retainers, which formed the outer defences of the* yashiki *or fortified mansions wherein dwelt the feudal nobles of Japan until the era of the recent Revolution in this country; and though now in many cases deserted, ruined and fallen into decay, time was when they played a conspicuous and honoured part in connection with the pomp and grandeur of the old feudal system which received its death blow only a half score years prior to the present date.*

McClatchie's article goes on to list how the amount of land available for the *yashiki* depended upon the income of the daimyō, as did the size and design of the building he might raise upon it. The rules are precise:

Kokushū daimyō – gate either detached, or else built into the nagaya; *two small side gates or posterns, one on either side, immediately adjoining it; two porters' lodges, situated just behind the posterns, built on stone foundations jutting out into the roadway for about three or four feet, and furnished with barred windows; roofs of lodges convex, formed of two slopes descending from a central roof ridge protruding at right angles from the wall of the* nagaya.

The outer wall of the Sanada mansion
The Sanada mansion gives us a good idea of the appearance of the daimyō's *yashiki* in Edo, none of which have survived. The outer wall is surrounded by a gutter, and windows project from the sides of the gateway.

There is nothing left in Tōkyō now, or even in Kanazawa, that gives us any indication of the appearance of these *yashiki*, which because of their associations are among the most important buildings of Edo Japan, but McClatchie's descriptions, and extant sketches of the buildings, are uncannily similar to a group of buildings in Matsushiro, a town in the mountainous Yamanashi prefecture. Matsushiro was the site of Takeda Shingen's Kaizu castle, of which the stone base alone remains, and was the fief

granted to the son of the Sanada, Nobuyuki, who served the Tokugawa. The complex of buildings which contain the Sanada mansion, its clan school and a fine garden, have survived almost perfectly, owing to their remoteness. Matsushiro is a sleepy little place a few kilometres from the city of Nagano, but has recently seen an influx of tourists, drawn there by a very successful television series called *Sanada Taiheiki,* which told the story of the division of the Sanada family referred to in a later chapter. The outer wall of the complex must be as near to the appearance of a *nagaya* as one can find, and in fact bears remarkable similarities to the actual *nagaya* depicted in a photograph of the Satsuma daimyō's *yashiki* in Edo, which was burned in 1868.

Further delights await visitors inside the grounds, as there is revealed to their eyes the perfect example of a daimyō's mansion, complete with landscaped garden. The nearby Sanada museum, with its rich collection of the daimyō's personal possessions, completes a unique time capsule of the Edo daimyō.

The journey of pride

The *yashiki* was a very private place, unsuited to ostentation or the flaunting of wealth, but nowhere was the pride and the good taste of a daimyō more on public display than when he travelled along the great highways of Japan to visit the Shōgun. The *yashiki* of Edo may have belonged to the daimyō, but he was only able to live in it one year out of two, the alternate year being spent back in his castle town. This *sankin kōtai,* the 'Alternate Attendance' system, was the most unusual, and the most successful, of all the means the Tokugawa *bakufu* were to devise for reducing the risk of rebellion from the warlords. In essence, the *sankin kōtai* was no more than kidnapping on a colossal scale, because the rule was that the daimyō's wife and children lived in the *yashiki* of Edo, while the daimyō himself alternated his residence between his fief and the capital. That was one aspect of it. The other was that the muster lists, which in times of war had regulated a daimyō's feudal oligations in terms of the supply of men and equipment for war, were continued into peace-time by prescribing the size and equipment of the retinue which the daimyō would be expected to have accompany him on his alternating trips. As stipends were fixed, and there were no fresh lands to conquer, the cost of the *sankin kōtai* kept the daimyō in a state of genteel poverty, and probably constant worry.

Certain daimyō with particular defence responsibilities were allowed a reduced commitment. The Sō daimyō on the island of Tsushima, which lies between Japan and Korea, only had to reside in Edo for four months in every two years. A similar concession applied to the little-known but strategically vital daimyō of the Matsumae family on the northernmost island of Hokkaido. In the early nineteenth century there were fears of expansion by Russia on to Japan's northern territories, and there was a tentative Russian incursion on to Matsumae's territory in 1807.

For other daimyō, the likelihood of any conflict was a remote possibility, but they still had to march at the head of a huge army, gorgeously dressed and ready for battle, either from their *han* to Edo or back again, once every 12 months. When the procession of the Maeda daimyō, the richest in Japan after the Tokugawa (their income was a staggering 1,250,000 *koku*),

The mansion of the Sanada daimyō
The azaleas bloom in the garden of the mansion of the Sanada family at Matsushiro, an outstanding expression of the aesthetic side of the daimyō's life. We are looking from the garden to the main set of rooms which comprise the mansion.

left Kanazawa in the years of the mid-seventeenth century, it consisted of no less than 4,000 samurai, but within a century the sheer financial burden forced a reduction in numbers to 1,500. There is a pathetic note in the account books of the Inaba daimyō referring to additional expenses encountered in 1852 after being overtaken by darkness in the Hakone Mountains. The daimyō suddenly found himself compelled to purchase 8,863 candles and 350 pine torches, as well as hiring extra porters and lantern bearers.

But if the *sankin kōtai* was a burden to the daimyō, it proved otherwise to his retainers. There was the prospect of a long, but not unpleasant journey, much of which, for most daimyō, would be along well-trodden highways. The two main roads linking Edo with Kyōto were Tōkaidō, which followed the Pacific coast, and the Nakasendō, which wended its way through the mountainous interior. As early as 1604, three decades before the *sankin kōtai* was introduced, a system of post-stations was introduced along the Tōkaidō, and by 1633 and efficient post-horse and courier system was completed, and reduced the travelling time for the 480-km (300-mile) journey from Nihombashi in Edo to Sanjobashi in Kyōto to a mere ten days. By frequent changes of horses, couriers could make the journey in three days. Needless to say, a daimyō's procession was conducted at a much more leisurely pace, making good use of the *Tōkaido Gojusan tsugi*, the 'Fifty-three stations of the Tokaido' made familiar from the prints of Hiroshige. (The Nakasendō had 69 post-stations.)

Each of the 53 post-stations acquired its own personality. Each had some famous site or historical association, such as an exceptionally long bridge, a hot spring or a dangerous river. Some towns were famous for their local delicacies, others for their inns, their girls and their porters. The porters, the *kumosuke,* were available for hire to carry baggage or palanquins. Whatever the weather these 'tough guys' wore only a loincloth. They were notorious for their rude songs, their drinking and their gambling!

To a daimyō's retainer, the annual march was not a risky voyage into the unknown, but a familiar journey repeated year after year, and with details familiar even to those who had never set foot along its length. Numerous wood-block prints and popular literature painted a picture of the great road for any who cared to enjoy it at second hand. There is very little left of the original Tōkaidō today, as Hiroshige's road has disappeared under railway lines and motorways, but, here and there, there are small sections, now no more than footpaths, which the determined traveller can find. I walked along such a short stretch near Yumoto, on the way into the Hakone Mountains in Odawara, and within seconds modern Japan disappeared from sight and from hearing. The traveller on the mountainous Nakasendō is more fortunate, and can walk a full 8-km (5-mile) stretch of the old road which once echoed to the feet of samurai. The path lies between the villages of Tsumago and Magome, high in the wooded mountains above the Kisogawa. Both villages, now bypassed by a modern road, are exceptionally well preserved by consent of the inhabitants, and give you the most vivid glimpse of old Japan available anywhere in that country today.

Street in Edo
A corner of the film set at the Toei Uzumasa Film Studios in Kyōto, showing a typical street of the Edo Period.

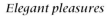

Elegant pleasures

One of the main attractions of the bustling city of Edo will be discussed in a later chapter, when we look at the notorious pleasure quarter of Yoshiwara. But there were other more seemly pleasures of which the daimyō and his family might partake during their sojourn in the capital. Where their appreciation of the arts differed from that enjoyed by their ancestors of the sixteenth century, who had invited artists and performers into their castles,

Garden of the post-station at Tsumago
This view is taken from within the main room of the post-station at Tsumago, looking out on to a simple, yet totally effective, Japanese garden. The ground cover is of moss, and the view is attractively framed by a split bamboo fence.

Masks for the Nō theatre
The Nō was the classical theatre of
Japan, and the form of theatrical art
that members of the samurai class
were expected to patronise, unlike
the vulgar kabuki. Nō actors wore
masks, and a selection are shown
here in this backstage photograph,
which the author was kindly
allowed to record.

was that the daimyō of the Edo Period could not claim much credit for patronage. The most notable cultural flourishing of the age occurred during the era-name of Genroku, which lasted from 1688 to 1703, and its impetus came largely from the newly wealthy merchant classes. The samurai class, and the daimyō in particular, may have pretended that the *chōnin* (townsfolk) were vulgar, of disreputable origin and with poor tastes, but by 1700 they had a century of tradition behind them, the wealth to enjoy artistic pleasures, and the confidence to commission them. So the culture which the daimyō enjoyed was one into which he was drawn, and which derived from a prosperous bourgeoisie devoted to amusement. The expression they used for it, *ukiyo*, the 'floating world', was a very telling one.

Hand in hand with the growth of *ukiyo* expression, 'samurai culture' went into something of a decline. There was little advance in architecture, probably because, as we noted above, the Shōgun's *bakufu* made rules for the size and shape of just about everything. Classical poetry all but disappeared, unable to compete for interest beside the vitality of the *ukiyo*.

The kabuki theatre

The year is 1713, and the renowned *kabuki* actor Ichikawa Danjurō II makes his dramatic entrance along the *hanamichi* as the hero Sukeroku during one of the first performances of the play *Sukeroku Yukari no Edo Zakura*. He wears a black *kimono* bearing the Sukeroku *mon*, while his *obi* bears in addition the actor's (Danjurō's) own family *mon*, a precedent followed by every actor in the role to this day. Sukeroku is an *otokodate*, a 'chivalrous fellow'. He is brave, charming and resourceful — all qualities that the townspeople looked for in a hero. In his characterisation of the flamboyant Sukeroku, Danjurō even went so far as to wear a head-band and socks dyed with a certain indigo dye which, because of the huge cost of obtaining it from China, only the Shōgun himself was accustomed to using.

On the stage the ladies of the town await their hero's arrival. The villain Ikyū is not so pleased to see him! Two members of the audience squabble while their companions watch the actor's every move.

The *kabuki* theatre provided the townspeople of Edo with the ideal vehicle for examining the morals and behaviour of the samurai class. Several of the most popular plays were based on actual incidents in history, often ones that had occurred very recently. Family feuds, such as those within the Data and Maeda families, were included in the repertoire, although names and characters were always changed, and the plot elaborated almost beyond recognition. *Meiboku Sendai Hagi*, for example, which is based on the Date feud, includes a villain who can change himself into a giant rat! *Kabuki* was banned by the Shōgunate on several occasions, but its popularity ensured its survival.

The last bastion of true samurai aesthetics was the *Nō* theatre, which continued under daimyō patronage. The *chōnin* had their own theatrical art-form, the flamboyant *kabuki*, which attracted the samurai in droves. *Kabuki* was banned, totally ineffectively, on six occasions, and always bounced back owing to public demand and the willingness of the authorities to turn a blind eye. Its rewriting of recent history and current events, both elements of which were absent from the *Nō*, appealed to the samurai every bit as much as it did to the *chōnin*. Much use was made in the *kabuki* of general incidents which would have been familiar to the samurai, either from their actual experience, or from the traditions in which they were educated. For example, the play *Ōmi Genji Senjin Yakata*, first performed in 1769, contains a famous scene of a head inspection. *Mekura Nagaye Ume ga Kagatobi* re-enacts a real-life quarrel that occurred in Edo between fire-fighters employed by the Maeda daimyō and the official Edo fire brigade. The other great theatrical art of the age was the *bunraku* puppet theatre, where each large doll was manipulated by three men, producing the most amazingly lifelike effects. The *bunraku* was regarded as even safer than the *kabuki* for satire and the riskier sort of plot, and several *kabuki* plays began life as dramas written for the puppets.

The *Nō*, by contrast, took all its plots from ancient legend. The first Tokugawa Shōgun, Ieyasu, had been a great patron of the *Nō*. He had invited leading companies to Edo castle, and *Nō* performances were a regular part of important State functions. Some of his descendants took part in *Nō* themselves, which certainly kept them away from *kabuki*, and then in 1700 the arch-moralist of the day, Arai Hakuseki, in a severe attack of pomposity, pronounced even this most stately and restrained of theatrical forms to be deleterious to morality and a danger to the State. At a Shōgunal banquet in 1711, ancient music was substituted for the *Nō*, and from that time on the *Nō* lost much of its official prestige and the larger part of its samurai popularity. The tea ceremony went much the same way, degenerating into an empty ritual, far too complicated for the *chōnin*, and unable to compete with other delights awaiting the samurai.

Perhaps the fate of *Nō* holds the key to understanding the apparent paradox. During the Sengoku Period, there was a genuine need for the reassurance of nobility against the evidence of his own barbarism that the daimyō accumulated. Aesthetics gave reassurance. It soaked up the reality of their deeds in the same way as the spiked board and the cosmetics transformed a ghastly severed head into an object for neutral contemplation. Without the cultivation of art, and gardens, and theatre, the samurai would have gone mad. Then, when wars had ceased, the samurai class had nothing to prove to anyone. Their social position was firmly established and, apart from a few rare exceptions, they did not kill. Instead, they were stultified within a stagnant culture, from which the new merchant classes, with none of their inhibitions, were to liberate them.

However, as we noted earlier, to the first daimyō there was no paradox. The two aspects of the samurai life not only could coexist, they had to coexist. One could not be a successful daimyō without both, as Hōjō Sōun wrote in the last words of his 'Twenty-One Articles':

It is not necessary here to write about the arts of peace and war . . . for to pursue these is a matter of course. From of old, the rule has been, 'Practise the arts of peace on the left hand, and the arts of the war on the right'. Mastery of both is required.

Notwithstanding the fact that the Hōjō had little time for practising purely aesthetic pleasures for their own sake, and that their emphasis on the arts of peace concentrated almost totally on good government, there is no better summary of the duties in peace and war of the cultivated warlord of Japan.

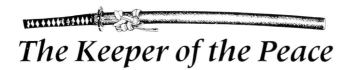

The Keeper of the Peace

During the Edo Period, one of the most important duties delegated to a daimyō, as part of the *baku-han* system, was the keeping of the peace and the administration of justice within the *han*. In this, the daimyō would find the reality of the streets of his castle town to be very different from the theoretical world of ordered and cultivated society which was the ideal. He would often find himself faced with a fire-trap of a city, where sub-servience to samurai was a myth, and where his own men would find

The daimyō presides
This page from the *Hōjō Godai-ki* neatly illustrates the daimyō's social position, as he receives gifts from his retainers. The daimyō sits on an elevated dais, while those lower squat on the *tatami*.

themselves in opposition to well-organised gangs of swordsmen every bit as well trained as well armed, and who owed equally firm allegiance to their own variety of Japanese warlord.

In theory, at any rate, this was a situation that could not possibly exist, because according to law, to established precedent and to a century of tradition, members of the samurai class were the only people allowed to carry swords. It was the wearing of swords that defined a samurai, as his privilege and his right. A series of edicts, beginning with Hideyoshi's famous 'Sword Hunt' of 1587, had set this trend in motion, and had theoretically disarmed all but the samurai class. In practice, swords, and other weapons, were readily obtainable and well used, sometimes by criminals, otherwise by desperate gangs of lower-class citizens upholding their rights and their lives against the abuse of power by samurai.

The samurai police

It was a very unusual daimyō, however, who failed to recognise the reality of life in Tokugawa Japan, and every daimyō was helped in his peace-keeping role by a well-developed police force. In common with many other institutions of Tokugawa Japan, the nature of the *baku-han* system allowed a successful system for the Shōgun's direct retainers in Edo to become the norm for the whole of Japan, and by 1631 the organisation of policing in Edo was replicated on a smaller scale in every *han* in the country.

As a daimyō spent much of his time travelling to and from Edo, he would delegate a major degree of responsibility within his own castle towns to magistrates, known as the *machi-bugyō*, who combined within their role

The seat of the Shōgun
In the Shōgō-In in Kyōto, this ornate audience chamber is preserved, with its characteristic raised dais.

the functions of chief of police, city mayor and presiding judge. In Edo there were two *machi-bugyō*, the need for two being similar to that which produced the system of two consuls in ancient Rome – each one kept an eye on the other! These two *machi-bugyō* worked a 'shift' system of one month on-duty, one month off-duty, though as the duties became more onerous in the expanding cities, particularly Edo, the 'off-duty month' became no more than a welcome quiet time for writing reports and seeing to other essential paperwork.

The Edo *machi-bugyō* had daily liaison with the Shōgun's senior councillors in Edo castle, which alone indicates the high status of the position. Even though the post of *machi-bugyō* was earmarked for comparatively lowly retainers of 500 *koku*, it carried an additional allowance of an extra 3,000 *koku*, and a court rank equivalent to that of some daimyō.

Under each of the two *machi-bugyō* were the *yoriki*, or assistant magistrates. There were 50 *yoriki* in all in Edo, 25 under each *machi-bugyo*. They were chosen from the Shōgun's direct retainers who had an income of 200 *koku*, and, in the case of the Edo *yoriki*, the appointment became hereditary within certain families, the position of *yoriki* passing from father to son. This resulted in a 'police force' that was very familiar with its territory, but also one that became very much a caste unto itself, living in a social limbo between the townspeople whose lives they controlled, and the samurai of the castle. The latter would have nothing to do with them because of the ancient Shintō fear of pollution from people who had a connection with death, as the *yoriki* had with the execution of criminals. In fact, the *yoriki* did not actually carry out executions; that was left to the outcast *hinin*, the 'non-humans', but the mere association with such practices, and their own fierce pride, kept the *yoriki* apart. The proud *yoriki* would wear a full samurai costume of the wide *hakama* trousers and the *haori* jacket, and wore the two swords of the samurai. They had a reputation for smartness in appearance, particularly in their hair-styles.

Serving under the *yoriki* were the *dōshin*, who played the role of the policeman 'on the beat'. They wore tight-fitting trousers rather than *hakama* and only carried one sword, though they were regarded as being of samurai status. In Edo, there were 120 *dōshin* under each *machi-bugyō*, and they were instantly recognisable by a distinctive side-arm that was a badge of office and a vital defensive weapon. This was the *jitte*, a steel rod fitted with a handle, and with one or two hooks along the edge of the 'blade'. Its purpose was to catch a sword stroke so that a felon could be taken alive.

The *dōshin*, accompanied by several assistants from among the townsfolk, who ranged from public-spirited citizens to paid informers, thus maintained the visible 'police-presence' on the streets of the castle towns, the *yoriki* being called to the scene of an arrest only if the situation warranted it. In this case, the *yoriki*, dressed in light body armour, would supervise affairs from horseback, with a spear kept as a last resort. The emphasis was always on taking the prisoner alive, which was no mean feat should the felon be an accomplished swordsman, as we shall see later in this chapter. Japanese ingenuity, however, allowed for the obvious danger and, in addition to the *jitte*, the *dōshin* were armed with a range of fierce-looking hooked and barbed spears, which kept the swordsman at bay, pinned him into a corner, or could usefully entangle items of clothing as he tried to escape. The determination of a cornered criminal was legendary, and many would sell their freedom as dearly as a samurai would sell his life.

The main street of Tsumago
The miraculously preserved main street of the village of Tsumago gives the best illustration of a village street from the Edo Period. It lies on the old Nakasendō road, which linked Kyōto and Edo (now Tōkyō) along the alternative mountain route.

Once the man was cornered and disarmed, he was rapidly tied up, and there existed a whole specialist area of 'martial arts' techniques for quickly and securely roping suspects. There is a famous wood-block print by Kuni-yoshi depicting the arrest of a criminal by *dōshin*, which James Field has used for his picture on page 88, that brings the whole process of justice vividly to life. It is an illustration to a scene from a popular novel, first published in 1814. The hero, Inuzuka Shino Moritaka, takes to the roof of the Hōryūkaku temple to avoid arrest by the *dōshin*. There are several versions of the scene, where Moritaka seizes one unfortunate *dōshin* by putting his arm round his neck, as his companions thrust their *jitte* at him, and blow whistles, while their more nervous companions wait below with bamboo ladders, ropes and sleeve entanglers.

Making an arrest

This plate is based on a vivid woodblock print by Kuniyoshi depicting the arrest of a criminal by *dōshin*. It is an illustration to a popular novel entitled *Nansō Satomi Hakkenden* by Takizawa Bakin (1767–1848). The plot of the novel concerns with the exploits of eight brothers, one of whom, Inuzuka Shino Moritaka, ends up on the roof of the Hōryūkaku temple. He is pursued by *dōshin* armed with *jitte*, the peculiar 'sword-catchers', and other devices designed to facilitate arrest. They are dressed in typical fashion, with fitted trousers rather than *hakama*, thus freeing their legs for such exploits as climbing roofs.

The popular image of the wandering lone samurai owes much to the activities of the criminal element in Edo society. The same is also true of the martial arts, which are often regarded as the preserve of the ruling samurai class. In fact many martial arts techniques owe their development to farmers and townsmen, deprived of the right to carry weapons, who turned to the use of simple weapons and bare hands to defend themselves against any abuse of power by their betters. (See *The Lone Samurai* by the present author for a detailed consideration of these points.)

The resulting punishments which the *machi-bugyō* had in their power to dispense ranged in severity up to death – including crucifixion, for such crimes as murder. For a samurai, the death penalty could, on occasions, be carried out by the convicted man himself in the honourable act of suicide, called *seppuku*. In certain cases, the execution of a condemned criminal could be a means of testing the quality of a sword blade – making a more realistic alternative to the more usual *tameshigiri* performed on a corpse. There is the story told of one such condemned man who went to his end with remarkable coolness, telling the sword tester that if he had been forewarned that this was how he was to die he would have swallowed some large stones to damage the samurai's precious blade. A much lighter punishment was exile, which had been used for centuries in Japan as a way of dealing with offences of a political nature.

Corporal punishment
A swift punishment for offenders from the lower social orders was a sound thrashing. Here, in an illustration to *Miyabu gaikotsu tobaka-shi*, the felon is held down securely while he receives his punishment under the watchful eye of the *yoriki*.

The great benefit of the *dōshin* system lay in its capacity for crime prevention. To the *dōshin's* local knowledge was added a topographical system that divided Edo into tightly controllable *machi*, or wards. This arose from the original design of the city, which was deliberately intended to make an approach to Edo castle difficult for an attacker. Like other big cities, the castle was surrounded by mazes of streets where the *chōnin* (townspeople) lived, and each *machi* was physically separated from others either by canals, walls or fences. It was thus a simple matter to control movement from one *machi* to another by means of gates which were fastened at night, and anyone passing through had to have appropriate authorisation.

The brave otokodate

If areas of a city, such as Edo, could be sealed off from outside, they could also be well defended from within, and it is not surprising to hear of the development of organisations of townspeople to provide protection against

House in Tsumago
One of the many houses of Tsumago which convey the feeling of a past age. The wooden slats filter the bright sunlight from the dusty street.

250

rivals, or against samurai who neglected their code of conduct. Against the *hatamoto-yakko*, or samurai gangs, there developed the *machi-yakko*. They became very well organised in the Edo Period, and their leaders, styled *otokodate*, became famous. The word *otokodate*, 'chivalrous fellows', implies the resistance to authority by those of lower class. In fact, some of the great *otokodate* were originally of the samurai class and had become *rōnin* for various reasons, and moved to find employment in distant towns. One such was Banzuin Chōbe'e, 'Father' of the *otokodate* of Edo.

Banzuin Chōbe'e was originally from Higo province in Kyūshū, and was a retainer of the Terazawa clan of Shimabara, the scene of the great Christian upheaval of 1638, known as the Shimabara Rebellion. Following the suppression of the revolt, he felt Kyūshū as a *rōnin* and went to Edo, where his talents were soon put to use. He became a *warimoto*, an agent who acted as a go-between for acquiring labourers. Once established in Edo, Chōbe'e took the name of Banzuin, which was the area where he lived, and set himself up as a 'Godfather' of *warimoto* who acted particularly as agents for supplying carriers and other labourers to daimyō undertaking their annual pilgrimage to Edo to pay respects to the Shōgun. Chōbe'e received 10 per cent of the labourers' earnings as commission, and in return provided for them in times of sickness. Banzuin Chōbe'e, therefore, came to exert the same authority over his followers as a daimyō did over his samurai, which came in very useful when the townspeople were oppressed by the samurai *hatamoto-yakko*.

In the enforced idleness of the Edo Period, boredom and poverty turned many samurai into criminals. Groups with names such as the *Shiratsuka-*

Retainer's house in Nagamachi, Kanazawa
In contrast to the simple houses of Tsumago, this town house in Kanazawa reflects the type of architecture that would have been enjoyed by the retainers of the Maeda daimyō of Kanazawa. This house, in the Nagamachi quarter, is one of the best known in the city.

gumi and *Jingi-gumi* formed and caused violence. The city people 'hated them like scorpions', according to one Japanese historian, and their unreasonableness against the townspeople became proverbial. Because such violence and perverseness among the samurai could not be crushed by the townspeople alone, former *rōnin*, such as Chōbe'e, became the natural nucleus for opposition. As their confidence grew, the *otokodate* of the *machi-yakko* began to walk openly in the streets in defiance of rules forbidding them swords. At the same time, they developed the art of combat with other weapons, such as the the long, 2-m (6-ft) staff, or *bō*, and the shorter 1.5-m (4-ft) long *jō*. They also became accomplished in the art of the *tantō* (dagger), which could be concealed under clothes, and the defensive use of implements such as the *tessen*, the iron war-fan.

Greatness has its penalties. Chōbe'e's fame was considerable, which brought him into direct opposition to the boss of the powerful *hatamoto-yakko* called the *Jingi-gumi*, one Mizuno Jūrōzaemon. Jūrōzaemon was of senior samurai rank, worth 2,500 *koku*, and had the reputation for being something of a dandy (the Japanese term is *datemono*) dressing in the finest clothes.

One day, according to a popular tale, it was rumoured that Chōbe'e was in the vicinity of Yoshiwara, where Jūrōzaemon's party was meeting. Jūrōzaemon desired some iced *soba* noodles and, as Chōbe'e was in a *soba* shop, he proposed, after some ritualistic bragging, that Chōbe'e should buy him some *soba*, knowing already that the shop had sold out of *soba* and did not have a steamer. It was a neat way of humiliating Chōbe'e, but, nothing daunted, Chōbe'e went downstairs and gave one of his followers a considerable sum of money, and ordered him to buy up all the cold *soba* that was available, which the *machi-yakko* members proceeded to dump unceremoniously in front of Jūrōzaemon. As the huge pile grew, Jūrōzaemon realised that he could not get the better of Chōbe'e and retired with considerable loss of face.

Not long afterwards, one of Chōbe'e's followers, called Iida no Nibe'e, caught three of Jūrōzaemon's men making unreasonable demands of a drunken townsman. He set on them and threw them into a ditch. This increased Jūrōzaemon's bad feelings for Chōbe'e, and resolved him to invite Chōbe'e into a trap. The treacherous means whereby Mizuno Jūrōzaemon planned to dispose of Banzuin Chōbe'e, and the latter's willingness to walk into the trap for the sake of his honour, forms the basis of the greatest of all legends of the brave *otokodate*. It is quoted as an example of how the honour of a townsman could be every bit as noble as that of a samurai. In fact, Chōbe'e's determination to carry out the inevitable drama reminds one of the decision of Kusunoki Masashige to fight the Battle of Minatogawa because it was the wish of the Emperor, even though he knew the situation to be hopeless.

The evil Jūrōzaemon invited Chōbe'e to come to his house for a drinking party as a way of saying 'thank-you' for the gift of *soba*. Chōbe'e guessed that it was a trap, but went along nonetheless. He was attacked by two of Jūrōzaemon's men as he entered, whom he defeated, but before they began to drink together Jūrōzaemon invited Chōbe'e to take a bath, a common enough courtesy to a visitor. Once Chōbe'e was in the bath-house, Jūrōzaemon's men began to stoke the boiler to raise the temperature of the hot tub and scald him to death. As the hot steam rose, Chōbe'e tried to break out, but Jūrōzaemon had locked the door. With his

The murder of Banzuin Chōbe'e
Banzuin Chōbe'e is the great hero of the *otokodate* of Edo, both from his championing the cause of the townspeople against unruly samurai, and his violent death in a bath-house, where he was treacherously murdered by Mizuno Jurozaemon, his great rival from the samurai.

252

rival cornered within, Jūrōzaemon's men thrust spears at him through the partition. One spear pierced his leg and broke off at the shaft. Chōbe'e had no weapons on him and was surrounded by about ten spears. One then struck him a mortal blow under the ribs and the pitiful Chōbe'e, a spear through his chest, ended his days in a bath-house, in a manner every bit as noble as the samurai he had once been.

The unofficial daimyō

Crime was by no means confined to Edo, nor was the capital the only place where non-samurai ruled as petty daimyō over their criminal or lower-class kingdoms. The eight provinces of the Kantō plain, the large area of flat land that nowadays accommodates metropolitan Tōkyō, Yokohama and the Chiba peninsula, and extends northwards towards Nikkō and the Pacific coast, acted as a cradle for the criminal element towards the end of the eighteenth century, when crime was on the decline in Edo itself. Hoodlums were rampant in the Kantō provinces, because police power was dispersed in the complexity of Crown land, daimyō land and *hatamoto* land. The *yakuza* (gangsters) gathered there for making money. Kōzuke in particular was a centre of *yakuza* activity.

The nature of the locality of Kōzuke had made it a centre of textile manufacturing, and it was also well known throughout the whole country

A gambling den
The provision of gambling places was one of the main reasons for the growth of criminal gangs in the Edo Period. Here, in an illustration from *Tsūjin san kyoku-shi*, a group of men settle themselves for a session, refreshed by tea and tobacco.

254

for its hot springs. In earlier days, the recuperative qualities of hot springs were privileges known only to the upper reaches of the samurai class, as we noted earlier in connection with the treatment of wounded, but as the Edo Period wore on, the wealthier among the merchants, who already knew the value of hot baths, gained access to these pleasures. The taking of baths in 'spa-towns', where the mineral waters had healing properties, thus became a popular way of relaxing, as it is today for all Japanese, and hot-spring resorts vied with each other in the quality of their mineral waters and the range of comforts and entertainments they could provide. The spas of Kōzuke were convenient places where the textile wholesalers and healing-spring guests could resort for relaxation and amusement, and one pastime appealed above all others – gambling.

The provision of gambling dens promised immense profit for those willing to take a risk and, as they were operating in a very shadowy area of legality, it is not surprising that controlling gambling became an activity for

A fight in a gambling den
This lively sketch from *Miyabu gaikotsu tobaka-shi* depicts the violent end to a gambling session. Coins fly everywhere, and a dagger is drawn in anger.

organised crime. The gangs acquired territories in which their law held sway, much the same as the Sengoku warbands had developed into daimyō territories. The leaders of these gangs acquired the airs of daimyō themselves. Some of these gang leaders, especially those of samurai origin, acquired such a reputation for swordsmanship and command that they were employed by the civil authorities to teach swordsmanship to samurai.

At that time, the great swordsmen of the day, who were not hereditary samurai retainers of daimyō could be divided into two types: those who worked for the existing authority, hiring to them their swords and their skills, and those who by choice or by pressure of circumstances lived outside the law as outlaws. The outstanding example of the former was a man called Ōmaeda Eigorō. He comes over as something of a 'Godfather' figure, like Edo's Banzuin Chōbe'e, attracting to his side many of the young men who were to make their names in the criminal world of the Kantō provinces. Like the samurai, these bosses worked on a well-established hierarchical model of a 'father-figure' at the top, to whom followers held allegiance.

Ōmaeda Eigorō was a native of Kōzuke province, and killed his first man at the age of 16, a person called Kugo no Shōhachi. He went on to become a dependable and charismatic leader who influenced a generation of swordsmen, yet he was always careful to operate within the law. He was certainly not a murderer, unlike some of his disciples, and did not needlessly start quarrels. The *han* authorities found him very useful, and were ready to co-operate with him to gain some share of the enormous influence he exerted. His service to the civil authorities was as reliable as any samurai of the Sengoku Period, and he deserved his leader's stipend. His duties included teaching swordfighting, as he was a fencing master of the Nenryū *dōjō*.

A later example of another successful 'unofficial daimyō' is Shimizu no Jirochō, who acquired the title of the 'First Boss of the Tōkai'. Like Ōmaeda Eigorō, he built his territory on gambling, and developed his remarkable leadership skills through evading the numerous traps set for him by *yoriki* and rivals alike, until he achieved a quasi-official position within his own province. He died in 1893, his life having encompassed the final days of the Japanese warlords, most of whom he outlived.

The outlaws

On the opposite side of the coin from Ōmaeda Eigorō and Shimizu Jirochō, both of whom either co-operated with the authorities, or learned how to handle them, stood characters such as Kunisada Chūji (1809–50). Chūji never sold out to the samurai, and his exploits in resisting authority, retold in numerous plays and novels, made him something of a 'Robin Hood' of Japan. He was certainly a popular subject for fiction, and the romantic gloss of works such as *'Yagi bushi'* disguising the unattractive reality of a long catalogue of extortion and murder for which he was finally arrested and crucified in 1850 at the age of 41.

Kunisada Chūji's criminal acts may have caused great problems to the civil authorities of the day, but at least his expressions of rivalry were on an individual level. Two other 'pupils' of Ōmaeda Eigorō collided on a much larger scale, one of which produced a virtual battle that brought back echoes of the samurai wars of the Sengoku Period. It happened in another

The Battle of the Tonegawa Dry-River-bed
Iioka no Sukegorō and Sasagawa no Shigezō were two rival gang-bosses in Shimōsa. Their feud exploded into violence in 1844, in an encounter on the dry river-bed of the Tonegawa. Blades flashed in the moonlight in a battle as fierce as many of the skirmishes of the Sengoku Period. (From a woodblock print in the author's collection.)

of the Kanto provinces where crime flourished – Shimōsa. Shimōsa bordered the Pacific Ocean, and the fishing industry predominated, exerting a similar economic influence as the textiles of Kōzuke. The fishing industry of Shimōsa was centred around the port town of Chōshi, at the mouth of the Tonegawa with its huge flat river-bed. Around Chōshi, two leaders had their spheres of influence. Their names were Iioka no Sukegorō and Sasagawa no Shigezō. Neither was a samurai, and their surnames merely refer to their localities, as the possessive adjective 'no' indicates. Sukegorō was based in the present-day town of Iioka, and Shingezō held authority in Tōshō by the Sasagawa.

Iioka was a prosperous fishing port on the coast. Tōshō was also a bustling river port, 19 km (12 miles) away on the Tonegawa. Sukegorō is referred to in a Japanese account of his life as a 'sumo delinquent' (!), and a vagrant, at one time employed by Iioka no Amimoto as a fisherman. In course of time, he pledged loyalty to a gang leader, called Chōshi no Gorozō, from whom he received an enormous stipend, and whose territory he inherited.

In contrast to Sukegorō, Shigezō was born and raised in a large farming family of the area. His sphere of influence was handed over from a leader called Shibajuku no Bunkichi of Hitachi. Sukegorō was, in general, the senior of the two rivals, and Shingezō also looked up to Sukegorō but gradually, as their spheres of influence grew, respect gave way to wariness. Their territories grew rapidly during the early 1840s, and eventually the two spheres of influence reached their limits. Both men were of equal standing. Sasagawa no Shingezō acted first, and like his contemporary Kunisada Chūji, hatched a plot to murder Iioka no Sukegorō. However, Sukegorō got to hear of the plot and acted first, attempting to destroy his

rival on a grand and dramatic scale by carrying out a night raid on the Sasagawa headquarters on the south bank of the Tonegawa in the ninth month of 1844. The sight of this frenzied mass swordfight by moonlight has inspired some fine wood-block prints, and one particular work of literature, *Tempō Suikoden*.

By all accounts the raid was a ferocious affair, with all the hallmarks of a medieval battle. It even had its fallen hero, in this case a certain Hirate Miki who was the *yojimbō,* or bodyguard, to the Sasagawa family. Hirate Miki is the popular person in the narrative of *Tempō Suikoden* who 'makes the blood flow at the Tonegawa dry riverbed'. Hirate Miki made a dramatic fight to the death as the samurai blades flashed in the moonlight. The overall purpose of the raid failed when they did not succeed in capturing Shigezō. This action is known to the world as the 'quarrel in the dry riverbed of the great Tonegawa'. Perhaps by virtue of it being so inconclusive, the battle set both sides at odds, until matters were resolved three years later when assassins from the Iioka side murdered Shigezō. This was a murder so underhand that even their own side did not admire the action, but it brought peace to the area.

Fire-fighting in Edo
The prevention and control of fires was one of the daimyō's most solemn obligations. For a daimyō to allow a fire to start in his own *yashiki* was an act of gross negligence. Here a daimyō's retainer, dressed in a fire-cloak and helmet, supervises operations.

258

The 'Battle of the Firemen'

The other demanding area of a daimyō's civil authority was the prevention and control of fires. Nowhere was this need more pressing than in Edo itself, and there was a considerable responsibility placed upon the daimyō owners of *yashiki*. If a daimyō allowed a fire to start within his *yashiki,* he was punished by a number of days confinement to his *yashiki,* but if the fire had not spread to other mansions, the punishment might not be carried out. Certain *yashiki* belonging to daimyō above 10,000 *koku* were allowed to have a look-out tower, the *hinomi*. The *hinomi* had mounted on it a bell and a striking-beam. Between 1704 and 1711, when orders were issued for the formation of fire brigades in Edo, the newly appointed commanders of the brigades, of *hatamoto* rank, were given leave to build *hinomi* 9 m (30 ft) high. There is the record of a certain Matsudaira samurai who 'having been charged, in the year 1810, with certain duties as to fires, he for the first time hung up a bell and a striking-beam, and during his term of office made use of the same'. Fire was of course an ever-present hazard in a city built largely of wood, and would spread so rapidly through it that if a fire started near Edo gaol, the prisoners were released on parole, with heavy fines if they did not return once the fire had been brought under control.

During the 250 years of the Edo Period, there were twenty large fires and three large earthquakes in the capital. In the fire of 1657, half the city was destroyed and over 100,000 people lost their lives. In 1772, half the city was again lost, and in 1806 nearly all the retainers' *yashiki* were swept

An earthquake
Earthquakes have always been a fact of life for the Japanese. Three major earthquakes hit Edo during the two and a half centuries of the Tokugawa. This rather poor-quality illustration from the *Gempei Seisu-ki* shows the effects of a tremor, which brings buildings crashing to the ground. The startled citizens run for cover.

away. The fire brigades were organised in a similar way to the *yoriki* and the *dōshin* who kept order in the city. They wore protective clothing made of leather and heavy cotton, and helmets similar to 'battledress' helmets, but with a cloak attached at the rear which buttoned under the chin. Cutting fire-breaks was the most effective means of controlling a blaze, and there are a number of exuberant wood-block prints which depict the firemen in action, using hooks to pull burning shingles off roofs (thatch was forbidden, for obvious reasons), and carrying buckets. Standing his ground, in the most visible position he dare occupy, is to be found the squad's standard-bearer. During the 1760s, water pumps were introduced and, with increased training, many potentially dangerous fires were averted.

There was, however, intense rivalry between the *hikeshi*, the fire brigades, which on one occasion erupted into serious violence. The greatest jealousy occurred between the members of the Edo *machi-hikeshi*, the 'city fire brigade', and the *daimyō hikeshi*, the brigades maintained by the individual daimyō in the city. The rivalry, which has great echoes of the violence between the *hatamoto-yakko* and the *machi-yakko*, probably had similar social origins, and the leader of the Edo *machi-hikeshi*, Shimmon no Tatsugorō, had the popularity and the airs of Banzuin Chōbe'e. He lived from 1800 until 1876, a time when memories of previous conflagrations made the citizens very frightened of the danger of fire, and ready to greet a successful fire-chief as the nineteenth-century equivalent of a conquering daimyō.

Tatsugorō's collision with the *daimyō hikeshi* took place with the fire brigade of the Arima daimyō of Chikugo. One night, Tatsugorō's *machi-*

The 'Battle of the Firemen'
One of the most extraordinary conflicts to have taken place in the streets of Edo was the battle between firemen of the Edo citizenry, the *machi-hikeshi*, and firemen of the Arima daimyō. At the end of the brief but violent argument, 18 men lay dead.

A water garden
A harassed daimyō, beset by the many duties which required his attention, would refresh his spirit by the contemplation of a garden, such as this beautiful example at a Zen temple in Okazaki.

hikeshi arrived at the scene of a fire to find the Arima brigade's standard flying over the scene. Tempers exploded, and the scene of the fire became one of carnage as the two groups of firemen attacked one another with their short swords and their fire-axes. By the time order had been restored, 18 men lay dead, a death toll higher than many of the celebrated vengeance feuds that scarred contemporary Japan. Tatsugorō took full responsibility for the lack of control among his men, and surrendered himself to the *machi-bugyō*. His resulting banishment was only temporary, and he was to end his life as personal retainer to the last of the Tokugawa Shōguns, Yoshinobu, during the civil war of the Meiji Restoration. He accompanied the doomed Shōgun during his flight from the imperial forces, and eventually died peacefully at the age of 75, as honoured as any warlord.

This was the world outside the samurai class which the daimyō was required to control, a world occupied by corrupt samurai, hereditary policemen, proud firemen, gambling bosses and bitter gangland feuds. The Edo Period may not have been scarred by the wars of the Sengoku era, but it can hardly be called an age of peace.

261

Sex and the Samurai

The great houses of daimyō of the Edo Period came into being by various means. Some were won, like the Hōjō, and then, unlike the Hōjō, were retained. Others were increased in the great shake-up after Sekigahara, or were created daimyō by the Tokugawa Shōgun. Yet, whichever way the houses were created, all shared the same desire – to found a dynasty that would carry the family name forward into the future, a noble name forged in the heat of battle, and made even nobler in the wisdom and virtue of successive generations of good government in peace-time. That was the ideal to which they all aspired, but the reality was to be that the maintenance of an honourable name was every bit as difficult in the age of peace as it had been in war. In wartime, daimyō houses could be wiped out in dramatic battles, but peace placed its own demands on behaviour, and sometimes these were more difficult to cope with. As well as the external pressures from administration and the suppression of crime, so much depended upon internal personal factors, upon the daimyō himself, upon his wife and concubines, and upon the quality of those who came after him.

A doll for the Boys' Festival
This display, set out in the living quarters of a temple in Kawachi-Nagano, for 'Boys' Festival Day' illustrates the value still placed on Japan's samurai past, and also reminds us that Japanese aesthetics are not always governed by restraint.

Two actresses from the Toei-Uzumasa Film Studios in Kyōto pose for the camera. They are wearing *kimono*, and their wigs are characteristic of the hair-styles of the eighteenth century.

Women and the daimyō

The relation of parent and child is limited to this life on earth; that between husband and wife continues into the after-life; that between lord and retainer continues into the life after that again.

This pious statement was quoted earlier as an illustration of the firm bond of loyalty between daimyō and vassal. We may now turn it on its head and examine its implications for the role of women in samurai society.

Women occupy a shadowy position in accounts of the Sengoku Period. When a woman comes into prominence, she is frequently cast either as an out-and-out villain or as a mere token, a pawn in a daimyō's game of power. There is no equivalent in the Sengoku Period for the only 'female warrior' in the whole of samurai history – Tomoe Gozen, wife of the Minamoto general Kiso Yoshinaka, who fought beside her husband in the campaigns of the Gempei War and met her death with him in 1184. Nor is there any woman remotely approaching the status of Masako, widow of the first Shōgun Minamoto Yoritomo, whom history presents as a bitter schemer, determined to destroy the Minamoto succession in favour of her own clan, the Hōjō.

In contrast, the daimyō of the Sengoku Period tended to use women as chattels, as objects who were useful for acquiring power through the de-

263

vice of *seiryaku kekkon*, the political marriage. So useful was marriage as a weapon that the making of political marriages was specifically banned on the rise to power of the Shōgun Tokugawa Ieyasu. In my *Samurai Warriors*, there is a description of the incredibly complex web of marriage alliances that linked the families of Takeda, Hōjō and Imagawa in the mid-sixteenth century; but it is to the more powerful daimyō that we must look to see how cynically marriage, or rather divorce, could be manipulated for political ends.

When Oda Nobunaga made his alliance with Tokugawa Ieyasu in 1561, following the Battle of Okehazama, he married his daughter to Ieyasu's son Nobuyasu. The girl fully understood that she was expected to act as a spy on her new family, which she did very successfully, and informed Nobunaga about a plot to kill him and replace him with Nobuyasu. The plot had been hatched, apparently, by her new mother-in-law. As the alliance with Nobunaga was very important to him, Tokugawa Ieyasu showed his good faith to Nobunaga by putting to death his son Nobuyasu and also his scheming wife.

Such channels of information could also be used for false intelligence. Oda Nobunaga was himself married to the daughter of his rival, Saitō Dōsan (1494–1556), and told his wife, quite falsely, that he was plotting with some of Dōsan's senior retainers to have Dōsan murdered. His wife dutifully conveyed the message to Dōsan, who obligingly put to death some of his most loyal men, greatly weakening his position against

A raid on a house
The women of a household flee in terror as a castle falls, and the enemy samurai gain access to their living quarters.

264

Nobunaga. It is not surprising that the wisdom of the age, enshrined in documents such as the *kakun,* or 'house-laws' of the daimyō, contained references to the dangers of trusting a woman, of which the most telling is one attributed to Takeda Shingen: 'Even when husband and wife are alone together, he should never forget his dagger.'

But no example of the political manipulation of women can quite compare with Nobunaga's use of his sister O-ichi, and her daughters. She was first married to Shibata Katsuie, Nobunaga's most senior retainer, but Nobunaga desperately needed a marriage alliance with the Asai family of Ōmi, so O-ichi was divorced from Katsuie and married to Asai Nagamasa, the heir of the family, in 1568. The alliance did not hold, and Nobunaga went to war against the Asai clan in 1570. When Nobunaga burned Nagamasa's castle of Odani in 1573, Nagamasa and his father committed suicide, having first returned O-ichi and her three daughters to Nobunaga. Nobunaga thereupon made O-ichi remarry her former husband, Shibata Katsuie.

In 1582, Nobunaga was murdered, and Shibata Katsuie led the opposition to a take-over of Nobunaga's domains by another of his generals, Toyotomi Hideyoshi. After his defeat at Shizugatake in 1583, Katsuie was besieged in his castle by Hideyoshi and he committed suicide, along with O-ichi. The daughters were again spared, and the victor, Hideyoshi, took the eldest as his wife.

This girl led the most unbelievably tragic life. She had already seen her father, mother and stepfather commit suicide and then be consumed by flames in blazing castles, and so much more was in store for her. As the Lady Yodo-gimi, the title she acquired on her marriage to the future dictator of Japan, she bore him a son, Hideyori, who was to inherit the whole of Japan as his kingdom at the age of 5, when Hideyoshi died in madness. Hideyori's succession was disputed by the newly victorious Shōgun Tokugawa Ieyasu, and in 1615 his heavy cannon bombarded Ōsaka castle, where the desperate Hideyori had taken refuge with his army, accompanied by the Lady Yodo-gimi. As Ōsaka castle fell, she too committed suicide, along with her son, as another Japanese fortress blazed around her.

The faithful wife

Nevertheless, in spite of being used in so many cynical ways, a wife was expected to show the same loyalty to her husband as he would towards his

---

A family commits suicide

The reader may recognise the inspiraton for this plate as being the dramatic scene in Kurosawa's film *Ran,* where the defeated warlord's family commit suicide in the blazing castle keep. A samurai wife was expected to show loyalty to her husband every bit as great as the loyalty he showed towards his lord. Hence such an act of mass suicide.

Two women are stabbing each other at the same moment, while in the background a man commits *seppuku,* assisted by a faithful retainer.

An understanding of the various motivations possible behind a decision to commit suicide is fundamental to an appreciation of *bushidō,* the code of conduct and honour of a samurai. The act of suicide could simply be one way of making a dramatic protest against

the conduct of one's lord. Alternatively it provided a means of 'wiping the slate clean' when one had failed, thus dying with honour. There are many examples of this from the battlefields of the sixteenth century. In the case of the family in this plate, the suicide is motivated by a desire to accompany the defeated lord in death, and serve no other master.

A daimyō's lady
The wife of a daimyō, as represented by this actress from the Toei-Uzumasa Film Studios in Kyōto, was expected to show the same devotion to her husband as he would towards his feudal lord.

wariord. 'A woman has no specific daimyō,' said a moral tome of the period, 'she looks on her husband as her lord', a neat summary of the actual status of woman in feudal society. On the question of adultery, there was one rule for a man, and another for a woman. The 'house-laws' of the Tokugawa family made the right of a husband to kill an adulterous wife and her partner into a duty every bit as solemn as the duty of vengeance for a slain master.

There was, however, no such thing as adultery on the part of a husband, provided that another man's wife was not involved. The taking of concubines was no more than a means of ensuring that a daimyō house would produce a son to inherit, and the more concubines, the greater the chances of success. One daimyō, Mito Mitsukuni, of a branch family of the Tokugawa, who was known for his virtue, had assigned his inheritance to his brother's son, and, although he kept many concubines, obliged each one to undergo abortion lest the production of an heir should imperil his nephew's chances. Even in less extreme cases than this, the concubine was vastly inferior to the wife in a feudal household, having a rank of no more than a servant. Not that an unmarried daughter was much better off. She hardly ranked as a relative within the blood-line, her only function being to marry and beget children for her husband.

The lowest point to which samurai society brought women was the selling into prostitution of daughters and sisters, often from impoverished farming families. Although this practice was virtually unknown and for-

Yoshiwara – the pleasure quarter of Edo
This 'street' at the Toei-Uzumasa Film Studios in Kyōto gives one a good impression of the notorious Yoshiwara, the pleasure quarter of Edo. The prostitutes would ply their trade from behind the wooden, slatted windows that opened on to the street.

bidden in the Kamakura Period, which ended in 1333, the urbanisation of the Edo Period, and deteriorating agricultural conditions, ensured a growing demand and a steady supply. The story of the revenge of the sisters Miyagino and Shinobu, recounted later in this book, has as its background the selling of daughters into the brothels of Edo.

The Tokugawa Shōguns took a very pragmatic view of prostitution, much as they did towards the *kabuki* theatre, that it was a necessary evil but needed regulating lest it get out of hand. It, therefore, set up 'pleasure quarters' in the great cities, of which the best known was Yoshiwara in Edo. The name, literally, meant 'the plain of the reeds', but had a pun in its pronunciation which made it also sound like 'lucky field', not that the district itself had much luck. It was founded in 1617, and suffered four disastrous fires during the following two decades. The inhabitants of Yoshiwara: the girls, the pimps, the brothel-keepers and the clients, form the raw material of half the romantic literature, the plays and the wood-block prints of the Edo Period. A man taking his pleasure in Yoshiwara could, if he chose, bankrupt himself with the highest-ranking girls – the *tayū*, each of whom had the right to refuse any customer she did not fancy – or merely enjoy a little 'window-shopping' along the narrow streets, where the girls of lower grades would sit behind wooden slatted grills on the ground floor of the houses.

Comrade loves of the samurai

It is impossible to leave the subject of the personal relationships of the samurai class without some reference to the practice of homosexuality. Indeed, the attachment of men for men could in many cases far surpass the love of women, though bisexuality was as common as homosexuality. Takeda Shingen, for example, who produced many children through wives and concubines, had a particular attachment for his retainer, Kōsaka Danjō Masanobu. The devoted Masanobu became one of his most trusted, and most skilled, military commanders, and was instrumental in saving Shingen from defeat at the cataclysmic fourth Battle of Kawanakajima in 1561. It was, however, left to a novelist from the merchant class, Ihara Saikaku, who was born in 1642, to put into words the homosexual nature of much of samurai society. His writings, tongue in cheek as they were for many observations of his supposed betters in the world of Edo Japan, tease the samurai, as in one preface when he writes, 'Our eyes are soiled by the soft haunches and scarlet petticoats of women. These female beauties are good for nothing save to give pleasure to old men in lands where there is not a good-looking boy.'

Such attachments were not merely tolerated, they were encouraged, in what was predominantly a male society, as being conducive to comrade-ship and self-sacrifice on the battlefield. A young boy, taken into the service of a daimyō as a page, could almost expect to be used as an object of sexual gratification. For some retainers, to be the favoured page of a member of the lord's family was a gateway to further advancement. Others were forced to manipulate this position when a patron's interest waned, as in the case of Ōtsuki Denzō, whose success caused a split within the Maeda family.

Popular history, as represented particularly by the plays of the *kabuki*

Kōsaka Danjō, the lover of Shingen
In a predominantly male society, homosexual attachments could be stronger than those of marriage. Kosaka Danjō Masanobu was the lover of Takeda Shingen, and his constant companion. His prompt action at the fourth Battle of Kawanakajima in 1561 almost certainly saved the Takeda from annihilation. This photograph is of actor Hiroaki Murakami, who played the part of Danjō in the 1988 television series, 'Takeda Shingen', and is reproduced by kind permission of NHK Television.

A boy of the samurai class
This young actor from the Toei-Uzumasa Film Studios is dressed in simple fashion. His hair is tied back in a queue, without the shaven front portion which would later denote his entry into manhood.

大月傳彦

Ōtsuki Denzō
Ōtsuki Denzō has been treated
unfairly as the epitome of villainy
in the *kabuki* theatre. He was, in
fact, a wise retainer, and suffered
from the jealousy engendered in the
other retainers by Maeda Yoshinori's
affection for him, for which he
eventually paid with his life.

theatre, has not dealt kindly with Ōtsuki Denzō. Of all the villains who
enter the stage in a family feud, he is the epitome of treachery – the
Japanese equivalent, one may say, of Shakespeare's caricature of Richard
III. Denzō was born the son of an insignificant retainer of the Kaga-han,
called Ōtsuki Shichiemon, and when he was 14, on account of his good
looks, he was summoned by Maeda Yoshinori, and employed as his page
with a considerable stipend of 2 ryō of gold. Denzō became very well
acquainted with Yoshinori, being a very handsome youth, and the affection Yoshinori showered on him rivalled that given to the favourite
children of the family.

Realising his good fortune, Denzō aimed at the chance of a successful
career in the administration of the *han*. However, Denzō had not been born
into the family's line, and it was made clear to him that he would be most
unlikely to succeed to a position of responsibility once Yoshinori's homo-

Kanazawa castle
Kanazawa castle was the seat of the Maeda daimyō, and the scene of the epic feud between Ōtsuki Denzō and Maeda Naomi, immortalised, and much embellished, in the 'soap operas' of the *kabuki* theatre. The outer wall and gateway are all that remain of the castle, which is now the site of Kanazawa University.

sexual preference for him began to wane. In fact, he rose to a high position within the family, and the mere existence of the stories that have grown up about Denzō's machinations tell us a great deal about the jealousies that could be aroused within a family.

According to the 'treachery' theory, Denzō devised a cunning, but very risky, plot. He stole a poisonous plant from the *han* medicinal herb garden, and poured it into Yoshinori's bowl of soup. At the very instant when Yoshinori was about to put it into his mouth, Denzō shouted 'My lord! Wait a moment' and, making it appear he was loyal, drank from the bowl. As soon as he had the taste of poison in his mouth, he vomited copiously and fell in convulsions. Yoshinori was enormously impressed by Denzō's acute awareness of danger and his outstanding loyalty, and promptly increased his stipend by 1000 *koku,* and appointed him to a senior rank. He became entrusted with Yoshinori's personal affairs, acting as a go-between for his feudal lord with beautiful women, and even though these stories are embellished, they give a good indication of the services a retainer was expected to perform for a daimyō, particularly an idle one.

Denzō's greatest coup came in procuring for Yoshinori, as a concubine, a celebrated beauty called O-tei. She was Yoshinori's second concubine, and inevitably provided a rival to his existing paramour, O-kiku, a situation exacerbated when both became pregnant at the same time. Eventually both gave birth, O-kiku producing Yoshinori's second son, O-tei his third. In reality, though, O-tei was to insist, her son had been born two days

273

earlier, while the other child's birth was the first to be notified. This had serious consequences for them both, because should Yoshinori's eldest son meet with an early death, then the third son would rank as subject to the heir. Ōtsuki Denzō took up her case.

Soon after, Yoshinori took a new concubine. O-tei was distraught, and entered into a plot with Denzō to have Yoshinori and his heir murdered, as a result of which Denzō would have undisputed power within the clan. The story goes on to relate how Yoshinori is ambushed while returning from Edo on the *sankin kōtai* visit, and stabbed as his horse is crossing a flooded river. His heir, Munetoki, is poisoned, and the servant girl, who is made a convenient scapegoat, meets a horrible end in a pit full of snakes, one of the most bizarre scenes in all the *kabuki* repertoire! Denzō is eventually found out and exiled to a distant place, where he commits suicide.

Historical reality is much more sober, but in its way far more tragic. Denzō did succeed to a high position within the Maeda family as a result of Yoshinori's attachment to him, and it is true that on Yoshinori's death, which was from natural causes, he was exiled to Gokayama in Etchū province and killed himself in 1745. Why should this have come about?

Needless to say the other retainers, and the family members in particular, were violently jealous of Denzō, in particular a certain Maeda Tosa-no-kami Naomi, who was a pillar of society, and his branch of the Maeda family counted as first among the eight families of Kaga. Naomi, who had a burning sense of duty towards great affairs of the family, was an exemplary player at power politics. History also tells us that Maeda Yoshinori was not a careless ruler, nor was Ōtsuki Denzō a bad, scheming person, but one who stimulated and enforced economy among the retainers, and raised funds by borrowing gold from Ōsaka merchants. He handled difficult economic affairs of the *han*, not by oppression, but from a position of wisdom and strength. Yet the whole affair shows how fragile such a position could be. Once Yoshinori was gone, Denzō could be removed by jealous family members. To a daimyō, family blood was thicker than water, and, inevitably, as a counter to Denzō's personification of evil in the *kabuki*, the indignant Maeda Naomi is presented as a shining example of the loyal samurai.

The servant girl in the pit of snakes
This illustration, which is taken from a nineteenth-century, wood-block-printed book cover, summarises the *kabuki* plot as the 'soap opera' of its day. The scene, rarely performed nowadays, is the bizarre climax of a play based loosely on the events of the Maeda family feud.

The divided sword

The universal acceptance of concubines may have ensured the birth of an heir, but numerous offspring could lead to rivalry within a family as bitter as the mistrust between Maeda Naomi and the outsider Denzō. Yet even though the wars of medieval Japan were civil wars, there are very few examples of families being split over allegiance in wartime, such as happened during the English Civil War. Such a split did in fact happen to the Sanada family, which greatly imperilled their future; yet it was the loyalty between them, and their recognition of samurai duty, that saved the Sanada as a daimyō family.

The Sanada were a family of Shinano province. The first to bear the name, Yukitaka, submitted to Takeda Shingen when he invaded Shinano. He went on to serve him together with his elder son, Nobutsuna, who was killed in 1575 at Nagashino. His younger son, Masayuki (1544–1608), inherited his father's position and, on the ruin of the Takeda with the death

Interior of the Sanada mansion
The simplicity of the Japanese domestic interior was a common thread that united all classes. From the simplest home to a grand house such as this, the Sanada mansion in Matsushiro, the straw *tatami* mats and the unpainted wood were characteristic of a deep and meaningful unity.

of Katsuyori in 1582, he was one of many Takeda retainers who were made to submit to Tokugawa Ieyasu. Masayuki grew to have little love for the Tokugawa. As a result of Masayuki's submission to Ieyasu, his elder son, Nobuyuki (1566–1658), was taken as a hostage to Hamamatsu, and eventually married the daughter of Ieyasu's great captain, Honda Tadakatsu; but Ieyasu went much further in his demands on the Sanada, and in 1586 tried to strip him of his territory to give to the Hōjō. So Masayuki rebelled, in spite of his son's presence with Ieyasu. The Tokugawa army advanced on Ueda and laid siege to the castle, but a truce was patched up, owing to the intervention of Hideyoshi.

When war came again in 1600, Masayuki instructed his son Nobuyuki to join Ieyasu, as that was where his duty lay. For Masayuki, and the other celebrated member of the family, Yukimura (1570–1615), their duty lay in opposing the rise of the Tokugawa. (Their emotional parting has long been a favourite theme for Japanese artists.) Ueda castle was strategically situated on the Tokugawa's most vital line of communication – the Nakasendō road, and as it had already withstood one siege by the Tokugawa army, Masayuki no doubt thought it could withstand another. The Sanada family, thereupon, contributed to the Sekigahara campaign by delaying the progress westwards of Ieyasu's son, Tokugawa Hidetada, which they did so successfully that the siege of Ueda in 1600 is regarded as one of the three classic sieges of Japanese history when the defenders were not defeated. A huge army was kept from Sekigahara, and had it not been for the attendant treachery on the field, their tactics may well have tipped the balance against the Tokugawa.

After Sekigahara, Masayuki and Yukimura were captured by the Tokugawa and faced almost certain death, but Nobuyuki interceded on their behalf and the sentences were commuted to exile. Nobuyuki was granted the castle of Ueda. Masayuki died in exile in 1608, and Yukimura returned from exile in 1614 to join the army that opposed Ieyasu once again from within the walls of Ōsaka castle. Here he was one of the most skilled of the defenders, and was finally killed in the Battle of Tennōji in 1615.

There seem to have been no bitter feelings from Masayuki to his son or vice versa. Each followed his duty as they saw it, and Nobuyuki carried on the family line, which to all of them was what really mattered. Through him the Sanada continued and prospered, and in 1622 he was transferred to Matsushiro, where they established the magnificent mansion which exists to this day.

A puppet from the Bunraku theatre
Like the *kabuki*, the plays of the puppet theatre would take their plots from contemporary events, such as family feuds. In fact the puppet plays tended to be more daring in their attempts at satire.

The Date family feud

The split within the Sanada family, mutually agreed by all parties as being in keeping with samurai honour and duty, is as nothing compared to the mighty rifts torn through the fabric of family loyalty in other great families, and there are several examples of daimyō families brought to the brink of ruin by corruption and feuding within their own blood-relatives. Unfortunately, as we have seen in the illustration of the Maeda family dispute, in the majority of cases, the facts behind these family feuds have been obscured by the treatment they received at the hands of novelists and dramatists, who used real-life stories of weakness and disaster among the rich and powerful as material for the 'soap operas' of their day. An excellent example is the near-disastrous rift within the Date family, daimyō of Sendai. The truth of the conflict is interesting enough as an example of the decline of loyalty and filial values, but the resulting story has been expanded out of all proportion.

Date Masamune (1566–1636) was one of the noblest daimyō to make the transition between Sengoku warlord and Edo daimyō, and the internal discord of the Date family arose entirely from the immorality of his grandson, the third generation daimyō Tsunamune. He devoted himself entirely to pleasure, with daily attendance in the red-light district of Yoshiwara. He was eventually condemned by the *bakufu*, an unusual and

A scene from **kabuki**
A wood-block print depicting a squabble between women of a daimyō's household. The scene is taken from the *kabuki* play *Meiboku Sendai Hagi*, which dramatises the events of the Date family feud.

very serious step for the Government to take, and as a punishment was made to underwrite the expense of the extension to the moat of Edo castle in 1660, an enormous civil-engineering project. But long before matters came to this pass, his retainers forced him to take early retirement in favour of his heir Kamechiyo (the future Tsunamura), who was still in his infancy.

The 2-year-old Kamechiyo's guardians were to be Date Hyōbu Munekatsu and Tamura Ukyō. Hyōbu was the tenth son of the *han* founder, Date Masamune, and Ukyō was Tsunamune's illegitimate elder brother. But Hyōbu Munekatsu was ambitious, and by and by clawed his way to absolute power, shielded from criticism by his relationship, through his son's marriage, to a powerful *bakufu* official. He dismissed senior retainers who opposed him, and promoted his particular favourite, a man called Harada Kai. Tamura Ukyō was gradually squeezed out of any control over the affairs of the *han*. In the 10 years of Hyōbu's office as guardian, he managed 120 retainers, and during that time had ordered 17 of them to commit suicide.

The story of the Date family feud forms the basis of the *kabuki* play *Meiboku Sendai Hagi*, which begins to diverge from reality at the point when Date Hyōbu is believed to have been plotting to murder the young heir, Kamechiyo, so that he could take over the domain. The child's nurse, Masaoka, tries to protect the boy by retiring to an inner room on the pretext of the child's illness. Two 'villains', acting on behalf of Date Hyōbu, bring cakes as gifts for the supposed invalid. The cakes are, of course(!) poisoned, and as a fine gesture of loyalty toward an infant lord, Masaoka's own son takes one to test it for poison. To avoid discovery of the fact that the cakes are poisoned, one of the villains stabs the boy to death.

In reality, the show-down with Hyōbu came from the person who was the next most powerful man in the family – one Date Aki Muneshige. The confrontation between Hyōbu and Aki made the Date feud grow more and more violent. Aki lodged a complaint with the *bakufu*, although he had little firm evidence on which to base his argument. Was there any more to the affair than Hyōbu's apparent incorrect treatment of land distribution? Aki stuck his neck out, and exposed fully Hyōbu's evil deeds and immoral acts as he saw them, accusations that forced the *bakufu* to intervene. The resulting investigation of Hyōbu's conduct and management took place in 1671 on neutral ground, at the residence of Sakai Ude-no-kami, the *tairō*, or chief retainer of the family, and therefore the most influential man outside the actual family.

Four people were questioned in turn about Date Hyōbu Munekatsu's conduct: Date Aki Muneshige, the retainers Shibata Geki and Yoshiuchi Shima, and Harada Kai. The accounts of the first three agreed totally, while Harada Kai's version differed wildly. Suddenly the investigation reached an unexpected climax when the enraged Harada Kai drew a short *wakizashi* sword and attacked Muneshige. Muneshige sustained two sword strokes and was severely wounded. The two other witnesses, Geki and Shima, chased after Harada and wounded him. Harada Kai was panting for breath, then lost his head completely and slashed indiscriminately at Geki and another retainer, called Haraya Yoshihiro, wounding them so badly that they died that evening.

But this sudden eruption into violence marked the end of the Date feud. Date Hyōbu Munekatsu's defence collapsed, and punishment was swift.

Harada Kai, villain of the Date feud
Harada Kai is the real-life villain of the feud within the Date family of Sendai. Here he is shown brandishing a blood stained knife at the residence of Sakai Ude-no-kami, where his fellow conspirator, Date Hyōbu, was impeached by the *bakufu* for mismanagement of the *han*.

The young heir, Tsunamura, was judged to have played no part in the upheaval of the *han*, and to have been powerless to prevent it on account of his youth. The *han* was, therefore, spared the confiscation by the *bakufu* of its wealth, which totalled 620,000 *koku*. As for Date Hyōbu Munekatsu, he was deprived of his stipend of 30,000 *koku*, and placed in the custody of the *han*. He was reduced to an insignificant rank, and died eight years later, in 1679, at the age of 51.

In the *kabuki* plays, Date Hyōbu Munekatsu and Harada Kai are the villains, while Date Aki Muneshige is presented as the finest of loyal family

members. However, this is in itself something of an exaggeration to make the play interesting. In reality, there was always factional strife among the loyal retainers of a large *han*, and to paint the combatants so clearly black or white is an oversimplification. The murderous outburst by Harada Kai, however, did actually happen, and is such a dramatic touch that one wonders why *Meiboku Sendai Hagi* has to be embellished so much, as, for example, in one scene when a sorcerer is introduced who changes magically into a rat!

The Kuroda feud

As a final illustration, let us examine the feud within the Kuroda family, which has received little embellishment. In this case, the dying lord, the great Kuroda Nagamasa (1568–1623), veteran of many battles including the invasion of Korea, hesitated before making his son Tadayuki his successor. There was much immorality in Tadayuki, Nagamasa reasoned, and he relied on his trusted *tairō*, Kuriyama Daizen, to remonstrate with him, even at the risk of his life. Nagamasa handed Daizen his famous helmet with water-buffalo horns and said, 'If Tadayuki gets foolish, put this helmet on and admonish him yourself.'

Legend says that Tadayuki had a favourite, Kurahashi Shudayu, whom he had originally procured as his personal retainer, and Tadayuki's debauchery continued in spite of Daizen's remonstrations against him. Shudayu, another bisexual, procured a beautiful girl called O-hide no kata for Tadayuki, who was carrying Shudayu's child in her womb, through whom he was planning to usurp the family. However, evil did not prosper and O-hide no kata was killed by a retainer. In disgust, the *tairō* Daizen left the service of Tadayuki and lodged a complaint with the *bakufu*. Daizen had Tadayuki placed in the temporary custody of the Nambu clan and Kurahashi Shudayu was exiled to Toishima. The *bakufu* recognised the loyal service to the Tokugawa of the previous head Nagamasa, and maintained intact the territory of the Kuroda, to which Tadayuki was later restored.

That is the tradition, but how much is true? There was a show-down between the two men, Tadayuki and Daizen, and the model of Shudayu is said to be a person called Kuraya Sodayu, who existed as Tadayuki's professional flatterer, but the Kuroda feud is just one more story of a fight between a stupid ruler and a stubborn old retainer, a feature common enough to the turbulent world of the warlords of Japan.

Death and the Daimyō

The nearness of death, and the awareness of the nature of the spirit world, was an omnipresent factor in the life of the warlord. We have noted twice already that the relationship between daimyō and retainer was regarded as extending beyond death, and that terrible gap between life and death was one that every samurai had to be willing to cross. If loyalty meant anything, it had to include dying for one's lord. Many years after wars had ceased, a samurai of the Nabeshima daimyō was to put this principle into words: 'The Way of the Samurai,' he wrote, 'is found in death.'

The supreme sacrifice

The 'way of the Samurai' was found in death, and this death could be brought about by an enemy sword, spear or bow, or even a gun – the means did not matter as long as the death was honourable, and for a death to be honourable it had to come about as a result of loyal service to one's lord.

Suicide on the battlefield
The daimyō's loyal samurai hold off the enemy while their master commits *seppuku*.

The loyal exploits of Sengoku Hidehisa
Death in battle was the ultimate expression of a warrior's loyalty, and on occasions was actively sought, but such self-sacrifice did not always lead to the daimyō's advantage. Here the hero Sengoku Hidehisa (1551–1614) performs valiantly, in a companion scroll to that depicted on the cover of *Battles of the Samurai* by this author. (Ueda castle museum)

In times of war, the achievement of such a death was prized as the ultimate proof of loyalty, and on occasions death could actively be sought for its own sake. There is a very fine dividing line between accepting the likelihood of death in reckless battle and actively seeking it out, which was effectively to commit suicide. An appreciation of the place of suicide in the concept of the loyal samurai warrior is essential for understanding the many acts of seemingly wasteful self-destruction we read of in the old war chronicles. What motivated this apparent eagerness for extinction, and how could destroying oneself ever be seen as loyal behaviour?

There were occasions when suicide was regarded as appropriate because of failure, and the samurai would commit *sokotsu-shi*, or 'expiatory suicide', the very act itself wiping the slate clean. Such a decision could be spontaneous and dramatic, like the action of the veteran warrior Yamamoto Kansuke at the fourth Battle of Kawanakajima in 1561. As Takeda Shingen's *gun-bugyō*, he had devised 'Operation Woodpecker', by which the Takeda were to surprise the Uesugi army. Realising his bold strategy had failed, Kansuke took his spear and plunged into the midst of the enemy army, committing suicide to make amends for his error. Minutes after Kansuke's suicide, he was joined in death by Morozumi Masakiyo, Shingen's 87-year-old great-uncle mentioned earlier. To Morozumi, a dramatic suicide was a way of dying honourably when faced with what he interpreted as certain defeat. In his case, there was no sense of personal failure, merely the culmination of loyalty in joining Shingen in his coming death. The tragedy of both these deaths is that their interpretations of the certainty of the destruction of the Takeda very soon proved incorrect. Reinforcements arrived, the army rallied, and a defeat was turned into

283

victory. Yet two experienced generals had been lost, both of whom would have served Shingen better by staying alive.

The motivation behind suicide is much less well appreciated than the means whereby it was carried out, which was usually the well-known act of *seppuku*. (If the two characters which make up the work *seppuku* are reversed, it produces *hara-kiri*, the word more familiar to Western ears.) *Seppuku*, which has been much described and much discussed, was a particularly painful act of suicide in that the samurai himself released his spirit from its seat in the abdomen by a swift and deep cut with his dagger. The rite was somewhat modified in later years to allow the presence of a second, who cut off the victim's head at the moment of agony.

The committing of *seppuku* was not always a voluntary activity. It could be allowed as an honourable alternative to execution for a condemned criminal of the samurai class, and we also noted earlier how Sasa Narimasa was 'invited' to commit suicide by Hideyoshi following his disastrous

Seppuku *on the battlefield*
This page from the *Hōjō Godai-ki* shows the act of *seppuku*, or ritual suicide, at its most poignant and dramatic – the mass suicide of a defeated army. One warrior receives the blessing of a second to cut off his head. Others discard their armour for the classic act of *hara-kiri*, while one throws himself on to his sword.

清水宗治御見事
花を惜しみ武士の
名を残し船中に於て
潔死す

The suicide of Shimizu Muneharu
One of the most dramatic acts of
suicide in samurai history was that of
the defender of Takamatsu castle,
Shimizu Muneharu, who took a boat
out into the artificial lake created by
Hideyoshi's siege operations, and
committed *seppuku* in front of the
besieging army.

handling of the territory Hideyoshi had given him. Sometimes a daimyō
was called upon to perform *seppuku* as the basis of peace negotiations, the
idea being that the surrender of a castle could be accepted without further
bloodshed, providing that the current daimyō committed suicide. This
would so weaken the defeated clan that resistance would effectively cease.
Toyotomi Hideyoshi used an enemy's suicide in this way on several
occasions, of which the most dramatic, in that it effectively ended a
dynasty of daimyō forever, is what happened when the Hōjō were defeated
at Odawara in 1590. Hideyoshi insisted on the suicide of the retired
daimyō, Hōjō Ujimasa, and the exile of his son Ujinao. With one sweep of a
sword, the most powerful daimyō family in the east ceased to exist, and
disappeared from history.

Alternatively, the victor could be satisfied with the death of his enemy's retainer, which would be most effective if the subordinate was in charge of the castle he was besieging. There are several examples of this from Hideyoshi's earlier campaigns on behalf of Oda Nobunaga. The most theatrical occurred when Hideyoshi besieged Takamatsu castle in 1582. It was a long siege, and only looked like being successful when Hideyoshi diverted a river to make a lake, which gradually began to flood the castle. Unfortunately it was during these operations that Hideyoshi received the dramatic news of the murder of Nobunaga, and knew that he had to abandon Takamatsu rapidly before any other of Nobunaga's generals found out and became his avengers instead. He hurriedly drew up peace terms with Mōri Terumoto, which included the clause that the valiant defender of Takamatsu, Shimizu Muneharu, should commit suicide. Shimizu Muneharu was determined to go to his death as dramatically as he had lived, and took a boat out into the middle of the artificial lake. When he was satisfied that Hideyoshi's men were taking careful note of what he was doing, he committed *seppuku.*

Sometimes such a suicide provided an honourable end only after extreme privations. Tottori castle, in Inaba province, held out for an incredible 200 days before it surrendered to Hideyoshi in 1581. Its commander, Kikkawa Tsuneie, inspired his men to this long resistance even though they were reduced to eating grass and dead horses. Tsuneie's suicide letter to his son survives to this day. It reads:

We have endured for over two hundred days. We now have no provisions left. It is my belief that by giving up my life I will help my garrison. There is nothing greater than the honour of our family. I wish our soldiers to hear of the circumstances of my death.

His suicide, along with that of two others, was the condition of surrender.

Another reason for committing suicide was the making of a protest. This is known as *kanshi.* Examples of this are rare, but it profoundly affected one of the greatest daimyō of the Sengoku Period. Oda Nobunaga inherited his father's domains at the age of 15 and, although he was a brave warrior, showed little interest in the administration of his territory. One of his best retainers, Hirade Kiyohide, tried in vain to persuade him to mend his ways, and when the young Nobunaga showed no inclination to listen to him, Kiyohide put all his feelings into a letter to his lord, and committed *seppuku* in protest. Nobunaga was greatly moved, and changed his ways for the better, with, of course, considerable consequences for the history of Japan.

Following in death

To return briefly to Shimizu Muneharu and his *seppuku* in the middle of the lake, there is a related anecdote which illustrates the one reason for committing suicide which did not meet with universal approval. This was the practice of *junshi,* or 'following in death'. In Muneharu's case, the loyal retainer actually preceded his lord in death, because Muneharu was invited to the man's room in Takamatsu castle the evening before his own suicide was due to take place. There his loyal retainer explained that, to reassure his master about the ease with which *seppuku* could be performed, he had himself committed suicide, and, pulling aside his robe, showed

秀吉の神慮

大宮父子が害心を識く殺さ〜む

Muneharu his severed abdomen. Muneharu was touched by the gesture, and acted as his retainer's second to bring the act to a speedy and less painful conclusion.

As noted above, there was a fine line between *junshi* and merely continuing a desperate fight. In the confusion of a battlefield, the circumstances of a retainer's death could never be clearly established. But when death from natural causes during times of peace provoked the performance of *junshi*, whereby a loyal retainer committed suicide to show that he could serve none other than his departed lord, it could only be regarded as utterly wasteful. During the Sengoku Period, such an act may have been approved of, and indeed some retainers did have little left to live for, but in times of peace *junshi* was a deliberate, premeditated and unnecessary act, noble, perhaps, in its sentiments, but scarcely helpful in maintaining the stability of a dynasty.

In the early Edo Period, as many as 20 leading retainers of an individual daimyō were known to have committed *junshi* on the deaths of their lords. For this reason, strong condemnation was made of *junshi*. A better way to serve one's departed lord, the *bakufu* argued, was to render equally loyal service to his heir. But *junshi* was firmly engrained in the Japanese mentality. It had been abolished originally by an imperial decree in the year AD 3 (!), yet still the tradition persisted, and as noted above, reached its peak in the Sengoku Period. A strong condemnation of it is found in the so-called 'Legacy of Ieyasu', the 'house-laws' left by the first Tokugawa Shōgun in

1616, but at the death of his grandson, the third Tokugawa Shōgun Iemitsu in 1651, five of the leading retainers of the Tokugawa committed *junshi*, a remarkable gesture against the law they themselves had formulated. A further attempt to ban it was introduced by the *bakufu* in 1663, and included the statement:

In the event that a lord had a presentiment that a certain vassal is liable to immolate himself, he should admonish him strongly against it during his lifetime. If he fails to do so, it shall be counted as his fault. His heir will not escape appropriate punishment.

Five years later, an instance of *junshi* occurred among the retainers of the recently deceased daimyō of the house of Okudaira, but little action was taken against the family because of the great service the Okudaira had rendered to the Tokugawa in previous years. (Their ancestor had been the defender of Nagashino castle at the time of the famous battle there.) The family of the actual performer of *junshi* was not so fortunate. His two sons were ordered to commit *seppuku*, and his two sons-in-law, one of whom was of the Okudaira family, were exiled.

Other daimyō finally took note, and from the mid-seventeenth century onwards, the practice of *junshi* effectively ceased, until it came dramatically to the attention of modern Japan in 1912. On the eve of the funeral of Emperor Meiji, General Nogi and his wife committed *seppuku*. Nogi had commanded troops in the Sino-Japanese War of 1894–95, and led the battle to take Port Arthur in the Russo-Japanese War of 1904–05. It was an

A Buddhist priest at prayer
A Buddhist priest of the Shingon sect kneels in prayer at the temple of Fudō-ji, on the site of the Battle of Kurikara.

act that astounded his contemporaries because of the bizarre disloyalty to the Emperor's wishes that the illegal act implied. It was also sobering evidence that the samurai spirit lived on in the Japan of the twentieth century.

The death of an enemy

In the Sengoku Period, the death of one's enemy was the aim, and the natural consequence, of the practice of war. Nevertheless, the recognition of an enemy death became surrounded by considerable ritual, of which the most bizarre, to Western eyes, were the practices surrounding the collection and inspection of heads. This is a feature found throughout samurai history, and was the surviving element of the ancient practice of sacrifice to the gods of war mentioned in a previous chapter. The heads would be washed, the hair combed, and the resulting trophy made presentable by cosmetics – all tasks performed with great delicacy by the women of the daimyō's court. The heads would then be mounted on a spiked wooden board, with labels for identification. If the ceremony were to be held with no time for this preparation, the heads could be presented on an opened war-fan, or on a paper handkerchief. Some leaves from a tree were recommended to soak up any dripping blood. The daimyō would sit in similar state to the one he had enjoyed when he had presided over the departure ceremony, and one by one the heads would be brought before him for comment. If a daimyō were otherwise engaged, the head ceremony could be delegated to a trusted subordinate, as in the *Hōjō Go-daiki*:

It is Nakayama Shurisuke that Hōjō Ujitsuna favours with [the right] to raise the flags and sit on the camp-stool at Kōnodai. This is a person who is known for his traditional virtues of military lore and loyalty by which he has destroyed enemies, carrying out strategy in numerous battles, and at the same time he is a samurai official. This person will be bugyō *for head inspection. He will record the relative importance of loyalties, and examine the details of contests when the heads were taken.*

Of course, not all the hundreds of heads taken during a battle were saved. The *Gunyōki* quotes the following document:

Tembun 2nd year (1533) 7th month, 6th day at the Hour of the Monkey. The list for [the Battle of] Ōyama. These are the heads that were taken:

Item: one head:	*Maekawa Zaemon*
taken by	*Kinichi Danjōshū and Shōshu Uemon*
Item: one head:	*no given name known*
taken by	*a* chūgen *[called] Genroku*
Item: one head:	*Arakami Jirozaemon*
taken by	*Nagao Gagaku Sukeshu and Masuda Danjochu*

The number of heads taken and discarded is not known.

One little-known feature of the head-inspection routine was that certain expressions on the faces of the deceased were supposed to be unlucky, and others lucky, namely:

1 *Eyes looking towards heaven – unlucky (and particularly disliked by the Takeda family).*
2 *Eyes looking towards the earth – generally lucky.*
3 *Eyes looking towards the head's left – lucky in enemies.*
4 *Eyes looking towards the right – lucky in allies.*
5 *Eyes closed – lucky, 'a head of tranquillity'.*
6 *One eye closed, gnashing teeth, etc. – unlucky.*

The mention of the heads of allies above refers to the practice of sending back to an enemy the heads of their noble dead.

A special privilege was reserved for the head of a defeated enemy general or a daimyō. It would be brought before the daimyō by two men, not just one, and, after the victorious army had given the shout of victory, the general would ceremoniously eat the same three dishes of which he had partaken before setting out, but with a difference – the head of the defeated general was allowed to share the *saké*. In a grisly ritual, some *kombu* (dried seaweed) was placed in the head's mouth, and *saké* poured on to it, with much dignity, from a long-handled cup.

As may be imagined, the expression on the face of a dead daimyō was very closely examined, as the chronicle *Ō-monogatari* tells us of the occasion when Oda Nobunaga viewed the head of his bitter enemy, Takeda Katsuyori, in 1582:

When Oda Nobunaga inspected the head of Takeda Katsuyori the right eye was

Oda Nobunaga views the heads
One of Oda Nobunaga's retainers is overcome by emotion as he contemplates the severed head of an enemy, during one of Nobunaga's head-viewing ceremonies following a victory.

closed and the left eye was enlivened with a scowl. Nobunaga was moved to sympathy at the sight of the dead head of the powerful general, and it is recorded that all concerned agreed that Nobunaga may have been victorious in battle, but had been defeated by Katsuyori's head.

The Japanese spirit world

The attitude of a samurai towards his own death, and that of his family, lord and enemy, was deeply coloured by his beliefs regarding the world of the spirits of the dead, to which the act of dying committed him. The religious beliefs of the Japanese relating to death and dying are not easy for non-Japanese to appreciate, as was brought home to the world's media in 1985 when the then Japanese Prime Minister Nakasone made an official visit to the Yasukuni Shrine in Tōkyō on 15 August, the fortieth anniversary of the end of World War II. There was considerable protest from overseas, particularly from the Chinese, who pointed out that war

The Mimakude Shrine
The Mimakude Shrine, where are enshrined the spirits of the Kusunoki family, is typical of thousands of such Shintō shrines throughout Japan. Note the characteristic *torii* gateway.

criminals, such as General Tōjō, were enshrined there. Analogies were drawn with President Reagan's equally unpopular visit to the West German military ceremony at Bitburg, where the remains of SS troops were buried. But there the resemblance ended. Bitburg contained human remains, while Yasukuni contained nothing at all – and there we have the key to understanding the notion of the Japanese spirit world.

A Shintō shrine, like Yasukuni, is neither a burial ground, nor is it simply a place of worship, like a Christian church, a synagogue or a mosque. It is also a spirit house, a gathering place for the spirits of the dead enshrined there. Since ancient times, the Japanese have believed that the spirit lives on after the death of a body, returning from time to time to the land of the living. The season of cherry blossoms is one of these times, when the *tama* (spirits) flock to the cherry-tree-covered hills of Yoshino. The midsummer festival of *Bon* is another occasion on which the spirits of the dead are welcomed back from the mountains or other sacred places where they live. In many parts of Japan, lanterns are floated on water to light the spirits' way home. In this Shintō scheme, the worlds of the dead and the living are coterminous. The spirits of the dead are always close at hand, and the theme of communication between the living and the dead is a strong theme running through Japanese tradition.

Shintō is, of course, not the only religion of Japan but, being so thor-

A Buddhist grave
A large stone *sotoba* marks the site of a Buddhist grave, where the cremated remains of a samurai are buried. Buddhism teaches that the soul is reborn after death in a state of reincarnation.

The Buddha of mercy and the vengeful judge

Two aspects of Buddhist cosmology are illustrated here. On one hand there is the beatific figure of the healing Buddha, Amida, who waits to welcome souls into his Western Paradise. On the other is one of the fierce judges of the underworld, whose judgement will decide into which of the states of transmigration the reincarnated soul will be born.

oughly grounded in traditional beliefs and folk practices, it has managed to absorb much of other religions within its own world view, so that even though the influence of Buddhism (introduced during the sixth century AD) encouraged the custom of preserving the ashes of the dead in family graves, the spirit has always been regarded as more important than the body. In most aspects of religious life, Shintō and Buddhism can be regarded as totally intermingled until the Separation Edict of 1868, which sought to make Shintō an 'Established Church'.

Sharing this acceptance of two apparently contradictory religions, the samurai believed that, 33 years after death, a person's spirit moved from the Buddhist temple where he or she was buried to a shrine, an idea totally contrary to the Buddhist doctrine of reincarnation, which saw the spirit existing in limbo, waiting to be reborn, and we read comments made to a dying samurai like, 'May you be reborn in bliss'.

This process of rebirth was not without its hazards. Where a spirit ended up depended on the person's actions during his life, and no one else's prayers made the slightest difference. There was a very strong belief in judgement during the sixteenth century. People believed that the Ten Kings of the Underworld, in Buddhist cosmology, passed judgement on each person's spirit after death. Seven days after death, the spirit was judged by King Shinkō; seven days later it was judged by King Shokō, and so on every seventh day until on the forty-ninth day, seven weeks after death, the verdict was handed down and the spirit was reborn in one of the six realms of transmigration – hell, the realm of Hungry Ghosts, the realm of the Beasts, the realm of the Asuras, or Titans, the human realm, or heaven. Above these six realms were the four states of enlightenment leading to final Buddhahood – the *sravaka*, the *prateya-buddha*, the *bodhissatva*, and finally, the completely enlightened *nirvana*. The spirit's individual 'case' was reviewed after a hundred days, a year, and three years. During the Tokugawa Period, the Buddhist memorial period for the dead was stretched from 3 years to 7, 13 and 17 years, until, finally, 33 years was accepted as the time of trial.

Shintō shrines were the homes for these spirits, and it is noticeable from old chronicles that the daimyō of the Sengoku Period would honour the fallen impartially, enshrining the spirits of friend and enemy alike. The act of enshrinement was very important, because it was believed that any-

The temple of Daitsu-ji, Nagahama
The Daitsu-ji is a large Buddhist foundation at Nagahama. Buddhism and Shintō are the two major religions of Japan, and have much in common. We are looking at the *hondō*, or main hall.

294

Parade of yamabushi
Yamabushi from the Shōgō-In in Kyōto march to their *goma* ritual.

one who had died unjustly or by violence, including on the battlefield, would become a *onryō*, or 'angry ghost', and haunt the living and cause misfortune. Even peaceful spirits at death could change their nature and become malevolent if neglected during the 33-year period. The samurai had a vivid concept of the nature of these unruly spirits. They saw the spirit right after death as having 'sharp edges'. If you enshrined it, it slowly lost its rough edges until it was 'as smooth as marble'. After the period of 33 years, these featureless spirits then gathered into one collective spirit – the 'god of the village'. Presumably the spirit of the war criminal General Tōjō is now 'as smooth as marble', owing to the safeguards of enshrining it

Yamabushi

This plate is an attempt to reconstruct the appearance of the members of the Shugendō sect, the *yamabushi*, as they would have appeared in the sixteenth century. They are on pilgrimage in the Yoshino mountains and are paying homage before a statue of Fudō. Fudō is always represented with a fierce expression and surrounded by flames. In his right hand he holds a

sword to strike down demons, and in his left he holds a rope with which to bind them. The *yamabushi* themselves look unkempt, which is supported by contemporary descriptions of them, but they wear their traditional skull-cap and carry staffs. These, with the details of the robe, symbolise various aspects of Buddhist doctrine.

Successive pilgrimages such as these, which included performing rituals of prayer and fasting at

anciently defined sites, were a form of initiation into the mysteries of Shugendō. *Yamabushi* were therefore regarded as the possessors of mystical powers. They were believed to be able to cast out demons, to talk to animals and to overcome fire. The sect was suppressed at the end of the nineteenth century, but has since undergone a revival, and annual pilgrimages are now undertaken.

correctly in 1978, 33 years after his death? Seen in this light, the existence of Yasukuni Shrine is not a glorification of the past, but a safeguard for the future.

However, a different Buddhist view of death was provided by the 'mass movement' Amidist sects that developed during the thirteenth century. According to the sect called Jōdo Shinshū, on death the believer's spirit left the world immediately for Amida's paradise, which explains the fanaticism of the *ikki* armies of the Sengoku Period, who vanquished daimyō forces, secure in their belief that death in battle ensured instant heaven. But even though such beliefs about the dead appear contradictory, they were regarded as complementary, and were firmly rooted in Japanese tradition. For example, the spirit of Taira Masakado, who was killed in AD 940, is enshrined in the Kanda Myōjin shrine in Tōkyō. Masakado was a rebel against the Emperor, and during the Meiji Period, when the institution of the Emperor was being strengthened against the memory of the overthrown Shōgun, it was decided to move Masakado's spirit from the main shrine to a subshrine. When this was done, local people refused to go to the main shrine, and boycotted its annual festival, the reason being, apparently, that it was wisest to keep an unruly spirit pacified, and that if Masakado's spirit was deprived of its proper shrine, then it would start causing trouble again.

Nagahama castle
A modern reconstruction of the keep of Nagahama castle, which was originally built for Toyotomi Hideyoshi.

The yamabushi *light the sacred bonfire*
The climax of the *yamabushi*'s *goma* is the lighting of a huge bonfire in the centre of the courtyard. Strips of wood, containing petitions, are flung into the billowing white smoke that ensues.

Communication with the spirit world

Although the living had a duty to perform to the recently dead, there were benefits to be gained from the departed spirits, who could pass the barrier between our world and theirs. The Japanese medium, or *miko*, allowed the spirit to possess his or her body, and transmitted messages to the living. Closely related to the *miko* was the notion of the ascetic who acquired special powers, the best known of whom were the *yamabushi*, the followers of the religious sect of Shugendō. *Yamabushi* means 'he who lies in the mountains', and the term has often been applied erroneously to the armies of warrior monks who plagued Kyōto during the twelfth century. Yoshitsune's companion, the warrior monk Benkei, disguised himself and his companions as *yamabushi* to avoid detection during their flight from Yoritomo's vengeance in 1185.

The figure of the wild-looking, wandering *yamabushi* is one that crops up regularly in Japanese art and literature, and we noted earlier how Hōjō Sōun recruited a *yamabushi* as his *horagai* blower. A *yamabushi* was endowed with magical powers, acquired as a result of fasting, onerous climbs of sacred mountains, and various ascetic exercises, such as standing naked under waterfalls. The initiate was believed to have the power to cast out demons, to talk to animals, and to overcome fire. By the recitation of prayers, *yamabushi* could overcome and exorcise any *onryō*, the above-mentioned 'angry ghosts', that were causing trouble in a locality.

The *yamabushi* thus reflected a blending of the Buddhist, Shintō and animistic traditions which were outlined above. To a *yamabushi*, a mountain was not just the abode of the *kami* (the gods of Shintō): it was a Buddhist mandala – a sacred space separated from ordinary space and time. His climb was a spiritual journey as well as a physical one, and the disciple passed symbolically through the ten worlds of transmigration. Each of these states was negotiated by means of a rite, the ordeal representing hell being vividly described during the sixteenth century by a former *yamabushi* who had become a Christian. The ritual, called *gōhyō*, or 'weighing one's karma', consisted of the disciple being tied and seated on a beam projecting over a cliff, with a large rock as a counterweight. In this terrifying position, he was required to confess his sins to his fellow *yamabushi*. If he confessed all, his karma was lightened. If he refused, he would be tipped off into the valley below. The rite of the Hungry Ghosts, which followed, was fasting; of the Beasts: abstinence from water; and of the Asuras: *sumō* wrestling. Following the final rite for heaven, a sacred dance, the climber received a form of baptism, confirming his powers as a *yamabushi*.

The rituals of the *yamabushi* lasted, with little change, right through the time of the samurai, but with some reduction in the severity of the disciplines. Shugendō all but ceased to exist with the Meiji Restoration, but has since been revived, and I was privileged to join some modern *yamabushi* on an ascent of their holy Mount Ōmine in 1986.

There are numerous references in war chronicles to daimyō consulting *yamabushi*, and more orthodox priests. It was, in fact, quite common for daimyō of the Sengoku Period to become monks while continuing the profession of warlord. Takeda Shingen and Uesugi Kenshin are the prime examples, and their banners with Buddhist prayers were among their most treasured possessions. Other daimyō took a more sceptical view of religion.

'Fearing neither gods nor Buddhas' is a frequent phrase used to describe such iconoclasts, as in the legend of 'Hideyoshi's Bridge':

On the sacred mountain of Kōya-san, where lie the mausoleums of numerous daimyō, there are three bridges on the road that leads to the tomb of the saint Kōbō Daishi. According to tradition, the third bridge cannot be crossed by anyone whose morals are unacceptable to Kōbō Daishi, and a sinful person could not proceed further. After Hideyoshi had risen to the highest position in the Empire he made a ceremonial pilgrimage to the tomb of Kōbō Daishi. Knowing that during his career he had committed many acts of violence, Hideyoshi went to the third bridge the night before and made a trial crossing. Nothing happened, and relieved of the anxiety that he would be publicly embarrassed Hideyoshi returned to the bridge the following day and marched over it in a grand and contemptuous manner.

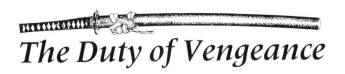

The Duty of Vengeance

If the loyalty due from a retainer to his daimyō was tremendous in life, it became all the more so after his death. But whereas *junshi* remained condemned for the larger part of samurai history, there was an entirely opposite requirement for revenge. Should one's lord die as a result of murder or other foul play, then a retainer's revenge was his by right. In fact, it went far beyond a right: it was a solemn duty, both sanctioned and practised at the highest levels of the samurai class.

The rules of vengeance

The notion of vengeance is inseparable from the ideals of the noble samurai. To the samurai, a man who took revenge was a man of honour; while he who shrank from this obligation was beneath contempt: a person to be despised more than the villain who had performed the original deed for which vengeance was sought. Such sentiments appear throughout samurai history, from the revenge of the Soga brothers at the time of the first Shōgun Minamoto Yoritomo in the twelfth century, to the classic epic of the Forty-Seven Rōnin (recounted in detail by me in *Samurai Warriors*).

The story of the Forty-Seven Rōnin, although the best-known outside Japan of any story of revenge, is not typical. The details, briefly stated, are that Lord Asano was required to commit *seppuku* as punishment for the crime of drawing a weapon within the Shōgun's palace, and wounding the

The revenge of the Soga brothers
The duty of revenge was found throughout samurai history, as illustrated by this wood-block print from the author's collection, which depicts the revenge of the Soga brothers during the twelfth century.

The Forty-Seven Rōnin
In this detail from one of many prints produced on the subject of the Loyal Retainers of Ako, the avenging rōnin engage the retainers of Kira in a fierce swordfight.

official who has been taunting him. His retainers, who survived him, hatched an elaborate plot of revenge in complete secrecy, turning to drunkenness and debauchery as a cloak for their intentions,which were achieved in a spectacular raid. Having taken the head of their lord's 'judicial murderer', they surrendered to the authorities, and committed suicide.

There are, in fact, very few examples in Japanese history of the murder of a daimyō and his subsequent avenging. Indeed, the Forty-Seven Rōnin is the only example of revenge being carried out in peace-time at such an elevated social level. This uniqueness probably accounts, to some extent, for the enduring popularity of the tale. It is also atypical in the secrecy with which the deed was carried out, which thereby put the avengers outside the law, and in the resulting condemnation by the authorities. The point illustrated by the Forty-Seven Rōnin is that, although revenge was central

The Forty-Seven Rōnin

The exploit of the Forty-Seven loyal retainers of Ako is vividly brought to life by this plate. They have arrived outside the gate of Kira's mansion. A dog is silenced for the split second before the enormous mallet crashes against the timbers of the gate. Their leader, Ōishi Yoshio, despatches men to the rear of the house.

Ōishi Yoshio was a pupil of the *bushidō* theorist Yamaga Sokō, and this expression of the loyalty to one's master due from a samurai is the best known practical illustration of *bushidō* in Japanese history. Yet even this famous raid was not without its critics. Yamamoto Tsunetomo, the author of *Hagakure*, a classic of *bushidō* writing which begins with the words 'The Way of the Samurai is found in death', praised the act of revenge on the grounds that it was the conduct to be expected, but went on to question the means whereby it was carried out. Yamamoto Tsunetomo was an adherent of the Wang Yang Ming school of Confucian philosophy, which taught that knowledge should always be accompanied by action, action that was swift and immediate. The revenge of the Forty-Seven Rōnin had been long in the planning, and Tsunetomo expressed surprise that it took so long for them to act. Dramatic acts of revenge were what appealed to men of such opinions, not a calculated and secretive plot such as that of the gallant Forty-Seven.

to the samurai philosophy, it must not be presumed that in carrying out revenge, a man was entirely free to do as he liked. Certainly, by the eighteenth century, the procedure of revenge was very clearly recognised.

If a deed was committed which required avenging, the avenger was required first to present a complaint to the daimyō, from whom he would get authorisation to search for and slay the enemy. This authorisation would be in the form of a letter certifying his identity, and indicating the name of his own *han* and the purpose of his search. After this, if everything had been carried out in perfect order, the particular way in which he slew his enemy was of no consequence, providing it was not attended by public disorder. Once the deed was done, the avenger was required to report immediately to the nearest authorities and explain the circumstances of his revenge. He would be interrogated on the details by the *machi-bugyō*, and asked the name of his family and of his *han*. He would then be required to present satisfactory proof that he had in fact been authorised to carry out the deed. Once his revenge was acknowledged as accomplished according to the rules, he was released from custody and walked away a free man, as in the account of the vengeance of the great swordsman, Miyamoto Musashi:

Miyamoto having encountered his enemy on the way, struck him and killed him. Having revenged himself in that manner, he narrated what he had done to the

Swearing vengeance before the lord's head
Retainers of a dead lord kneel in reverence before his severed head, swearing vengeance on his killer. Vengeance was the samurai's privilege and solemn duty.

The Mountains of Iga
The misty Mountains of Iga shelter
the town of Iga-Ueno, scene of the
Igagoe Vendetta.

*daimyō of the province, who instead of blaming him, congratulated him and sent
him back in security to his lord's territory.*

The duty of vengeance received its solemnest expression in the collection
of laws and recommendations referred to as the 'Legacy of Ieyasu', attributed to the first Tokugawa Shōgun, who died in 1616. The section dealing
with revenge is a later addition, but sums up beautifully the requirements
of the vendetta:

*In what is concerning the revenge to be exercised against the man who killed your
father or lord, it is expressly written by Confucius that you and your enemy cannot
live together under the same heaven.*

*In consequence of that, the man who has an act of revenge to do must first notify
it to the Court of Criminal Justice, which must neither prevent him from
accomplishing his desire, nor obstruct him in its execution. Whatever be the case, it
is prohibited to kill his enemy by raising troubles or in a riot.*

*The individual who revenges himself without notifying it to the Court of Criminal
Justice, must be considered as a wolf, and his punishment or pardon will depend on
the circumstances.*

The Igagoe Vendetta

Even though revenge for the death of a daimyō is a very rare event, there
are, however, many examples where a daimyō was intimately concerned

with a blood feud among his own retainers. The best example of this is the Igagoe Vendetta, which we shall study in some detail, because of the illustration it provides of the legal requirements surrounding the vendetta which we have outlined above.

The city of Ueno lies about 97 km (60 miles) due east of Ōsaka, among the wooded mountains of Mie prefecture. It is commonly called 'Iga-Ueno' (Iga being the name of the pre-modern province of which Ueno was the provincial capital) to distinguish it from the better-known Ueno, which is a district of metropolitan Tōkyō. Nowadays, Iga-Ueno is a mecca for tourists interested in the famous *ninja*, bands of whom had their headquarters in these remote valleys; but this is a modern phenomenon, and for centuries Iga-Ueno was known for a very different reason: as the site of one of the most dramatic acts of vengeance in Japanese history – the Igagoe Vendetta.

The Igagoe Vendetta has its origin in the incident when a certain Watanabe Gendayū was murdered by Kawai Matagorō, a retainer of the Okayama *han*. The Okayama *han*, which was under the control of the Ikeda family, had for some time been troubled by dissension among the samurai retainers, and between the retainers and the daimyō. The murder of Gendayū, which was in a sense the culmination of these troubles, happened on the night of the lively *Bon Odori* festival in 1630 in Okayama, the castle town which was the *han* capital, hundreds of kilometres from Iga-Ueno on the shores of the Inland Sea. That night, Matagorō, accompanied by some companions, was visiting Kazuma, a retainer of his comrades. Kazuma's younger brother, Gendayū who was keeping him company, was absent at that precise moment. Somehow a brawl developed. Matagorō and his associates mortally wounded Gendayū and took flight. Gendayū died very shortly afterwards, while Kawai Matagorō ran away from Okayama and went to Edo.

At this point in the story, we note the involvement of the daimyō. Watanabe Kazuma, who now had the responsibility of avenging his brother, was only 16 years old, and at first seems to have hoped that the Ikeda daimyō would bring Matagorō to justice on his behalf. But relations within the *han* had become so strained that Matagorō was safe in Edo, where a comrade, called Andō Jiemon, eagerly sheltered him. Even the daimyō himself, Ikeda Tadao (1602–32), could not enter unannounced, but hoped that, by employing various stratagems, he could capture Kawai Matagorō, who had caused him a great deal of trouble in the past. A raid was, in fact, carried out, but was seriously bungled. The attackers overcame Andō Jiemon but let Matagorō escape.

Before long, Ikeda Tadao died of a disease, smarting from the humiliation caused him by this public evidence of dissension among the retainers. Such was his tenacity of purpose that his dying wish is supposed to have been: 'For my memorial service, above everything else offer on my behalf the head of Kawai Matagorō.' His younger brother, Ikeda Teruzumi (1603–63), took to heart his elder brother's dying wishes, and relations among the retainers, some of whom openly supported Matagorō, increasingly took a dangerous turn. The be-all and end-all was the existence of Watanabe Kazuma, who sought revenge, and whose unfulfilled desires acted as a goad.

Eventually, the *bakufu* stepped in and officially ordered the exile of Kawai Matagorō. As it was the Shōgun's orders, a samurai had to submit, and by this preserve the honour of the Okayama *han*. This was Kazuma's

Araki Mata'emon
Araki Mata'emon, a swordsman of
the Yagyū Shinkage-ryū, became the
hero of the Igagoe Vendetta when he
helped his brother-in-law, Watanabe
Kazuma, to track down and kill
Kawai Matagorō.

opportunity. He was now 18 years old and able to save his own honour as
well as that of the Okayama *han*, so he applied to the Ikeda family for
discharge and, with official approval, began to search everywhere for
Kawai Matagorō.

Kazuma left the service of the Ikeda family in the ninth month of 1632.
At the end of much hardship and long journeying, he located Kawai
Matagorō, in the eleventh month of 1634, in the neighbourhood of Iga-
Ueno. By now Watanabe Kazuma had been joined in his revenge by his

sister's husband, Araki Mata'emon, one of the foremost swordsmen of the day. We know that Araki Mata'emon was a swordsman of the celebrated school of fighting called the 'Yagyū Shinkage-ryū' and had been taught by Yagyū Mitsuyoshi. He served the Matsudaira family of Yamato-Koriyama and gave instruction in *kenjutsu*, and seems to have combined good intelligence with swordfighting skill, as related by an anecdote about Mata'emon fighting a swordsman called Yamada Shinryūkan. This Shinryūkan's favourite weapon was the *kusari-gama*, which consisted of a very sharp sickle, to the handle of which was attached a long weighted chain. The skill in using the *kusari-gama* was to whirl the chain at high speed, thus either keeping a swordsman at bay or entrapping his sword. The weight could also be spun to catch the opponent's leg and pull him over. When faced by this weapon, Araki Mata'emon enticed his enemy into a bamboo grove, where the *kusari-gama* could not be used effectively, and overcame him.

Sometime during the period of Kazuma's quest for revenge, Araki Mata'emon took his leave of the Matsudaira *han*, and volunteered his services as his brother-in-law's 'second'. The alliance caused great consternation among Matagorō and his followers, for one of their number had once been defeated by Mata'emon in a fencing match.

On the seventh day of the eleventh month of 1634, Watanabe Kazuma,

The Kagiya crossroads at Iga-Ueno
The scene of the Igagoe Vendetta is marked nowadays by this stone at the Kagiya crossroads in Iga-Ueno.

Araki Mata'emon and two others waited for Kawai Matagorō's faction in Iga-Ueno. They had been reliably informed that Kawai Matagorō was *en route* from Ōsaka to Ise, a journey that would take them through Iga-Ueno. That morning the road was frozen. At the Hour of the Dragon (8 am), Mata'emon and followers entered a shop belonging to a certain Yorozu Yakiemon at the Kagiya Crossroads in Iga-Ueno, and waited for Matagorō's party to arrive along the road from Ōsaka. One man of their party stood guard. The time passed very slowly. Apparently Matagorō's uncle, Kawai Jinzaemon, complained of a chill, and their pace had slackened, so they entered Iga town later than Mata'emon had anticipated.

In one of several novels written about the incident, Mata'emon's guard whispers 'They have come!', keeping his voice as low as possible. Mata' emon and his followers leave the shop and line up at the crossroads; then in a gesture towards samurai honour, Mata'emon returns alone to the shop to settle the account of one *sen*. No doubt this incident is included to show the great swordsman's attention to the mundane, and to demonstrate his desire not to be troubled by money during such a great affair. It is also a fact that by this gesture of honesty towards his host, thereby disregarding the chance of being killed within the next few minutes, he would show himself as a samurai who was a defender of the law. This was of crucial importance. The whole of the vendetta had to be carried out according to the spirit and the letter of the law.

The Igagoe Vendetta
A vigorous wood-block print depicting the vengeance of Watanabe Kazuma at Iga-Ueno.

The six-hour blood feud

The law prevailed right through the conflict that followed. Mata'emon first struck the old Jinzaemon, and also killed the followers who were surrounding Matagorō. (The story as it has grown puts the number slain by Mata'emon at 36). But Mata'emon had decided that he did not intend to kill Matagorō. Kazuma was the one to do that, as the law demanded, so Mata'emon pushed Matagorō to Kazuma's side. He himself patiently joined his companions and did not invite them to join in. The Igagoe Vendetta was, in essence, a duel between Kazuma and Matagorō, and nothing must inconvenience it, nor must there be unnecessary deaths.

The duel between Kazuma and Matagorō continued for six hours until the Hour of the Ram (2 pm). Both became so weakened in mind and body that they could not even see their opponent. Nevertheless Mata'emon did not intervene. In a hoarse voice, he encouraged Kazuma, and at one point was able to head off Matagorō from˝ scaping. Discipline was also maintained by Matagorō's side, who had supported him during his exile. There was an equal need for their side to be seen to be behaving according to the law and the dictates of samurai honour. If Matagorō behaved in accordance with the wishes of the Emperor, he might regain the daimyō authority following a victory. So he made a desperate effort. Much more than samurai honour was at stake.

By now the sun was sinking in the west, and the area around the Kagiya crossroads was dotted with corpses, and only Kazuma and Matagorō's

The Erin-ji
The temple of repose of Takeda Shingen, one of the greatest of the Warlords of Japan, as seen from its magnificent garden.

violence could be heard. But a resolution of the combat was not far away. Kazuma hit home on Matagorō, and just before Matagorō responded, Kazuma's sword cut the artery in Matagorō's left arm. Half of Matagorō's body was dyed with blood, and as he fell Kazuma dealt him a decisive and final blow to the neck.

To the bitter end, the law had priority, and the duel at the Kagiya crossroads became famous as a legal duel, ending as it had begun. Mata'-emon and the others carried out the appropriate procedures afterwards, and surrendered themselves to the local Tōdō han. They had fulfilled the legal requirements to the very end. There was no riot, and Mata'emon and the others had not killed people indiscriminately. Their operation had been conducted within the limits laid down by law.

The Kameyama Vengeance

One important aspect of the Igagoe Vendetta is that the revenge killing was actually carried out by the immediate kin of the murdered man. Should this prove impossible – the passage of time, for example, preventing such an act from taking place – then the duty of revenge passed from that man to his son, and on, theoretically, until the final generation, when revenge could be gained. The outstanding example of this is the Kameyama Vendetta, which, unlike the Forty-Seven Rōnin and the Igagoe Vendetta, is virtually unknown outside Japan.

On the morning of the ninth day of the fifth month of 1701, beneath the

---

The flags of the Takeda family

In this plate are shown the flags of Takeda Shingen and those of his 'Twenty-Four Generals' of which details have survived.

They include the large standards of the Takeda family, passed from father to son (which are described in the text), the centipede flag of the messengers, Shingen's personal *uma-jirushi* of three 'flowery-edged' *mon*, and the flag with three *mon* which identified Shingen's personal retainers.

The blue flags of Anayama Baisetsu (d. 1582) (drawn to scale) illustrate the range of flags available to one of Shingen's generals. As Anayama is in the *shinrui-shū*, i.e. the 'relatives', the large *sashimono* worn by his mounted samurai and the smaller one worn by those on foot bear the Takeda *mon*. The long *nobori* and *uma-jirushi*, however, have the same coloured ground, but an individual device. The same would apply to the others of the 'Twenty-Four Generals' illustrated here who were family members, namely the two Takedas. Itagaki and

Ichijō. With the others we may assume that the device that appears on the *uma-jirushi* appears also on the *sashimono* and the *nobori*.

The other flags are the personal *uma-jirushi* of the 'Twenty-Four Generals'. As noted in the text, the term is not a contemporary one, nor were they all active over the same period. In some cases the colours of the flags are controversial. Reading from left to right:

Top row: Kōsaka Danjō Masanobu, Omari Torayasu (killed at Ueda, 1548), Takeda Nobukado (brother of Shingen; design also shown as black on white), Takeda Nobushige (killed at Kawanakajima 1561) and also his son Nobutoyo, Yamamoto Kansuke (killed at Kawanakajima 1561)

Second row: Tada Mitsuyori (d. 1563), Tsuchiya Masatsugu (killed at Nagashino 1575), Obu Toramasa ('red regiment', executed 1565), Obata Toramori (d. 1561), Okiyama Nobutomo (killed 1575)

Third row: Oyamada Nobushige, Sanada Yukitaka (d. 1574), Yokota

Takatoshi (killed 1550), Saigusa Moritomo (killed at Nagashino 1575), Obata Masamori (son of Toramori, d. 1582)

Fourth row: Ichijō Nobutatsu (Shingen's brother), Itagaki Nobukata (killed at Ueda 1548), Anayama Baisetsu, Hara Masatane (killed at Nagashino 1575), Sanada Nobutsuna (son of Yukitaka, killed at Nagashino 1575)

Fifth row: Yamagata Masakage (brother of Obu Toramasa, who inherited the 'red regiment', killed at Nagashino 1575), Naitō Masatoyo (killed at Nagashino 1575), Baba Nobuharu (killed at Nagashino 1575; alternative design has flag black on white, as shown in frontispiece), Hara Toratane (died 1564)

Not illustrated here are the flags of Takeda Katsuyori, Shingen's heir, who had two *uma-jirushi*, each bearing the character ō meaning 'great', one white on black, the other reversed, and Morozumi Masakiyo. whose flag was light blue with the family *mon*.

313

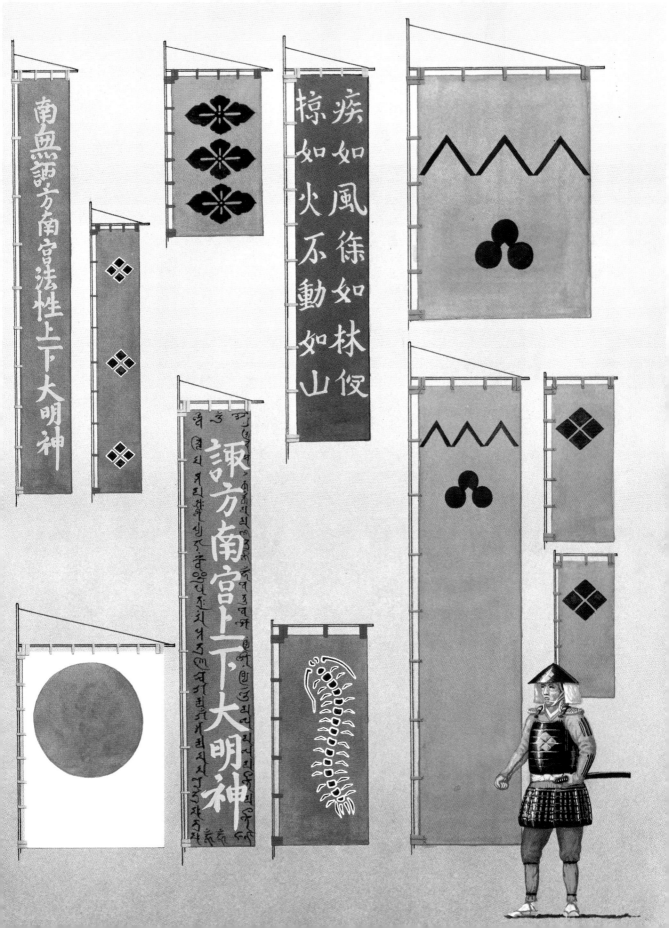

Ishigaki gate inside Kameyama castle, Akabori Sui-no-suke, a retainer of Itagaki Shigefuyu, the keeper of Kameyama castle, was heading for guard duty when his attendant heard the voices of two men, and a sword stroke was brought down from his forehead to his neck. As he fell, the two men gave him a finishing stroke. After this, they tied a message by a cord to Sui-no-suke's *hakama*, and departed calmly, the deed having been accomplished. Some retainers of the Kameyama *han* spotted them and chased after them, but the two men got away. According to the message, the two men who murdered Akabori Sui-no-suke were Morihei, a sandal bearer, and Hanemon, an attendant, and it became clear that they had killed the man who had killed their father. They had carried out this vengeance, they wrote, in accordance with the traditions of the samurai class, and after a wait of an amazing 28 years!

Their late father, one Ishii Uemon, was a samurai who received a stipend of 250 *koku* as a retainer of the keeper of Komoro castle, in Shinano. On the twenty-ninth day of the third month of 1662, his overlord agreed that he should become the warden of Ōsaka castle, and he moved to Ōsaka together with his four sons. This Uemon was a friend of a *rōnin* from Otsu in Ōmi province, called Akabori Yugen, and he was asked if Yugen's adopted son, Gengoemon, might come and study in Ōsaka. Uemon gave his whole-

Journey on the Nakasendō
To seek vengeance, a samurai would wander for years along the roads of Japan in search of his quarry.

316

hearted consent, and summoned Gengoemon to Ōsaka, on the understanding that he applied himself diligently to the martial arts.

However, this Gengoemon was an arrogant young man, and showed little progress in skill when he began instruction in spear fighting with the assembled pupils. On being reprimanded by Ishii, Gengoemon got very angry and challenged him to a contest. Ishii Uemon reluctantly agreed to a contest with wooden swords, but Gengoemon used a real spear, yet was easily defeated. As a result, Gengoemon lost face with his fellow pupils and, when the opportunity presented itself, he murdered Uemon and fled.

Uemon's son, Hyōemon, was 18 years old at the time, and personal retainer to the daimyō Munetoshi. That night he was on guard duty, and on learning of his father's death he applied for leave of absence, and set off in search of revenge. However, the enemy was nowhere to be seen. A long search began, and that winter Hyōemon killed Gengoemon's father Akabori Yūgen in Otsu, hoping thereby that Gengoemon would make an appearance; but he did not turn up. That act made Gengoemon also thirst for revenge for *his* father, and he tracked down Hyōemon to a bath house. Gengoemon attacked him suddenly from behind. Hyōemon drew his sword at the same time and thrust for his thigh, but a deep wound from the first swordstroke led to his death.

The defence of Chihaya castle
One of the most celebrated acts of defiance in samurai history was the defence of Chihaya castle by Kusunoki Masashige and his tiny army. In this section from a painted scroll, owned by the Nampian Kannon-ji at Kawachi-Nagano, the defenders set fire to a bridge.

Thereupon, the duty of revenge passed to his younger brother, and Uemon's second son, Hikoshichiro, set out on a quest for vengeance, but ill luck led to his early death. Two young children were left, who were being cared for by a relative called Aki. The third son, Genzō, was 6, and the fourth son, Hanzō, only 3. Gengoemon felt a sense of relief because the remaining sons were just young children, but a relative who was a retainer of Itagaki, the keeper of Kameyama castle, nevertheless recommended vigilance, and proposed that he should enter the service of the Itagaki. Gengoemon was given a stipend of 150 *koku*, and changed his name to Akabori.

Through Aki, Genzō and Hanzō nurtured their desire for revenge, and through him also heard of their enemy's change of name and that he had become a retainer at Kameyama. Genzō was not yet 14, but wanting to comply with the wishes of his family, he sent Aki on a quest for revenge. He came to Kameyama and sighted Sui-no-suke, but there was no way to sneak into the castle, and he spent an ineffective day. In 1688, the youngest son, Hanzō, became 17, and the brothers felt confident enough to take matters into their own hands. Leaving Aki behind, the two went to Edo, and studied the comings and goings of the Itagaki clan on the *sankin-kōtai*, disguised as pedlars. Then they got the chance to serve Hirai Zaiemon, a senior retainer of the Itagaki daimyō. At the time, when Zaiemon was to accompany his overlord on the *sankin-kōtai*, the two Ishii brothers went along as *chūgen*. No sooner had they begun to rejoice on being able to enter the castle than Zaiemon unfortunately died a natural death, and they saw their enemy departing for Edo, while they were unable to prevent it. However, their lowly service had at least brought them within the circle of the Itagaki retainers. Genzō changed his name to Morihei, and Hanzō to Hanemon, and impressed the *bugyō* by their soberness. Soon they grew to have the confidence of the castle family. The two frequently met and talked about their revenge, and as fellow retainers they kept watch on their enemy, Akabori Sui-no-suke.

Then came the day of realising their ambition. In the morning of the ninth day of the fifth month of 1701, at the Hour of the Dragon, 8 am, Akabori Sui-no-suke was making his way under the Ishigaki gate, accompanied by his sandal bearer. The brothers came up from behind and shouted simultaneously, 'We are the sons of Ishii Uemon, Genzō and Hanzō, and you are our father's enemy Akabori Gengoemon. Fair Play!' They cut him from forehead to neck. Sui-no-suke unsheathed at the same time, but the wound was too severe, and he fell. Sui-no-suke's sandal bearer fled. The two brothers tied the message to his *hakama*, fled from Kameyama and wrote a letter to their family, expressing satisfaction at the outcome. Then they went to Edo via the Nakasendō, and reported to the *machi-bugyō*, but neither received any punishment for their deed. Instead, because of the talent they had shown, they were enlisted by Aoyama Tadashige, keeper of Hamamatsu castle in Tōtōmi, and were each given a stipend of 250 *koku*.

The Revenge of the Daughters

Let us conclude this account of the duty of vengeance by noting that its requirements were by no means confined to the male line of a family. Once again, the most celebrated example is practically unknown outside Japan.

A woman's revenge
The duty of revenge was not confined to the male line of a family. On occasions, as shown by this illustration from the *Ehon-Taikō-ki*, a woman could revenge her lord in dramatic fashion.

The courtyard of the Keitoku-In
The site of the passing of the last of the Takeda warlords, Katsuyori, the Keitoku-In shows many characteristics of the styles of dwellings with which the daimyō would have been familiar.

319

This is the vengeance of the two daughters, Miyagino and Shinobu. Popular accounts of this affair exist in many versions. The *kabuki* play *Gotai eiki shiro ishi banashi* is the result of the joint work of three persons, and, like most *kabuki* plays, is much embellished, particularly with romantic detail.

The factual basis of the story concerns a samurai, called Shiga Daishichi, who was on the run because of a misdemeanor and hid in a paddy-field in a village near Shiro-ishi-banashi, in Mutsu. By chance, he was observed by a farmer, Yomosaku, who had been transplanting rice seedlings, and in his surprise Shiga Daishichi panicked and killed the farmer. Yomosaku had two daughters, the eldest of whom, Miyagino, had (according to the more romantic versions of the tale) been engaged to be married, but through poverty had been sold into prostitution and become a *tayū*, a courtesan of the highest status in Yoshiwara, in Edo. The younger daughter, Shinobu, intending to tell her elder sister about her father's death, went to Edo from far away, and, not being familiar with the topography, she was helped by a person at the Kaminari gate of Asakusa. By chance, he was the master, Muneteru of the Okurosha, where Miyagino was employed. Shinobu was taken by Muneteru to the Okurosha, where she was teased by the girls for her naïve provincialism. Her Mutsu accent revealed her to her sister, so the girls met, and Shinobu recounted their father's untimely last moments.

In the *kabuki* play, she says: 'The man who did it has been captured by our uncle the village headman.' Miyagino, too, when she knew of her father's death, said: 'Such an event brings my tears, . . . let us pray that our requests be granted. . .' The audience expresses sympathy at this scene, one of the great tear-jerkers of the *kabuki* stage. At all events, the two daughters, Miyagino and Shinobu, secretly slipped away from Yoshiwara in order to seek revenge for their father's death, and began to study the martial arts under the guidance of Miyagino's samurai fiancé. They were eager in their pursuit of knowledge, and the result was the vengeance on their father's enemy, Shiga Daishichi, in 1649.

The girls were determined to carry out the revenge themselves. When the time was ripe, they went through the formalities of asking their daimyō overlord for authorisation to avenge the death of their father. There was, in this case, no need for a long search for the enemy, as he had remained in the daimyō's service. The lord accordingly ordered him to be brought before him, and, according to the popular accounts, the girls set on him there and then. Miyagino was armed with a *naginata,* the long curve-bladed polearm which by the Edo Period had become the traditional weapon for women. Shinobu wielded a *kusari-gama,* the sharpened sickle to which was attached a long weighted chain. With the aid of the chain, Shiga Daishichi's sword was rendered ineffectual, and the other sister finished him off with her *naginata.*

This remarkable duel, carried out in front of the approving daimyō and his senior retainers, has proved a popular theme for wood-block prints. In the *kabuki* play *Shiro-ishi-banashi,* Miyagino is freed from servitude as a courtesan and is united with her fiancé, and lives happily ever after.

Exposure of heads
Wax dummies at the Toei-Uzumasa Film Studios remind us of the surest proof of a samurai's loyal service: to bring back the severed head of his enemy.

The end of vengeance

The above examples serve to illustrate how the notion and duty of revenge

Vengeance
This crude fragment from a *kawaraban*, or broadsheet, depicts a revenge killing, probably that of Miyagino and Shinobu. *Kawaraban* were the forerunners of modern Japanese newspapers, and often featured vendettas in their accounts of contemporary life.

was a feature of samurai culture from the earliest times. The Meiji Restoration dealt the death-blow to the tradition of samurai revenge, as it was to do to so many aspects of the warrior tradition. The imperial decree forbidding revenge was issued in February 1873, and went as follows:

Assassination being absolutely prohibited by the law of the Empire, the Government's duty is to punish any individual who kills another.

According to ancient habits, it was an obligation on a son or a younger brother to revenge a father or elder brother, nevertheless, personal interest must not lead one to transgress the law and despise the public powers by revenging himself. Whoever so acts cannot be pardoned, the more especially because in that case it is impossible to know who is in the right and who in the wrong. Therefore from this day, no one shall have the right to avenge or pass judgement for himself. If unfortunately someone has done wrong towards a member of your family, take your complaint and explanations to the authorities, but do not follow the ancient custom, or you will be punished according to law.

There were many more decrees to come: the abolition of the wearing of the pigtail, the restriction of the wearing of swords to the armed forces, and soon the actual abolition of the name and class of samurai itself; but of all the new laws that took Japan into the modern world, none so eloquently reversed the duties of a previous age, and set at nothing the values of the 'Warlords of Japan'.

APPENDIX I
The 1559 Hōjō Register

The typical daimyō's retainer band was commonly divided into three main parts, namely: family members and relatives (which might include others regarded as equivalent to family because of a long and close relationship); *fudai*, the hereditary retainers of the family; and 'outsiders', either the surviving retainers of conquered enemies, the inhabitants of newly gifted lands or simply newcomers whose loyalty had yet to be tested. Allied families were usually placed in this category. There is often a separate unit for the daimyō's bodyguard, but its members tended to be recruited from the *fudai*.

The balance of evidence seems to be that only the troops furnished by the 'family members' category bore the family *mon* on their *sashimono*. The *fudai* and allies fought under the flag of their commander, and the daimyō's bodyguard and messengers usually had their own distinctive appearance.

The Hōjō register, the *Odawara-shū shōryō yakuchō*, listed the military

The Hōjō bodyguard
A samurai wearing the *sashimono* of the personal guard to the head of the family.

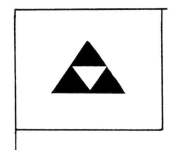

The personal standards of the Hōjō family (not to scale)
Upper left: the Hōjō *mon* in black on a very large white banner of *shihō* type (horizontal dimension exceeds vertical), used by Hōjō Ujiyasu; *right*: a long inscription (practically untranslatable!) in black on white, used by Hōjō Ujimasa; *lower left*: 'hachiman' in black on pale yellow, used by Hōjō Tsunanari.

322

The character mu

The character *mu*, which means 'nothing', is a popular device in Japanese heraldry. It appears within a black ring on the *uma-jirushi* of Sengoku Hidehisa (1551–1614), and here as the *uma-jirushi* of Hōjō Ujinao (1562–1591). According to Takahashi, an identical banner was used as a *sashimono* by Uesugi Kenshin up to about 1555. He presented it to Usa Sadayuki, his general in charge of the messenger unit, following one of the Battles of Kawanakajima (probably the second, in 1555).

obligation of the retainers of the Hōjō in 1559, under the third daimyō Hōjō Ujiyasu. There would also be a sizeable contribution to the army from the daimyō lands, which were not registered. Each of the retainers counted below would have had to supply men in accordance with the current compilation, which gives roughly 10,000 men. (The notes are the present author's observation.)

Unit Name	Notes, and prominent members	No. of retainers
Gokamon	('relatives', inc. heir Ujimasa, 2nd son Ujiteru, 3rd son Ujikuni)	17
Go-umawari-shū	('the daimyō's bodyguard')	94
Takoku-shū	('allies')	28

Units identified by geographical location —

Tamanawa-shū	(inc. Hōjō Tsunanari, Ujiyasu's adopted brother)	18
Miura-shū	(inc. Ujiyasu's 4th son Hōjō Ujimitsu)	32
Kotsuke-shū	(inc. Ujiyasu's 5th son Ujihide, adopted by the Uesugi in 1563)	29
Tsukui-shū	(inc. Naitō family)	57
Izu-shū	(inc. Kasawara family)	29
Matsuyama-shū	(inc. Kano family)	15
Edo-shū	(inc. Toyama family)	103
Odawara-shū	(inc. Matsuda family)	34

Other units

Ashigaru-shū		20
Temple land		28
Shrine land		13
Shokunin-shū	(craftsmen)	26
Total retainers listed		560

APPENDIX II
The 1575 Uesugi Register

This list is particularly interesting as, in addition to similar information to that for the Hōjō in Appendix I, it shows the various weapons to be supplied. The totals, from 39 names of retainers (simply classified as *ichimon*, family; *fudai*, inner retainers; and *kuni-shū*, country units) are as follows:

Mounted samurai	*600*
Foot-soldiers	
Spearmen	*4,899*
Flag bearers	*402*
Arquebuses	*360*
Reserves (inc. servants etc.)	*610*
Grand total:	*6,871*

The fine detail shows how the above proportions of one mounted to ten foot-soldiers are maintained throughout the army. As examples, for the family (*ichimon*) and family equivalent (*kakushō*), they appear as:

Name	Spears	Reserve	Arquebuses	Flags	Horsemen	Total
Uesugi Kagekatsu	250	40	20	25	40	375
Nagao Kagetori	106	15	10	10	15	156
Nagao Kagenobu	54	10	4	5	8	81
Sambonji Sadanaga	50	10	2	3	6	71
Kamijō Masashige	63	15	2	6	10	96
Murakami Kunikiyo	170	20	25	15	20	250
From among the eleven fudai *families*						
Matsumoto	101	15	13	13	16	158
Honjō	150	30	15	15	30	240
Yamayoshi	235	40	20	30	52	377
Naoe	200	30	20	20	35	305

Name	Spears	Reserve	Arquebuses	Flags	Horsemen	Total
From the kunishū, *well-known names are:*						
Nakajō	80	20	10	15	15	140
Irobe	160	20	12	15	20	227
Takemata	67	10	5	6	10	98
Kakizaki	180	30	15	15	20	260
Saitō	153	20	10	12	18	213
Shibata	135	20	10	12	17	194
Yasuda	60	15	5	5	10	95
Shimojō	32	10	2	3	5	52
Shimazu	58	10	6	7	10	91

The proportions and the overall numbers are very similar to an earlier, but less detailed, Uesugi Register of 1559. Combining this with contemporary accounts of the Fourth Battle of Kawanakajima it is possible to reconstruct the divisions of the Uesugi army at this encounter. (See my *Battles of the Samurai* for a detailed account of the fighting).

Forward troops
Vanguard: Kakizaki, Shibata, Shimazu
Second rank: Suibara, Takemata, Saitō
Third rank: Suda, Matsumoto, Shimojō

Headquarters troops
Takanashi, Ōgawa, Ayukawa, Inoue, Murakami, Watauchi
Irobe (*gun-bugyō*), Usa (messengers)

Flanks
Right: Yamayoshi, Shibata, Kaji
Left: Nagao, Yasuda, Honjō

Rear-guard
Nakajō, Koshi, Ozaki

Support
Amakazu (who held the ford at Amenomiya), Naoe (supplies)

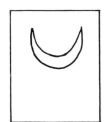   

 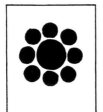  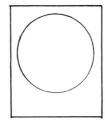

   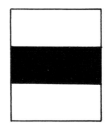

  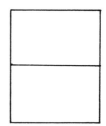

The personal standards of the Uesugi generals

Depicted here are the remaining known designs of flags used by Uesugi Kenshin's generals which are not shown elsewhere in the plates in this book. All are in black and white except where noted. Reading from left to right:

Top row: Suibara (white on red), Saitō, Takemata, Matsumoto

Second row: Nagao (dark blue on white), Yasuda, Usa, Irobe (red on white)

Third row: Yamayoshi (red disc, black inscription), Ayukawa, Inoue, Amakasu

Fourth row: Naoe, Nakajō (retainers' *sashimono*), Murakami, Sambonji (white over red)

APPENDIX III
Takeda Shingen

The following list is taken from the *Kōyō Gunkan*, showing the obligation to the Takeda Shingen by family, hereditary retainers and newly acquired vassals:

Name	No. of horsemen	Name	No. of horsemen
Family members		Ōyamada Nobushige	250
Takeda Nobutoyo (son of Nobushige)	200	Amari	100
		Kurihara	100
Takeda Nobukado (brother of Shingen)	80	Imafuku	70
		Tsuchiya	100
Takeda Katsuyori (heir)	200	Akiyama	50
		Hara Masatane	120
Ichijō Nobutatsu (brother of Shingen)	200	Ōyamada Bitchu no kami	70
Takeda Nobuzane (brother of Shingen, killed at Nagashino)	15	Atobe	300
		Others (four names in total)	255
Takeda Zaemon (cousin of Shingen)	100		
Nishina	100	*Ashigaru taishō*	
Mochizuki	60		
Katsurayama	120	30 names, commanding 255 horsemen, 785 *ashigaru* in all	
Itagaki Nobukata (killed at Ueda, 1548)	120		
		Semposhū (by province)	
Kiso	200	Shinano (includes Sanada family)	2020
Anayama Baisetsu	200		
		East Kozuke	1035
Fudai		Suruga	430
		Totomi	320
Baba	120	Hida	150
Naitō	250	Etchu	170
Yamagata	300	Musashi	180
Kōsaka	450		

Navy (41 ships, no numbers of crew given)

Shingen is also said to have had a bodyguard of 6,373, though whether these were drawn from the above or were his direct retainers is difficult to say. It seems a very large figure, even for such an important daimyō.

APPENDIX IV
Hashiba Hideyoshi

In 1573, following the defeat of the Asai family, Hashiba (later Toyotomi) Hideyoshi achieved a certain degree of independence from Oda Nobunaga by being granted in fief the castle of Nagahama. The details of his troops and their heraldry are interesting in providing a 'snapshot' of the future *Taikō* at one stage of his rise to glory. Unfortunately there are no numbers or weaponry given.

His *uma-jirushi* was a single golden gourd. Takahashi Ken'ichi, in his book *Hata Sashimono*, devotes several pages to a discussion of whether or not Hideyoshi ever did adopt the famous 'thousand-gourd standard', and notes that as late as 1575 only one gourd is to be seen. (This is on the famous painted screen of the Battle of Nagashino.)

His retainer band organisation follows the pattern common to many daimyō. There are the *ichimon-shū* (relatives), the *fudai-shū* and the *shinzan-shū* (literally 'newcomers'). This latter group is divided geographically by province, giving the Omi, Mino and Owari-*shū*, and includes such names as Ishida Mitsunari (Omi) and Yamauchi Kazutoyo (Owari).

The *fudai-shū* included a seven-man contingent who formed Hideyoshi's personal bodyguard known as the 'yellow *horō-shū*'. (Compare Nobunaga's use of black and red *horō* in his army.) Their numbers were later raised to 22.

Hideyoshi's messengers, 29 in all, were distinguished by an identical gold-coloured flag (see illustration).

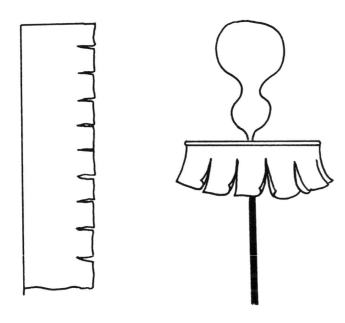

Hideyoshi's flags
These sketches illustrate the golden gourd standard, with its golden flag, and the style of flag used as a *sashimono* by Hideyoshi's messengers.

APPENDIX V
The Ii 'Red Devils'

The troops of Ii Naomasa and his son Naotaka, the most loyal of the Tokugawa *fudai*, formed an important part of the Tokugawa army at Sekigahara and at Ōsaka, and provide the most striking illustration of a *fudai* contingent adopting its own distinctive colours. The *Iika Gumpō*, quoted by Takahashi, gives the full regulations for the appearance of this army, to a degree of detail that is quite unique. Takahashi gives no date for the document, but it probably dates from the early seventeenth century.

Item, the standard is a 5-shaku [1 shaku = 1 foot] length of four widths of silk. On a red ground, the mon, *which is the character 'i' in gold in the centre. The pole is lacquered black.*

*Item, personal large banner [*nobori?*] is two widths of silk, 1 jō [9 feet] long. The* mon *on red ground. By invitation, on a 7-shaku length, on a red ground, the characters 'Hachiman Dai Bosatsu' in white. The pole is lacquered black.*

Item, the uma-jirushi *is a gold fly-catcher, with a black-lacquered pole.*

Item, mounted samurai, on a 5-shaku length of two widths of silk, on a red ground the surname written in gold.

Item, retainers' personal flags the same, excepting that by invitation the family mon *in white on a red ground.*

Item, ashigaru's back-flags, three, each of one width of silk, 5 shaku long, immediate ashigaru *a red field with no* mon, *retainers the* mon *of the family of birth in white.*

Item, armour, harness, saddle and stirrups to be red, with the exception that retainers may display in gold the mon *of their family of birth.*

Note how much the heraldry adopted depends on the nature of the relationship, such as being a retainer or a warrior directly commanded by the lord. The regulations fit almost exactly with the figures depicted on the painted screen depicting the Ii army at Ōsaka. Using a rule of thumb of two mounted and twenty foot-soldiers per 1,000 koku the Ii contingent at Ōsaka would have consisted of about 20 and 200 men respectively, plus their own followers. On the screen appear the 19 mounted samurai, of whom 9 wear red *horō*. There are 123 samurai on foot, mostly armed with long spears. Nearly all have inscriptions in gold, which must be the surnames referred to above, though one or two have *mon*. There are 50 *ashigaru*, of whom 19 have arquebuses.

Bibliography

Ackroyd, Joyce, 'Women in Feudal Japan', *Transactions of the Japan Society of London*, 1957.

Asakawa, Kan'ichi, *The Documents of Iriki*, Yale University Press, 1929.

Baba, Ichiro, *Heike Monogatari Emaki*, Taiyō special edition, winter 1975, Heibonsha, Tokyo, 1975.

Birt, M.P. 'Samurai in passage: the transformation of the sixteenth century Kanto' *Journal of Japanese Studies*, 1985 **11**: 369–399

Birt, M.P. *Warring States: A Study of the Go-Hojo Daimyo and Domain*, Ph.D. Thesis, Princeton University, 1983

Brownlee, J.S. 'The Shokyu War and the political rise of the warriors' *Monumenta Nipponica*, **24**: 59–77

Caron, François, *A True Description of the Mighty Kingdoms of Japan and Siam*, C. R. Boxer, London, 1935.

Elison, G. & Smith, B.L. *Warlords, Artists and Commoners*, University of Hawaii Press, 1981

Hall, J.W. (ed.) *Japan Before Tokugawa*, Princeton University Press, 1981

Inoue, Toshio, *Kenshin to Shingen: Nihon Rekishi shinshō*, Tokyo, 1977.

Kobayashi, Keiichiro, *Kawanakajima no tatakai*, Nagano, 1985.

Kōsaka Danjō (attributed to), *Kōyō Gunkan*, in *Sengoku shiryō-shū*, series 1, Vols. 3–5.

Kuwada Tadachika (editor), *Sengoku Bushō no shōkan*, Tokyo, 1968.

Kyūan, Rōjin, *Uma-jirushi*, Edo, 1655.

Matsumoto, Tamotsu, *Kassen Enki Emaki. Taiyō Classics and Picture Scroll Series IV*, Heibonsha, Tōkyō, 1979.

Miura Jōshin (attributed to), 'Hōjō Godaiki', in *Hōjō Shiryō-sō-shō*, series 2, Vol. 1.

Nakamura, Shinju, 'Taiheiki', illustrated in *Taiyō Monthly*, 178, February 1978.

Sachiya H., and Yamamoto, S., 'Kūki to shite no Yasukuni', *Shokun*, April 1986.

Sadler, A.L., 'Heike Monogatari', *Transactions of the Asiatic Society of Japan*, Vol. 46, No. 49, Yokohama, 1918 and 1921.

Sanford, J.H. 'Shakuhachi zen' *Monumenta Nipponica*, **32**: 411–440

Sasama, Y. *Zukai Nihon Katchu Jiten*, Tokyo, 1973

Sasama, Y. *Zuroko Nihon no Katchu Bugu Jiten*, Tokyo, 1978

Sasama, Y. *Buke senjin sahō shu¯sei,* Tokyo, 1968.

Sugiyama, H. 'Sengoku daimyo' *Nihon no Rekishi,* Vol. II Tokyo, 1971

Sugiyama, Hiroshi, *Hōjō Sōun,* Odawara, 1976.

Sugiyama, Hiroshi, *Sengoku daimyō (Nihon no Rekishi 11),* Chuo Koronsha, Tokyo, 1971.

Sugiyama, Kyushiro, 'Yasukuni no kiso chishiki jūhachi', *Shokun,* April 1986.

Takahashi, Ken'ichi, *Daimyōke no kamon,* Akida Shōten, Tokyo, 1974.

Takahashi, Ken'ichi, *Hata Sashimono,* Akida Shōten, Tokyo, 1965.

Takahashi, Ken'ichi, *Kamon, hatamoto, hachiman-ki,* Akida Shōten, Tokyo, 1976.

Takahashi, Masato, *Buke no jirushi,* Iwasaki Bijutsusha, Tokyo, 1979.

Turnbull, S.R. *Samurai Armies 1550–1615,* Osprey, 1979

Turnbull, S.R. *The Book of the Samurai,* Arms and Armour Press, 1982

Turnbull, S.R. *The Mongols* Osprey, 1980

Turnbull, S.R. *The Samurai – A Military History,* Osprey, 1977

Turnbull, S.R. *Warlords of Japan,* Sampson Low, 1979

Turnbull, S.R., 'Shorthand of the Samurai – the Use of Heraldry in the Armies of Sixteenth Century Japan', *Proceedings of the Japan Society,* London, 1989.

Turnbull, S.R., *Battles of the Samurai,* Arms and Armour Press, London, 1987.

Turnbull, S.R., *Samurai Armies 1550–1615,* Osprey, London, 1979.

Turnbull, S.R., *The Book of the Medieval Knight,* Arms and Armour Press, London, 1985.

Turnbull, S.R., *The Book of the Samurai,* Arms and Armour Press, London, 1982.

Turnbull, S.R., *The Lone Samurai,* Arms and Armour Press, London, 1990.

Turnbull, S.R., *The Mongols,* Osprey, London, 1980.

Turnbull, S.R., *The Samurai – A Military History,* Osprey, London, 1977, 1988.

Turnbull, S.R., *Warlords of Japan,* Sampson Low Library of the Past, 1979.

Varley, H.P. *The Onin War,* Columbia University 1967

Yoshida, Taiyo, *Kamon kakei jiten,* Shōbunsha, Tokyo, 1979.

Index

abortion, 268
abumi (stirrups), 1
adoption, 73–4
adultery, 268
Ainu, 10
Akamatsu
  Masanori, 60
  Mitsusuke, 48, 51
Akasaka, Siege of, 36, 41
Akechi Mitsuhide, 95, 96
Alternate Attendance, *see sankin-kōtai*
Ama-shogun, 29
Amakazu Kagemochi, 325
Amako, family of, 191
Amida, 293
Anayama Baisetsu, 201, 313–15, 327
Anegawa, Battle of (1570), 86–90
Arai Hakuseki, 242
Arai, Battle of (1518), 180
Araki Mata'emon, 309
archery, 9, 10, 26, 36
architecture, 227–36
armies:
  size of, 212, 324
  organisation of, 197, 209–22, 322–9
armour, construction of, 10, 16, 20, 25, 30, 48, 78, 82
armour, development and styles of (for definitions see text)
  dangaie-do, 100
  do-maru, 10, 14, 18, 22, 26, 55, 60, 75
  hara-ate, 44, 51
  haramaki, 36, 52, 66
  hotoke-do, 100
  mogami-do, 80, 82, 96
  namban-do, 116
  nuinobe-do, 96

okegawa-do, 68, 84
tanko, 16
tatami-gusoku, 92
yoroi, 1, 10, 22, 30, 32, 36, 144
armour, parts of
  agemaki (ornamental bow), 20, 36, 48, 100
  do (body armour) *see* Armour, styles of
  eboshi (cap worn under helmet), 1, 10, 22, 44
  fukigayeshi (helmet turnbacks), 14, 64
  hachimaki (headband), 88, 135
  haidate (thighguards), 36, 52, 55, 60, 80, 96, 144
  hoate (face-mask), 64
  kabuto, see Helmet
  kohire (padding for shoulders), 80
  kote (sleeve armour), 1, 10, 22, 44, 55, 63, 92
  kusazuri (plates suspended from *do*), 18, 55, 68, 100
  kuwagata ('horns' on helmet), 1, 36
  kyubi-no-ita (tying cord protector), 10, 48
  maedate (helmet badge), 80
  mempo (face mask), 80, 144
  nodowa (throat guard), 55, 66
  obi (belt), 17
  sashimono (banner on armour), 68, 75, 80, 100
  sendan-no-ita (tying cord protector), 10, 48
  sei-ita (back plate), 52
  shikoro (neck guard), 14, 48, 64, 92
  sode (shoulder plate), 14, 20, 48
  suneate (leg armour), 36, 60, 80, 96, 144

tabi (socks), 36
tehen (hole in crown of helmet), 10
tsurubashiri (breastplate of leather), 10
waraji (sandals), 36, 80
yodarekake (throat guard), 80, 144
yoroi-hitatare (armour robe), 22

arquebus, 84, 92, 95
arresting techniques, 246–7
art, appreciation of, 227–43
Asai
  Nagamasa, 80, 87
  Asakura Yoshikage, 87
Asai, family of, 80
ashigaru (footsoldier, 16th century), 62, 75
ashigaru, 186, 218–19, 329
ashigaru-taisho, 161, 186
Ashikaga
  Chachamaru, 178
  Masatomo, 178
  Takauji, 42, 44
  Yoshiaki, 83, 183
  Yoshiharu, 66
  Yoshikazu, 51
  Yoshimasa, 52, 176
  Yoshimitsu, 50, 176
  Yoshimochi, 51
  Yoshinori, 48, 176
  Yoshitane, 60
Ashikaga, family of, 42, 176
Azuchi, 230

Baba Nobuharu, 68, 161, 313–15, 327
baku-han (Shogun and local government), 124, 189
bakufu (Shogun's government), 26, 28, 34, 190, 239

banshō, 215
Banzuin Chōbe'e, 251–4
battle-cry, 211
Bishamon-ten, 201, 202
bodyguard, 220, *see also yō jimbō*
bō, 252
Buddhism, 293
bugei (martial arts), 9
bugyō, 198
Bunraku puppets, 242, 276
bushido (warrior's code), 17, 265, 303
call to arms, 206–7

cannon, 122
castle town, 231–6
castle, 70, 90–100, 124
   design, 186, 229–34
   building of, 179
cavalry, 186
ceremonies:
   of departure, 210–11
   of head inspection, 289, 290
   of victory, 222–6
Chihaya, 36, 41–3
chonin (townsman), 140–2, 239, 240
Christian samurai, 84–6, 102–8, 116, 130–4
chūgen, 289
club, iron, as weapon, 55
colour, use of in heraldry, 215, 216, 222, 326, 328–9
communications, 126–30
conch, *see horagai*
concubine, 268
corporal punishment, 250
crime prevention, 250
crime, 244–61
crucifixion, 250

daimyō (feudal lord), 55, 62, 63, 66, 67, 68–78, 124
   as administrator, 244–61
   as aesthete, 227–43
   as commander, 183, 187, 207, 209–26
   as focus of loyalty, 191, 208
   criminal equivalent of, 245–56
   definition of, 169, 173, 190
   rise to power of, 177
Dan-no-Ura, Battle of (1185), 26
Date feud, 239, 277–80
Date, family of, 277–80

Date:
   Aki Muneshige 118
   Hyōbu Munekatsu, 278
   Masamune, 277
   Tsunamune, 278
   Tsunamura, 278
death, beliefs about, 289–98
doso (merchant), 64
dōshin, 246
drum, 211, 227

earthquakes, 259
Edo, 115–6, 182, 232, 245–56
emishi (Barbarian), 10–13
Emperor, institution of, 25, 30
Erin-ji, 226
execution, 246, 287

fan, signalling, 86, 96
festivals, 204, 209–11, 216–20, 226, 262
fire, 258–61
firearms, 187, 223
firebombs, 38
firemen, 242, 258–61
flags, 75, 80, 84, 88, 119, 124; *see* heraldry
food, 197, 206, 211
footsoldiers, 22, 26, 30, 44
'Forty-Seven Rōnin', 302–5
fudai-daimyō, 190
Fuji, Mount, 176
Fukane, 224
Fukeshu, 152, 154
fundoshi (loincloth), 68

gambling, 254–8
games, 198
gang warfare, 250–61
gardens, 233, 238, 261
gekokujō, ('the low overcome the high'), 70–2, 174, 178
Gempei War, 18
Genroku Era, 239
geta, 175
Gifu, 82, 88
go, 198
go-hatamoto, 215
gun-bugyō, 206
Hachiman, god of war, 29
hairstyles, 140, 280
Hajikano Masatsugu, 161, 201, 221
hakama (trousers), 130, 132, 146–7, 156, 247

Hakone mountains, 174
Hakone Pass, 34
han (*daimyo*'s domain), 124, 189
haori (jacket), 72, 130, 142, 175
Hara Masatane, 68
hara-kiri, see suicide
Hara:
   Masatane, 175, 327
   Toratane, 218, 313–15, 327
Harada Kai, 278–9
Harumoto, 67–8
   Katsumoto, 60
   Masatomo, 60
   Sumimoto, 60
   Tadaoki, 128
Hashiba *see* Toyotomi
hatamoto-yakko, 251
head, revering a, 305
heads, collecting and ceremonies, 30, 34, 210, 222–5, 289
Heavenly King, 51–5
Heiji Monogatari emaki (scroll of Heiji War), 14
helmet, styles of, 1, 10, 14, 36, 92, 103, 124, 128

Imagawa, 71–8
   Ujichika, 178
   Yoshimoto, 71–8
   Yoshitada, 178
Inabayama, 82, 99
Inari, 233
Inuyama, 230–1
Inuzuka Morilake, 247–9
iro-iro odoshi (multicoloured armour braids), 100
Irobe Katsunaga, 206, 325–6
Ise Shinkurō Nagauji *see* Hōjō Sōun
Ishida Mitsunari, 119
Ishii Uemon, 316
Ishikawa gate, Kanazawa, 234, 273
Ishiyama Hongan-ji, 67, 90–2
Itagaki Nobutaka, 313–15, 327
Itakura Shigemasa, 132
Itsukushima, Battle of (1555), 71
Izu, invasion of, 173

jinbaori (surcoat), 103, 161
jingasa (footsoldier's helmet), 144, 222
jitō, 176
jitte, 246
Jokyu War, 30–6
jō, 252

jō shu , 198
Jōdō Shinshū, 298
jōkamachi, see castle town
junshi , 287

kabuki (theatrical art), 139, *239, 240–2*
kabuki as popular history, 272–4, 277–81, 320
Kagiya crossroads, 312
kago (palanquin), 127
kagura, 243
Kakitsu Rebellion, 52
Kakizaki Kagaie , 218
Kamakura, 20, 28, 34, 42–3, 176, 179
Kameyama, 98
Kameyama Vengeance, 313–17
kami (spirit of god), 22
kami-kaze (divine wind), 39
kami-shimo (samurai's formal costume), 146–7, 148, 192
kana, 216–17
Kanazawa, 186, 232–6, 273
kandaka, 198
kanjō, 224
kanshi, 286
Kantō, 174, 176
karō, 199, 215, 232
kashindan see retainer band
kataginu (type of jacket), 146, *192*
katana (standard fighting sword), *see* sword
Kato Kiyomasa, 100, 103
Kawagoe, 215
Kawai Matagorō, 308
Kawanakajima, Battle of (1561), 185, 201, 220, 325
Kawanakajima, Battles of (1553–64), 71
kebiki-edoshi (close-spaced lacing on armour), 25, 75
Keitoku-In, 319
kesa (monk's scarf), 64, 72
Kikkawa Tsuneie, 286
kimono (robe), 132, 146–7, 192
Kitabatake Mitsumasa, 51
ko-bakama (short form of *hakama*), 148
ko-uma jirushi, 195
Kobe, 25
Kofuku-ji, 24
koku (dry measure of volume, c.180 litres), 135, 197

komuso (wandering, flute-playing monk), 156
Kongo-san, 41
Konjaku Monogatari, 14
Korea, 103, 112–14
Koya-san, 84
Kōkokuji, 178
Kōnodai, Battle of (1538), 180
Kōnodai, Battle of (1564), 184
Kōsaka Danjō, 270, 313–15, 327
Kōyō Gunkan, 186, 200, 225, 327
Kōzuki, 195
Kublai Khan, 36
kumosuke, 238
Kunisada Chūji, 256
Kurikara, Battle of (1183), 24
Kuriyama Daisen, 280
Kuroda Nagamasa, 112
Kuroda:
  Nagamasa, 280
  Tadayuki, 280
kusari-gama, 310, 320
Kusunoki
  Jiro Masahide, 52
  Masashige, 36, 41
  Masatsura, 46, 50
  Mitsumasa, 51
Kusunoki Masashige, 177, 205, 317
Kusunoki, family of, 36
Kyōto, 43, 176
kyuba-no-michi (Way of Horse and Bow), 17
kyusen-no-michi (Way of Bow and Arrow), 17

land surveys, 197–8
Later Three Years' War, 10
Lotus Sect, 63
loyalty, 191–208, 265, 282
luck, belief in, 290

machi-bugyō, 245
machi-yakko, 251
Maeda
  Naomi, 274
  Toshiie, 234
  Yoshinori, 272
Maeda feud, 239, 270–4
Maeda Toshiie, 106
Maeda, family of, 236
Magome, 127, 238
maku (curtains round camp), 96
Manju-ji, Prince, 52
mansions, 234–6, 275

marriage, 73–4, 178, 264–5
Masa-ko, 28
Matsumae, family of, 236
Matsushiro, 235–7, 276
Matsuura, family of, 198
medium, communication through, 300
Meiboku Sendai Hagi, 239, 280
messengers, 220–2
Miidera, 22, 46
Mikata-ga-Hara, Battle of (1572), 91, 199
miko, 300
mikoshi (portable shrine), 22
Minamoto
  Kugyo, 30
  Noriyori, 28
  Sanetomo, 29
  Yoriie, 28–9
  Yorimasa, 22
  Yoritomo, 20, 26, 28, 29
  Yoshinaka, 14, 20, 24
  Yoshitsune, 1, 20, 24, 26, 28, 29
Minamoto, family of, 176
Minamoto, family of, 18, 20, 28–30
Minatogawa, Battle of (1336), 46–50, 177
Mito Mitsukuni, 268
Miura Yoshimoto, 91
Miura, family of, 180
Miyajima, 18
Miyamoto Musashi, 305
Miyoshi Yoshitsugu, 83
Mizuno Jūrōzaemon, 252
mon (family badge), 5, 87, 103
mon, 205, 215, 216, 239, 240
Mongol Invasion, 32, 36–9
Mori
  Motonari, 70
  Morinaga, Prince, 39
Mori, family of, 70–1
Morozumi Bungo-no-kami
  Masakiyo, 201, 283, 311
Mōri, family of, 194
Murakami Kunikiyo, 325–6
murder, 252, 256, 279, 308, 317, 320
musha-bashiri, 231
music, 227

Nagahama, 299
Nagakute, Battle of (1584), 98
Nagamachi, 234
Nagashima, 88–92

Nagashino, Battle of (1575), 84, 92, 217, 229
nagaya, 236
naginata (glaive), 14, 18, 52, 186, 320
Nagoshi Takaie, 41, 42
Naitō Masatoyo, 161, 311–13, 327
Nakae, 92
Nakajō Fujikashi, 202, 325–6
Nakasendō, 34, 237
Nambokuchō Wars, 50, 176
Nanjō Gemba-no-suke, 216
Naoe Kanetsuge, 325–6
Naruse Masakazu, 231
Nasu Munetaka, 26
Nihongi (early chronicle of Japan), 9, 10
ninja (hired assassin), 74, 95, 140, 143, 308
Nitta Yoshisada, 42–3
no ('noh') (formal play), 139
no-dachi (extra-long sword), 48
nobori, 212–22
Nozokito, 218
Nō, 228, 239, 242

O-ichi, 265
Obata:
    Masamori, 68, 313–15, 327
    Toramori, 313–5, 327
obi, 240
Obu Toramasa, 222, 313–5, 327
Oda
    Nobunaga, 75, 79-95
    Nobutada, 80
    Yuraku, 119
Oda Nobunaga, 188, 194, 213, 222, 264, 290, 328
Odaigahara, Mount, 54
Odani, 91, 229
Odawara, 80, 108, 112, 161, 178
Ōishi Yoshio, 303
Ōishi, 218
okegawa-dō, 222
Okehazama, Battle of (1560), 75–8
Okiyama Nobulomo, 313–15, 327
Ōmaeda Eigorō, 256
Omari Torayasu, 313–315
Ōnin War, 58–60, 177, 178
onryō, 295
organisation of armies, 74–5
Ōsaka, 194, 213, 222
Ōsaka Castle, 119, 122–3, 156
otokodate, 240, 250–4

Ōtsuki Denzō, 270–4
Ouchi Yoshitaka, 70
ō-uma jirushi, 213
Oyamada Nobushige, 201, 313–15, 327

pilgrimage, 300
piracy, 36
police, 245–50
post-stations, 127, 237
pottery, 228
poverty, 270
prisoners, treatment of, 195, 287
prostitution, 268–70

quiver, 22, 36

rake, used as weapon, 173
Regalia, Imperial, 26, 40, 50, 52, 54
reincarnation, 294
religious beliefs, 210, 291–301
Rennyo, 66
retainer band, 178, 195–200, 322–9; failure of, 205
revenge, 302–21
rewards, 222–5
rice, cultivation of, 174, 196
rockets, 214
Rokkaku Yoshisuke, 84
rōnin, (masterless samurai), 138, 251, 302 148, 151
Ronin, the, 47, 142–8
roshō, 215

Saigo Takamori, 154–6
Saigusa Moritomo, 313–15, 327
Saito, family of, 79–83
Sakai, Battle of (1567), 84
saké , 206
samurai, definition of, 9
samurai, elite status of, 9, 14, 25
Sanada
    Masayuki, 274
    Nobutsuna, 313–15
    Nobuyuki, 236
    Yukimura, 119, 274
    Yukitaka, 68, 274, 313–15
Sanada Taiheiki, 236
Sanada, family of, 235, 274–6, 327
sankin kōtai (Alternate Attendance System), 128, 135, 142, 236–8
Sasa Narimasa, 205
Sasagawa no Shigezō, 257
Sasaogawa, 161

sashimono, 161, 204, 209–22
Satomi Yoshitaka, 183
Satsuma Rebellion, 156
Sekigahara, Battle of (1600), 115, 119–22, 275
Sendaigawa, Battle of (1587), 100
Sengoku Hidehisa, 283, 323
sengoku-daimyō, 169
seppuku see suicide
sex, 262–71
shakuhachi (bamboo flute), 156
Shibata Katsuie, 84, 107, 110, 265
shield, 38
Shijo-Nawate, Battle of (1348), 46, 50
shikken (Regency of Hojo family), 29
Shimabara Rebellion, 130–4
Shimazu Norihisa, 218
Shimazu, family of, 197
Shimizu Muneharu, 285
Shimizu no Jirochō, 256
Shimmon no Tatsugorō, 260
Shimojō Saneyori, 202, 325–6
Shintō, 291–9
Shiro-ishi-banashi, 320
Shizugatake, Battle of (1583), 96–8
Shizuka Gozen, 29
Shogun, 26, 50, 96, 123, 154
shoya (village headman), 132, 138
Shoyuki (An old chronicle of Japan), 17
shō, 227
shōgi, 161, 201
Shōgun, 176
shōshō, 215
shrines, 291
shugo, 176–8
siegecraft, 41–2, 102, 106, 110, 111, 215, 285, 286
signalling, 211–12
Soga brothers' revenge, 302
sohei (warrior monk), 18, 22, 32, 34
Sōun-ji, 183
spirit world, belief in, 291–9
spying, 264
strategy, 185
Suda Chikamitsu, 202, 325
sugake-odoshi (wide-spaced lacing on armour), 78
suguroku, 198
Suibara, family of, 325–6
suicide, 24, 26, 43, 48, 83, 144,

178, 265–7, 282–8
  as condition of peace, 285
  as protest, 286
  as punishment, 302
  'following in death', 286
  to make amends, 285–6
  to save honour, 283
Sukeroku, 239, 240
Sunomata, 99
sword, 10, 13, 17, 52, 62
'Sword-Hunt', 245
sword-making, 140
sword-testing, 128

Tachibana Muneshige, 124
Tada Mitsuyori, 313–15
Tadano Samon, 213–14
Taiheiki (Chronicle of 14th century), 40
Taira
  Atsumori, 25
  Kiyomori, 25
  Korehira, 18
  Masakado, 14, 17
  Muneyori, 18
  Tomomori, 38
Taira Masakado, 298
Taira, family of, 18, 20
tairō, 280
taisho (general), 22
Takamatsu, 95, 111, 285
Takanashi Masayori, 202, 325
Takayama Ukon, 103–11
Takeda
  Saburo, 73
  Shingen, 64, 72–4
Takeda, heraldry of, 216–22
Takeda, retainers of, 200–4, 216–22, 327
Takeda:
  Katsuyori, 195, 311, 327
  Nobushige, 216, 313–15, 327
  Nobutoyo, 216, 313–15, 327
  Shingen, 161, 185, 199, 220–1, 313–15, 327
Takemata Hirotsuna, 325–6
Tame, family of, 215
tanto (dagger), 1, 10, 48
tasuki (sash), 156
tea ceremony, 228
tengai (basket-like hat worn by komuso), 156
'tenka-fubu' (Oda Nobunaga's motto), 83

teppo (arquebus), 84
textile trade, 255
Toda-Gassan, 193
Tōkaidō, 34, 237–8
Tokugawa
  Ieyasu, 79, 96, 115–31, 189
  Keiki, 151
  Yoshimune, 144
Tominaga Masaie, 215
Tonegawa, Battle of (1844), 257
Tottori, 286
Town-planning, 233–6
Toyotomi
  Hideyori, 122
  Hideyoshi, 82, 95–14, 179, 189, 195, 205, 213, 265, 285, 286, 301, 328
tozama-daimyō, 190
travel, 236–8, 316
Tsuchiya Masatsugu, 313–15
tsukai-ban (messenger corps), 68; *see* messengers
Tsumago, 238, 247, 248
Tsurugaoka Hachiman Shrine, 20, 29
'Twenty-Four Generals', 200–4, 311, 327

Ueda, 275
Ueno, Battle of (1867), 154–6
Uesugi
  Kagekatsu, 73
  Kagetora, 73
  Kenshin, 64, 95, 188, 206, 322
Uesugi, family of, 179
Uji, First Battle of (1180), 22–4
Uji, Second Battle of (1184), 24
Uji, Third Batle of (1219), 34
ukiyo, 239
uma-jirushi, 212–22, 176–9
Usa Sadayuki, 204, 322

vendetta, *see* vengeance
vengeance, 302–21
  abolition of vendetta, 321
  regulations for, 307
  women's, 318–20

wakizashi (short sword), 114
war-fan, 173
warimoto, 251
warrior Monks, *See sohei*
Watanabe:
  Gendayū, 308

Kazuma, 308
water supply, 215, 234
women, position of, 263–70, 318
wounded, treatment of, 226

Yagyū Shinkage-ryū, 309–10
yakudaka, 197, 322
yakuza, 254
yamabushi, 211, 295, 296
Yamaga Sokō, 303
Yamagata Masakage, 68, 222, 313–15, 327
Yamamoto Kansuke, 64, 283, 313–15
Yamamoto Tsunetomo, 303
Yamana Sozn, 52, 60
Yamanaka Shika-no-suke, 191–5
yamashiro, 229
Yamato-takeru, Prince, 13
Yamazaki, Battle of (1582), 96, 108
yashiki, 232–6
Yashima, Battle of (1184), 25
Yasukuni Shrine, 291
Yi Sun Sin, Admiral of Korea, 112–14
Yodo-gimi, 265
Yokota Takatoshi, 313–15
yoriki, 246
Yoshino, 50
Yoshiwara, 269–70
yōjimbō, 258

Zen, 228

Illustrations

All the black and white photographs used in this book are by the author, except for p.114, the *wakizashi*, which was supplied by courtesy of Christie's. All the colour plates, line illustrations and maps were specially prepared by James Field; the maps were annotated by Chartwell Illustrators. The author would like to thank the following individuals and organisations who gave permission for works in their possession to be photographed: Mr I. Bottomley; Mr T. Watanabe; the Nampian Kannon-ji, Kawachi-Nagano; Fudo-ji, Kurikara.